EVIL OR ILL?

F

A

In *Evil or Ill?*, Lawrie Reznek writes about excuses in general and the insanity defence in particular. Reznek aims to understand the concept of an excuse and explain why our moral and legal systems contain the excuses that they do. He draws from famous legal cases to explain that a person is not responsible if that person was not in control of his actions, or was ignorant of what he was doing.

Reznek shows us that these excuses derive from Aristotle's excuses of ignorance and compulsion. *Evil or Ill?* argues that there is a third excuse ignored by Aristotle and subsequent philosophers – the excuse of character change. Reznek explains that the excuse of character change demonstrates that the idea of an 'evil character' lies at the heart of our legal and moral systems, and that the notions of responsibility and excuses (as well as the whole institution of punishment) is based on the overall aim of punishing evil characters and excusing good ones.

Reznek, using careful and clear philosophical analysis, arrives at a fresh understanding of age-old notions and institutions, ranging from law to philosophy and psychiatry to criminology.

Lawrie Reznek is both a trained philosopher and psychiatrist. He teaches psychiatry at the University of Toronto. He is also the author of *The Nature of Disease* (Routledge, 1987), *The Medicine Men* (Collins, 1990), and *The Philosophical Defence of Psychiatry* (Routledge, 1991).

PHILOSOPHICAL ISSUES IN SCIENCE
Edited by W.H. Newton-Smith
Balliol College, Oxford

EVIL OR ILL?

Justifying the insanity defence

Lawrie Reznek

London and New York

First published 1997
by Routledge
11 New Fetter Lane, London EC4P 4EE

Simultaneously published in the USA and Canada
by Routledge
29 West 35th Street, New York, NY 10001

Typeset in Palatino by Routledge
Printed and bound in Great Britain by
T J International, Padstow, Cornwall

British Library Cataloguing in Publication Data
A catalogue record for this book is available from the British
Library

Library of Congress Cataloguing in Publication Data
Reznek, Lawrie.
Evil or ill? : justifying the insanity defence / Lawrie Reznek.
Includes bibliographical references and index.
1. Insanity–Jurisprudence. 2. Criminal liability. I. Title.
K5077.R39 1997
345´.04–dc21
97–11034
CIP

ISBN 0–415–16699–3 (hbk)
ISBN 0–415–16700–0 (pbk)

For my father
Joel 'Koffie' Reznek
A most remarkable man

CONTENTS

vii

CONTENTS

CONTENTS

PREFACE

This book is about excuses in general and the insanity defence in particular. It explores the justification for the insanity defence, and asks when we should excuse a person rather than punish him. Central to the book is the attempt to draw the distinction between those who are evil and deserve punishment, and those who are mentally ill and deserve treatment. The book explores the clash of fundamentally opposed views of evil behaviour – the medical view that it is caused by a disease, and the legal view that it is the product of our choices.

No book is a solo effort. I would like to thank William Newton-Smith for his philosophic and editorial assistance. I would also like to thank my mentor, Vivian Rakoff, for his help and support. Alex Greer helped with an earlier draft and made many useful comments, and the Reader for Routledge also provided a most insightful review. I would also like to thank my colleagues at the University of Toronto and the Toronto Hospital, especially Paul Garfinkel and Gary Rodin, without whose support the book would not have been written. I am grateful to Churchill Livingstone for providing me with a copy of their excellent *Principles and Practice of Forensic Psychiatry* at an affordable price. My thanks to my secretary, Rosanne Davidson, who helped keep me organized. Lastly, I must thank my wife Eleanor and my children Sam, Jess and Will for tolerating frequent visits to my Macintosh.

I have dedicated this book to my physician father who taught me more than anyone about what it is to be a good man and a good physician – about both morality and medicine – which are the subjects of this book.

INTRODUCTION
The diagnosis of evil

MAD OR BAD?

From 1978 to 1991 Jeffrey Dahmer killed seventeen young men, mostly homosexuals, by luring them to his apartment with the promise of money for posing in nude photographs. There Dahmer plied them with drinks spiked with the sedating drug Halcion. Once asleep, he strangled them, cut them open, and had sex with the exposed body parts. He was only able to have an erection if his partner was unconscious. He kept some of the dead victims in his apartment for days, repeatedly sexually assaulting them. He boiled their skulls in hydrochloric acid, painting them for a shrine which he hoped would give him 'special powers'. The skulls aroused him, and he frequently masturbated in front of them. He ate parts of his victims after tenderizing them, responding with an erection. He explained his cannibalism by saying that he wanted his victims to come alive in him. He tried to turn some of his victims into walking zombies – sex slaves – by performing frontal lobotomies. He drilled holes in their heads and injected muriatic acid. Some died instantly but others managed to walk around for days after the operation.

Was he mad or bad? The matter was put to the courts. Dahmer was charged with fifteen murders and pleaded not guilty by reason of insanity (NGRI). The ensuing trial became a battleground of experts. Psychiatrists for the defence testified that Dahmer suffered from necrophilia to such a degree that he was unable to control his behaviour. They recounted that his fascination for death began early in life when he searched for animals along the side of the road, experimenting with their dead bodies and bleaching their bones with acid. He dissected

1

fish to see their insides, and once nailed a dog's carcass to a tree, mounting its severed head on a stake. At the time he started masturbating, he became engrossed in dissecting animals at school, and began to fantasize about their dissected bodies while masturbating. This obsession with death continued until fantasy alone had not been sufficiently gratifying. That was when he lost control, so his psychiatrists argued, and the killing began.

Psychiatrists for the prosecution were unimpressed. They agreed that Dahmer had necrophilia, but denied that he was unable to control his impulses. When the police found one of his potential victims staggering naked in the street, Dahmer lied that the 14-year-old boy was a drunken 19-year-old house guest. The police officers were convinced and left the apartment. Straight afterwards Dahmer strangled the boy and had sex with the corpse. This was not the behaviour of a man in the grip of an uncontrollable impulse. The experts notwithstanding, Dahmer's sanity was decided by twelve lay people, and they concluded he was evil and not ill. Before sentencing, Dahmer addressed the court: 'I believe I was sick. The doctors have told me about my sickness, and now I have some peace . . . I hope God has forgiven me. I think He has. I know society will never be able to forgive me . . . I am so very sorry.' He was sentenced to 957 years in prison, but was subsequently murdered in prison (Schwartz, 1992).

Was Dahmer suffering from a mental illness undermining his responsibility, or was he an evil man responsible for his deeds? Did his necrophilia constitute an excuse? Is there something special about mental disorder that allows it to excuse? Does his having a mental illness preclude his being an evil man? If his behaviour was determined by abnormal biological factors, does this mean he was suffering from a mental disorder, or are these factors the biological basis of evil? Does explanation imply exculpation? What sort of explanation, if any, of his evil acts implies he was not evil? Should we offer him humane treatment for his mental disorder, or should we punish him for his evil deeds? These are the questions the book aims to answer.

PUZZLES AND PARADOXES

To understand whether Dahmer's illness transforms him from an evil man into an innocent victim, we must understand the notions of responsibility and excuses. This requires us to understand the whole institution of punishment and its justification, and this in turn the notion of an evil person. There is a circle of concepts, one of which cannot be understood without the other. The concept of mental illness, although seemingly peripheral in this network, is just as crucial as the other concepts. Only with an understanding of the nature of mental illness will we be able to fully understand such concepts as responsibility, excuse, punishment, and evil. Seemingly peripheral concepts often illuminate more central notions because they force us to draw the boundaries of the concept carefully. For example, ant hills are not paradigmatic cases of living things. However, they have the property of being able to maintain their own structure. Whenever the hills are damaged, the ants rebuild them. This property is in fact a feature of all living cells – they have DNA and a cellular metabolism that enables them to take energy from their environment to rebuild their structure in the fight against decay. Since we know many living things cannot reproduce (like mules), these sorts of cases suggest that the essence of living things is that they can maintain their own structures. Only by thinking about such cases can we understand the central cases of life more deeply. Similarly, I hope to show that mental illness illuminates the whole notion of responsibility.

In the process of showing this, we will encounter many problems. The first is the *Ultimate Issue Problem*. Should psychiatrists give 'ultimate issue' testimony, that is, testimony that a defendant is insane? Should they go beyond making diagnoses of mental illness and infer sanity or insanity? Should they have testified whether Dahmer was insane? This issue turns on whether judging insanity is something that falls within their expertise, and this on whether insanity is a factual or scientific matter. Is it a factual matter whether Dahmer has an excuse? On the one hand, whether he has an excuse depends on whether he was mentally ill, and whether he was able to control himself, which seem to be factual matters. On the other hand, whether Dahmer has an excuse depends on whether we ought to blame him, and whether he ought to have controlled himself, which are normative matters. Is insanity a psychiatric concept like schizophrenia, the criteria for which are factual and objective, or is it a normative or evaluative notion implying that someone deserves to be excused from blame and punishment, which cannot be decided by the examination of the facts alone? If the matter is ultimately a factual one, then psychiatrists are in the best position to judge whether Dahmer has an excuse. But if the question is a normative one, a jury is better placed to decide. We need to settle this to understand the role psychiatrists ought to play in the courts.

The second problem is the *Relativity Paradox*. The second edition of the Diagnostic and Statistical Manual (DSM II), the American Psychiatric Association's (APA) disease taxonomy, classified homosexuality as a disease, but the next edition did not. This change was not the result of any scientific discovery, but the result of a change in values effected by political pressure from organizations like Gay Liberation (Bayer, 1987). Let us suppose that necrophiliacs successfully lobby for the removal of necrophilia from DSM V. They argue, like homosexuals did, that necrophilia is a 'way of life'. If being a disease is settled like this, and if Dahmer's responsibility depends on having a disease, then whether he is responsible is relative to our disease classification. We would be forced to say that prior to DSM V, he was not responsible, but subsequently he is, which is absurd. If this sounds far-fetched, a situation actually arose in the District of Columbia when psychiatrists classified psychopathic personality disorder as a disease, but then over a weekend changed their classification. As Burger, a circuit judge, noted: 'We tacitly conceded to St. Elizabeth's Hospital the power to alter drastically the scope of a rule of law by a weekend change of nomenclature' (Moore, 1984: 229).

The third problem is the *Demarcation Paradox*. Our legal system presumes we are sane and therefore responsible for our actions. In this way, it draws a sharp boundary between mad and bad. But if deviant behaviour, including crime, is due to a disease, and this exculpates, this distinction collapses. As Moore (1984: 201) puts it: 'If to be ill is to deviate from some sort of norm, and to passively suffer such deviation rather than actively cause it, badness becomes one kind of illness.' Diamond (1962: 189) predicted over thirty years ago that 'within 10 years biochemical and physiological tests will be developed that will demonstrate beyond a reasonable doubt that a substantial number of our worst and most vicious criminal offenders are actually the sickest of all. And if the concept of mental disease and exculpation from responsibility applies to any, it will apply more appropriately to them.' Does science show that criminals are ill and should be excused? Is it, as Peck (1983: 127) argues, that 'evil is the ultimate disease' and that 'the evil are the most insane of all'? If mental illness is defined in terms of a departure from some ideal, then it may swallow up the whole category of evil. Lord Devlin (1959: 53) has noted: 'The concept of illness expands continually at the expense of the concept of moral responsibility.' If we define the norms of illness too broadly, evil may disappear. One psychiatrist defined mental health as the 'ability to live happily, productively, without being a nuisance' (Wootton, 1959: 98). Menninger (1968: 77) defines mental illness as 'a certain state of existence which is uncomfortable to someone . . . The suffering may be in the afflicted person or in those around him or both.' In terms of these definitions, crime becomes a disease, the distinction between mad and bad is obliterated, and responsibility becomes, in Menninger's terms, a 'metaphysical fiction.'

The mad–bad distinction is also threatened if we see everyone as responsible. Szasz (1960: 1965) argues there is no such thing as mental illness, and therefore there is no such thing as a mental illness that excuses. As Szasz (1973: 91) writes:

When a person does something bad, like shoot the president, it is immediately assumed that he might be mad, madness being thought of as a 'disease' that might somehow 'explain' why he did it. When a person does something good, like discover a cure for a hitherto incurable disease, no similar assumption is made. I submit that no further evidence is needed to show that 'mental illness' is not the name of a biological condition whose nature awaits to be elucidated, but is the name of a concept whose purpose is to obscure the obvious.

Wootton (1981: 78) makes an epistemological argument: 'Neither medical nor any other science can ever hope to prove whether a man who does not resist his impulses does not do so because he cannot or because he will not.' Lord Parker agrees: 'The step between "he did not resist his impulse" and "he could not resist his impulse" is incapable of scientific proof. A fortiori there is no scientific measurement of the degree of difficulty which an abnormal person finds in controlling his impulses' (Williams, 1983: 692). If we can never discover these sorts of facts, we can never draw the line between mad and bad.

5

The fourth problem is the *Determinism Paradox*. We hold someone responsible for his actions if he could have done otherwise. According to G.E. Moore, someone could have done otherwise if he would have done otherwise had he wanted to (Austin, 1970). But what if he cannot want otherwise (Edwards, 1958)? What if a person's character is determined in such a way that he cannot want otherwise? If his character is determined by factors outside his control, and his actions are determined by his character, is he really in control of his actions? If we say he is, we seem to face a deeper paradox:

> If I suffered from a compulsion neurosis, so that I got up and walked across the room, whether I wanted to or not, or if I did so because somebody else compelled me, then I should not be acting freely. But if I do it now, I shall be acting freely, just because these conditions do not obtain; and the fact that my action may nevertheless have a cause is, from this point of view, irrelevant. For it is not when my action has any cause at all, but only when it has a special sort of cause, that it is reckoned not to be free. But here it is objected that, even if this distinction corresponds to ordinary usage, it is still very irrational. For why should we distinguish, with regard to a person's freedom, between the operations of one sort of cause and those of another? Do not all causes equally necessitate? And is it not therefore arbitrary to say that a person is free when he is necessitated in one fashion but not when he is necessitated in another?
>
> (Ayer, 1954: 276)

We know that those with a psychiatric illness are five times more likely to commit acts of violence than those without (Swanson *et al.*, 1991), and that delusions or hallucinations are what makes the mentally ill violent (Link *et al.*, 1992). But as Morris (1968: 520) argues:

> Why not permit the defence of dwelling in a Negro ghetto? Such a defence would not be morally indefensible. Adverse social and subcultural background is statistically more criminogenic than is psychosis . . . You argue that insanity destroys, undermines, diminishes man's capacity to reject what is wrong and to adhere to what is right. So does the ghetto – more so.

If all our behaviour is caused, we need to know why some causes excuse and some do not.

We are led straight into *Wootton's Paradox*: If abnormal conditions are classified as disorders, and this implies a lack of responsibility, then those with the most bizarre desires will be the most innocent. Wootton (1978: 231) writes: 'If a man's crimes are by ordinary standards only moderately objectionable, we are prepared to regard him as wicked, and therefore a suitable subject for punishment; but if his wickedness goes beyond a certain point, it ceases to be wickedness at all and becomes mental disorder.' The more extreme the behaviour, the more inclined we are to consider that the behaviour is the product of a deranged mind. If being mentally disordered undermines responsibility, it is impossible for extreme evil to exist, which seems absurd.

Finally, we face the *Paradox of Evil*: The law considers a person responsible if his evil deeds are the consequence of his character (Radden, 1985). An evil person is someone who does not care sufficiently about the well-being of others in the pursuit of his own selfish interests. Many crimes require the offender to be indifferent to the needs of others. If committing such crimes is symptomatic of a personality disorder and this qualifies him for an excuse, there will be no criminals at all. This paradox threatens to eliminate the categories of evil and crime altogether and thereby undermine our whole moral and legal system.

THE LEGAL AND MEDICAL PARADIGMS

During the course of an insanity trial over which he was presiding, Judge Levin commented on the clash between two paradigms:

> Psychiatry and law approach the problem of human behaviour from different philosophical perspectives. Psychiatry purports to be scientific and takes a deterministic position with regard to behaviour. 'Its view of human nature is expressed in terms of drives and dispositions which, like mechanical forces, operate in accordance with universal laws of causation.' Criminal law is, however, 'a practical, rational, normative science which, although it draws upon theoretical science, also is concerned to pass

judgment on human conduct. Its views of human nature asserts the reality of free choice and rejects the thesis that the conduct of normal adults is a mere expression of imperious psychological necessity.'

(Moore, 1984: 353)

In courts of law, psychiatric and legal conceptual systems lock horns. Psychiatrists talk of manic-depression and schizophrenia, lawyers of insanity and diminished responsibility. Psychiatrists make deterministic assumptions and explain behaviour in terms of serotonin levels and frontal lobe damage, while lawyers assume free will and explain behaviour in terms of desires and beliefs. Psychiatrists analyse the causes of the behaviour, and lawyers look for the reasons. How do these different concepts and theories relate to one another? Is there a way of reconciling the assumptions of determinism and free will? Is insanity a moral or legal concept with no relation to psychiatric concepts? Or is insanity a scientific concept, the presence of which is settled by the facts?

Our moral and legal systems adopt Folk Psychology which makes the following assumptions: (1) Intentional behaviour is the product of an agent's desires and beliefs, and (2) Agents are (by and large) rational. An agent is rational if he has a set of rational beliefs, a set of desires, an ordering of these desires based on a set of values, the ability to figure out the options, the ability to understand the consequences of these options, the ability to weigh up the pros and cons of each option, and the ability to choose the one that most satisfies his most important desires. Churchland (1986: 299) explains:

> Folk psychology is commonsense psychology – the psychological lore in virtue of which we explain behaviour as the outcome of beliefs, desires, perceptions, expectations, goals, sensations, and so forth . . . As philosophers have analyzed it, the preeminent elements in folk psychological explanations of behaviour include the concepts of *belief* and *desire*.

Whether we praise or blame a person depends on how we explain his behaviour. If Peter kills Paul by running over him in his car, before we can blame him we need to know whether he did it deliberately (for monetary gain) or accidentally (without knowing he was under the car), whether he believed the man was trying to kill him or whether he had lost control of his behaviour. These explanations are drawn from Folk Psychology. When the explanation consists in the person believing he is doing evil and freely choosing to do it, we conclude he deserves punishment. If psychiatry challenges this sort of explanatory theory, it will undermine the whole of morality.

There are two paradigms of human behaviour which provide different rationales for different criminal justice systems (Packer, 1969). The legal paradigm makes these assumptions:

1 Intentional human behaviour is explained in terms of reasons (desires and beliefs).
2 Agents are generally rational and free.
3 If an agent is rational and free, he is responsible for his actions.
4 Agents who break the law but suffer from exculpatory ignorance or compulsion should be excused.
5 Lay people are best placed to decide who is responsible and how a defendant should be disposed (punished, treated or freed).
6 Someone found guilty should be punished.
7 Punishment is effective in deterring, reforming, and incapacitating.

The (strong) medical paradigm (Jeffrey, 1993; Menninger, 1968) assumes:

1 Intentional human behaviour is explained by physiological events.
2 Agents are irrational and unfree.
3 Since every event has a cause, no one can do otherwise and no one is responsible.
4 All agents have excuses since all their behaviour is caused.
5 Psychiatrists are best placed to decide how the offence was caused and how the person should be disposed (confined, treated or freed).
6 Those with reversible causes of crime should be treated while the rest should be confined.
7 Since punishment is ineffective at deterrence and reform, treatment should be considered instead.

A weak version of the medical model changes assumptions 3 and 4:

3* Agents are responsible if their behaviour is not caused by disease.

4* Crime is due to a neurological disease.

Jeffrey (1993: 303) writes:

> Major changes must be made in the legal system, which assumes free will and moral responsibility. If we are to follow the medical model, we must use neurological examinations in place of the insanity defense and the concept of guilt. Criminals must be placed in medical clinics, not in prisons.

Deciding what paradigm to adopt is one of the tasks of this book. If these two paradigms are to be reconciled, a middle road between Free Will and (Hard) Determinism, and between Folk Psychology and Neuroscience, will have to be found.

Both versions of the medical paradigm regard the insanity defence as part of an outmoded theory. The strong version believes we should jettison the whole notion of responsibility, while the weak version argues we should replace the insanity defence with the neurological defence. As Restak (1991: 20) puts it:

> In reducing deviant behaviour to brain dysfunction and the genetic, dietary, social and environmental factors that lead to it, neurologists threaten to eliminate the humanistic concept of the person as a rational being endowed with rights and responsibilities. The shift from the insanity defence to the neurological one would resolve the traditional tension between the mad and the bad by defining away the bad.

Should we replace the insanity defence? Is Fenwick (1993: 572) right when he says that 'the concept of a guilty mind belongs to a non-scientific era'? We will see.

INSANITY DEFENCE

Aristotle articulated two basic excuses – a cognitive and a volitional category, or what he called ignorance and compulsion. A person deserved to be excused when he was unaware he was doing wrong (ignorance) or when he was unable to control himself (compulsion). He ignored a third sort of excuse that is neither cognitive nor volitional – one I will call the excuse of character change. It will be the major task of this book to argue for this new category, and show that this demonstrates what is at the centre of all excuses – the need to punish evil characters and protect society from them. The cases that demonstrate this new category of excuse most clearly are those where the offender is suffering from a mental illness. It is the injustice of punishing mentally ill offenders that shows the way to accepting this novel excuse. Matters at the periphery of the whole institution of excuses will turn out to be central.

Paralleling these excuses, there are a number of insanity defences. By insanity defence, I mean a legal device for excusing a defendant on the basis of his mental illness. It usually implies that the defendant is completely excused, but I will also discuss devices that partially excuse a defendant on the basis of mental illness. First, there is the *Cognitive Defence*: A person is NGRI if and only if (1) he is suffering from a mental illness, and (2) the mental illness causes him to be ignorant of what he is doing. This defence says: 'I'm not guilty because I didn't know what I was doing.' Second, the *Volitional Defence*: A person is NGRI if and only if (1) he is suffering from a mental illness, and (2) the mental illness causes him to lose control of his impulses. This defence says: 'I'm not guilty because I lost control.' Third, the *Causal Defence*: A person is NGRI if and only if (1) he is suffering from a mental illness, and (2) the mental illness causes his behaviour. This defence says: 'I'm not guilty because my behaviour was caused by a mental illness.' I will argue for a fourth defence – the *Character Change Defence*: A person is NGRI if and only if (1) he is suffering from a mental illness, and (2) the mental illness causes a change of moral character. This defence says: 'I'm not guilty because I wasn't myself when I committed the offence.' While I will argue this is a new excuse, it is already in use in our legal system. It is implicit in many of our insanity judgements, and points the way to a new understanding of the whole institution of excuses. If justice is to be preserved, we must accept this novel defence. A final category of excuse only partially excuses – the *Diminished Capacity Defence*: A person is not as guilty by reason of mental illness if and only if (1) he is suffering from a mental illness, and (2) the mental illness diminishes his responsibility. This defence says: 'I'm not as guilty because mental illness reduced my responsibility.' We need to see whether we ought to retain both an insanity defence and a diminished capacity defence, retain only one, or abolish both.

THEMES AND OUTLINE

It is easier to follow an argument if one knows beforehand where it will go. For this reason, I will outline the principle direction of the book. I wish to show that the best way to understand the whole institution of excuses is with the notion of moral character. A person's character consists of character traits, and a character trait is an enduring disposition to behave (in particular situations) in a certain way. For example, cowardice is one of Dennis's character traits because when faced with any dangerous situation, he (usually) runs away. A trait is part of a person's moral character if the disposition is one that inclines him to act in moral or immoral ways. For example, altruism is one of Theresa's moral character traits because when she is faced with situations where she can help others, even at the expense of her own needs, she (usually) does so. I will argue that the best way to make sense of excuses is that these are features which show that even though the person did a harmful thing, he is nonetheless a good character.

While the notion of intentionality is central to the criminal law, the notion of character is especially important to the understanding of who deserves punishment. I will try to show this in a number of ways. First, it is the notion of evil character (and not evil intent) that best explains why we accept the excuses we do. Second, the idea of evil character also explains why we accept certain conditions as aggravating (rather than excusing) the offence. Third, traditional accounts of the insanity defence are inadequate in that they do not take into account the fact that mental illness can temporarily transform character. Once again, we will see that someone can be excused because of his underlying good character in spite of his intention to commit a harmful act. Fourth, the excuse of character change most clearly shows that the notion of evil character is central to what counts as an excuse. Fifth, from the epistemological point of view, character is important. Someone who knocks over another person by accident has an excuse. But how do we know that he did it accidentally? The best evidence is if such acts are 'out of character', showing once again that character and not intent is central (I owe this point to Alex Greer). Finally, I will show that both Retributivism and Utilitarianism justify this position. This is particularly interesting since Retributivism is essentially backward-looking, being concerned with what the agent has done and deserves, and Utilitarianism is essentially forward-looking, being concerned with preventing future crimes.

I will be using the terms 'evil', 'bad' and 'wicked' (when qualifying people) as synonyms. Some readers may see this as linguistic legislation because, for them, terms like 'evil' have a spiritual meaning. However, when I use the term, I am not implying that the person is possessed by the Devil or governed by some hypostatized Evil Force. Instead, I want to naturalize the concept and define an evil person by his propensity to harm others in the pursuit of his own selfish interests. I will use the term 'harm' to refer to changes where a person's interests have been adversely affected. Of course, the concept of evil might once have carried this spiritual meaning, but so did the concept of disease once imply spirit possession (Ackerknecht, 1982). This does not mean that it cannot now be used free of this connotation. At one time, evil might have implied the existence of the Devil, but now it does not carry such an implication. To illustrate that we use the concept free of theological implications, I glanced at the *Globe & Mail* at the time of writing this section (22 April 1995). There was an article on the terrorist bombing in Oklahoma City, entitled 'Evil and violence no stranger to the weeping Heartland.' 'Evil' is used free of any theological implications. The article quotes Wichita State University historian Craig Miner: 'When something evil happens we always want to believe it happened because of some alien force. We want to believe that those terrorists are from Iran, or at least New York City.' While we might be driven to place the source of evil outside ourselves by postulating the existence of the Devil or an Evil Force, I will stick to this naturalized and common usage.

A word about my usage of the word 'irrationality'. I do not use the word to imply a complete absence of reason, as some philosophic usage does. If someone fails to follow the rules of reason – if, for example, he is inconsistent, or violates modus ponens in his reasoning, or fails to reject a hypothesis when it is falsified – I will call him irrational. Like many things, excepting pregnancy and the like, I will argue that irrationality comes in degrees. An insane person will end up being more irrational than a sane person on this view, but it may turn out that sane people are also irrational, but to a lesser degree. I will not assume it is a necessary truth that most people are rational most of the time, and will leave it open for us to discover that we are pervasively irrational in certain areas.

Chapter 1 examines the history of the Anglo-American concept of insanity. Without history, philosophy is blind. Chapter 2 gives a taxonomy of defences. Chapter 3 examines the excuse of ignorance, Chapter 4 the excuse of compulsion, and Chapter 5 the excuse of automatism. Chapter 6 justifies the existence of excuses in our conceptual system by exploring two theories – Retributivism and Utilitarianism. We will see that both Retributivism and Utilitarianism demonstrate the centrality of character in the criminal law. Chapter 7 asks whether causes excuse. Chapter 8 examines the Reductionist Theory – the theory that mental illness excuses only in virtue of the traditional excuses of ignorance and compulsion. I will show that this theory is incomplete. Chapter 9 examines the Irrationality Theory – the theory that mental illness excuses because of irrationality. This theory too is flawed. Chapter 10 explores the concepts of disease and mental illness. Chapter 11 examines the novel idea that character change excuses. Not only will we see that we have reason to accept this new excuse, but I will show that the reason why other theories failed was because they did not take this feature into account. Chapter 12 explores the clash of the legal and medical paradigms, and Chapter 13 shows how the insanity defence functions in practice. The Conclusion shows that we need an understanding of evil character before we can understand excuses in general and insanity in particular.

1

A HISTORY OF CRIMINAL RESPONSIBILITY

BAD DEEDS AND EVIL MINDS

Understanding the concept of insanity requires knowing its conceptual history. Anglo-American law is constitutively historical: past procedure and decisions determine how the present law functions (Smith, 1981). For this reason, understanding the history *is* to understand the law. According to Anglo-American law, a person is guilty of a crime if two conditions are satisfied. He must commit a criminal act and have a criminal mind. These two components are called the *actus reus* and *mens rea* respectively – the bad deed and evil mind. The idea that evil intent is necessary for a crime is cited as far back as Bractin in his thirteenth-century treatise *On the Laws and Customs of England*: 'a crime is not committed unless the will to harm be present.' This is the doctrine of *mens rea*: *Actus non facit reum nisi mens sit rea*: The act does not make a man guilty unless his mind is guilty. The requirement that a particular state of mind be present for a crime to exist has a fundamentally important consequence: it opens the possibility of excuses in general, and in particular the possibility that abnormal states of mind can exculpate. The history of the insanity defence is the history of what states have counted as excuses and why.

Little has changed in 150 years. When M'Naghten was found NGRI in 1843, there was a public outcry. The *Illustrated London News* noted that 'within the previous three years there had been five assassination attempts, three against the sovereign, and not a single criminal had been duly punished'. The House of Lords was moved to draw up the M'Naghten Rules defining insanity. In 1981, Hinckley was found NGRI, provoking a similar outcry.

President Reagan, who had been wounded, instructed the Attorney General to propose new legislation to reform the insanity defence and 'restore the balance between the forces of law and the forces of lawlessness'. These reforms led to an insanity defence that was none other than a rewording of the M'Naghten Rules!

THE EMERGENCE OF LEGAL INSANITY

There are two sorts of insanity. A person can be judged insane when he is out of touch with reality (because he is deluded or hallucinating), or when he is considered to be so mentally ill as to lack responsibility. The former is a medical concept and the latter a legal one. 'Insanity' is nowadays used only to refer to the legal concept, and I will follow this usage. But initially the word had a medical usage too. The earliest case illustrating the distinction arose when Edward Arnold, known locally as 'Crazy Ned' for his bizarre behaviour, shot and wounded Lord Onslow in 1724. He believed Onslow had sent imps and devils to disturb his sleep and appetite. Arnold planned the crime, buying shot and powder, announcing: 'God damn him, if I see him I will shoot my Lord Onslow.' In his trial, Mr Justice Tracy followed the bible of criminal law, Hale's *History of the Pleas of the Crown*:

> [S]ome people that have a competent use of reason in respect of some subjects, are yet under a particular dementia in respect of some particular discourses . . . [T]his partial insanity seems not to excuse . . . The best measure that I can think of is this: such person as, labouring under melancholy distempers, hath yet ordinarily as great under-standing as ordinarily a child of fourteen years hath, is such a person as may be guilty of treason or felony.
>
> (Walker, 1968: 38)

Being deluded or suffering from 'partial insanity' (a medical concept) did not amount to exculpatory insanity (the legal concept). The law stated that in order for mental illness to excuse, it had to reduce understanding to that of a 14-year-old. This age was chosen because in English common law, a child under that age was presumed to be unable to distinguish right from wrong. This made the insanity defence cognitive: Someone

16

is NGRI if they were unable to distinguish right from wrong. In his final address to the jury, Mr Justice Tracy instructed them thus:

> If he was under the visitation of God, and could not distinguish between good and evil, and did not know what he did, though he committed the greatest offence yet he could not be guilty of any offence against any law whatsoever: for guilt arises from the mind, and the wicked will and intention of the man . . . [I]t is not every frantic and idle humour of a man that will exempt him from justice . . . it must be a man that is totally deprived of his understanding and memory, and doth not know what he is doing, no more than an infant, than a brute or wild beast, such a one is never the object of punishment.
>
> (Walker, 1968: 56)

The cognitive test Tracy articulated became known as the 'Wild Beast Test' of insanity, and the jury used it to convict Arnold. He was sentenced to death, but Lord Onslow intervened and the sentence was commuted to life imprisonment. Arnold was clearly insane in the medical sense but was judged legally sane.

On 15 May 1800 Hadfield stood up in the Drury Lane theatre and fired a pistol at King George III, missing his head by a foot. He was labouring under the delusion that God would destroy the world unless he sacrificed himself. Believing that suicide was a mortal sin, he decided to shoot at the king, knowing that attempted regicide was punishable by death. He was tried six weeks later, having the brilliant lawyer, Thomas Erskine, as his counsel. Erskine had evidence that Hadfield was mentally ill – he had received a penetrating head wound in the war against the French making him deranged, but Erskine knew Hadfield did not pass the Wild Beast Test. Although Hadfield was deluded (or medically insane), he knew he was breaking the law. In fact, it was precisely because the act was illegal that he had performed it. Erskine's tactic was instead to argue that madness could be partial and not reduce men to helpless idiots, but still excuse. The jury was convinced and Hadfield was acquitted.

Acquitting the mentally ill created the problem of disposition. Prior to 1800, mental asylums were few and most insane offenders were sent to jail. Of those ending up in asylums, most were discharged after 12 months, even if uncured. The vagrancy legislation of 1744 allowed two judges to order the detention of an offender as a dangerous lunatic, but the common law only allowed his detention until he had recovered. This led to dangerous lunatics being released during 'lucid intervals', and the Attorney General pointed to 'several instances of His Majesty's subjects having lost their lives for want of a due provision in this respect' (Walker, 1968: 78). Hadfield's judge, Lord Kenyon, did not want him released early:

> The prisoner, for his own sake, and for the sake of society at large, must not be discharged; for this is a case which concerns every man of every station, from the king upon the throne to the beggar at the gate; people of both sexes and of all ages may, in an unfortunate frantic hour, fall a sacrifice to this man, who is not under the guidance of sound reason; and therefore it is absolutely necessary for the safety of society that he should be properly disposed of.
>
> (Walker, 1968: 78)

As a result of this decision, an act of parliament hastily established the existence of the special verdict – NGRI – allowing Hadfield to be committed indefinitely to Bethlem. Hale's view that 'partial insanity' cannot excuse had been overturned.

The existence of the statutory special verdict was important for a number of reasons. Walker explains:

> From the jurisprudential point of view, the statutory special verdict was an attempt at a compromise between two traditional alternatives. It purported to be an acquittal, for it used the words 'not guilty'. On the other hand, it was an acquittal in name only, for it tacitly admitted that the doctrine of *mens rea* could not safely be applied to the insane. A criminal lunatic might be as morally innocent as a man who had done harm by accident or in self-defence, but the danger of *treating* him as innocent was too great. The solution was to pay lip-service to his innocence but use the law to make sure he remained in custody . . . From the judicial point of view, Hadfield – or rather Erskine – established the doctrine that in order to be excused on the grounds of insanity the accused need not be shown to have lacked all understanding, or the ability to distinguish

between right and wrong, but could be proved to have suffered from a delusion which prompted his act.

(Walker, 1968: 81)

Contra Walker, the insanity defence was not an acquittal in name only – until the death sentence was abolished, it enabled a defendant to escape the gallows. In any event, Hadfield's case established that the presence of a delusion could be sufficient to undermine criminal responsibility.

The best known of all insanity trials is that of the Scottish wood-turner, Daniel M'Naghten, who in 1843 fatally wounded Edward Drummond, private secretary to the English Prime Minister, Sir Robert Peel. He believed the Tories, orchestrated by Peel, had been persecuting him for six years. He bought a pair of pistols and on 20 January, mistaking Drummond for Peel, followed him up Whitehall to his bank and shot him in the back. Drummond died five days later. When examined at Bow Street, M'Naghten gave this statement to the police:

> The Tories in my native city have compelled me to do this. They follow and persecute me wherever I go, and have entirely destroyed my peace of mind. They followed me to France, into Scotland and all over England; in fact they follow me wherever I go . . . They have accused me of crimes of which I am not guilty; in fact they wish to murder me. It can be proved by evidence. That's all I have to say.
>
> (Walker, 1968: 91)

On 3 March, M'Naghten went on trial, defended by one of the most able counsels of the time, Alexander Cockburn, with Chief Justice Tindal and two other judges presiding.

In his opening address, the Solicitor General favourably cited Hale on insanity, and dismissed Erskine's reasoning in Hadfield's trial as a misleading statement of the law – if a delusion did not lead to an inability to distinguish right from wrong, it was no defence. Cockburn's task was difficult – M'Naghten's statement to the police indicated he knew precisely what he was doing and that it was illegal. Cockburn enlisted the testimony of Dr Monro of Bethlem, who argued that M'Naghten's illness was 'sufficient to deprive the prisoner of all self-control'. Cockburn argued that M'Naghten was insane because he lacked self-control:

I trust that I have satisfied you by these authorities that the disease of partial insanity can exist – that it can lead to a partial or total aberration of the moral senses and affections, which may render the wretched patient incapable of resisting the delusion, and lead him to commit crimes for which morally he cannot be held responsible.

(Walker, 1968: 94)

All this did not impress Judge Tindal, who reminded the jury that they should find M'Naghten guilty if he had been able to distinguish right from wrong.

The jury returned a verdict of NGRI, and the public outcry that followed led the House of Lords to call upon fifteen judges of the Queen's Bench to clarify the legal position regarding the criminal responsibility of the mentally ill. The House of Lords put five questions to the judges: (1) What is the law pertaining to persons acting on delusions who know they are acting contrary to the law? (2) What are the proper questions to be put to the jury? (3) In what terms should the question of the person's state of mind be put to the jury? (4) If a person is deluded as to the facts, is he thereby excused? And (5) Can a psychiatrist who never saw the person prior to the trial be asked his opinion as to the state of the person's mind at the time the crime was committed? Lord Chief Justice Tindal gave the views of the judges on questions (1) and (4):

[W]e think he must be considered in the same situation as to responsibility as if the facts with respect to which the delusion exists were real. For example, if under the influence of his delusion he supposes another man to be in the act of attempting to take away his life, and he kills that man, as he supposes, in self-defence, he would be exempt from punishment. If his delusion was that the deceased had inflicted a serious injury to his character and fortune, and he killed him in revenge for such supposed injury, he would be liable to punishment.

(Walker, 1968: 99)

Tindal answered questions (2) and (3) together:

[E]very man is to be presumed to be sane, and to possess a sufficient degree of reason to be responsible for his crimes, until the contrary be proved to their satisfaction; and that to establish a defence on the ground of insanity, it must be clearly proved that, at the time of the committing of the act, the party accused was labouring under such a defect of reason, from disease of the mind, as not to know the nature and quality of the act he was doing; or, if he did know it, that he did not know he was doing what was wrong.

(Walker, 1968: 100)

Finally, he answered question (5):

[W]e think the medical men, under the circumstances supposed, cannot in strictness be asked his opinion in terms above state, because each of those questions involves the determination of the truth of the facts deposed to, which it is for the jury to decide, and the questions are not mere questions upon a matter of science, in which case such evidence is admissible.

(Walker, 1968: 102)

This last answer carefully differentiated medical from legal insanity – a psychiatrist might be qualified to decide the former factual matter, but the latter evaluative issue was a matter for the courts.

These answers, establishing a purely cognitive test, have become known as the M'Naghten Rules. They establish a complex relationship between medical insanity and legal insanity, as the answer to questions (1) and (4) outline. Medical insanity does not imply legal insanity, but medical insanity does not have to reduce understanding to that of a 14-year-old to qualify as legal insanity. Curiously, the jury used a volitional test in finding M'Naghten NGRI. Erskine conceded that M'Naghten knew what he was doing, but argued that he could not stop himself acting on his delusions. Even more curiously, had the M'Naghten Rules been followed in M'Naghten's case, the jury would have found him sane! Nevertheless, the M'Naghten Rules have dominated legal thinking on both sides of the Atlantic for 150 years, preventing non-cognitive tests of insanity being recognized.

THE INVENTION OF DIMINISHED RESPONSIBILITY

Until the notion of Diminished Responsibility (DR) was introduced, Anglo-American law operated with a dichotomous system. If someone intentionally committed the offence, he was either sane and guilty, or insane and not guilty. There was no room for intermediate verdicts such as a little insane and a little guilty. The Scots were the first to introduce the notion of DR, and it has since been entrenched into English law, supplanting the use of the M'Naghten's Rules (Dell, 1984).

Although the Scots were 'ahead' in this respect, many English commentators were aware of the defects of the Rules and criticized their exclusively cognitive definition. A mentally ill person who was unable to control his behaviour – who suffered from 'irresistible impulses' – was legally sane according to the Rules. Talk of irresistible impulses offended lawyers, as the young barrister Fitzjames Stephen explained to the Juridical Society in 1855: 'There may have been many instances of irresistible impulse of this kind, although I fear there is a disposition to confound them with unresisted impulses' (Walker, 1968: 105). However, when Stephen embarked on the codification of English criminal law, he was convinced that it should exempt an offender who had been 'prevented by disease affecting the mind . . . from controlling his own conduct.' In his *History of the Criminal Law of England*, he felt that the M'Naghten Rules were an incomplete statement of the law:

> If it is not, it ought to be the Law of England that no act is a crime if the person who does it is at the time . . . prevented either by defective mental power or by any disease affecting his mind from controlling his own conduct, unless the absence of the power of control has been produced by his own default.
>
> (Walker, 1968: 106)

In this respect, he followed Cockburn's defence of M'Naghten. Stephen actually suggested that 'the law ought . . . where madness is proved, to allow the jury to return any one of three verdicts: Guilty; Guilty, but his power of self-control was diminished by insanity; Not Guilty on the ground of insanity' (Walker, 1968: 147). If his suggestion had been adopted, the defence of DR would have been introduced into English Law 70 years earlier than it was.

The landmark case in Scotland arose when Dingwall, an alcoholic who suffered from attacks of delirium tremens, married an older woman who tried to temper his drinking. Things came to a head on New Year's Eve, 1866. After consuming his daily allowance of whisky (a glass before each meal) he went out to drink half a dozen more glasses with neighbours – on Hogmanay, Scottish custom dictates that households offer whisky to whoever presents themselves at the door. He returned with a bottle of whisky, but when his wife hid it, a quarrel followed and he stabbed her. She died several days later. At his trial, Lord Deas instructed the jury:

> The prisoner appeared not only to have been peculiar in his mental constitution, but to have had his mind weakened by successive attacks of disease . . . The state of mind of a prisoner . . . might be an extenuating circumstance, although not such as to warrant an acquittal on the ground of insanity.
>
> (Gordon, 1978: 338)

The jury found Dingwall guilty of culpable homicide and sentenced him to 10 years of penal servitude. By this innovation, Lord Deas had allowed an intermediate verdict for those suffering from mental illness not amounting to insanity. Lord Alness explains:

> Formerly there were only two classes of prisoner – those who were completely responsible and those who were completely irresponsible. Our law has now come to recognize in murder cases a third class who, while they may not merit the description of being insane, are nevertheless in such a condition as to reduce the quality of their act from murder to culpable homicide . . . [T]here must be a state of mind which is bordering on, though not amounting to, insanity; that there must be a mind so affected that responsibility is diminished from full responsibility to partial responsibility – in other words, the prisoner in question must be only partially accountable for his actions. And I think one can see running through the cases . . . that there must be some form of mental disease.
>
> (Gordon, 1978: 392)

The Scots had admitted a distinct insanity test allowing an intermediate verdict and an intermediate sentence. Mental illness could be a partial excuse and constitute a partial insanity defence.

In England Lord Atkin chaired a committee to examine the suitability of the M'Naghten Rules in view of such innovations. The British Medical Association recommended that the Irresistible Impulse Test be added to the Rules. The Atkin Committee favoured this but the Government ignored the recommendation. After World War II, the Royal Commission on Capital Punishment took up the issue again, but its recommendations were ignored. Finally in 1957 the Government introduced DR into English law via the Homicide Act:

> Where a person kills or is party to the killing of another, he shall not be convicted of murder if he was suffering from such abnormality of mind (whether arising from a condition of arrested or retarded development of mind or any inherent causes or induced by disease or injury) as substantially impaired his mental responsibility for his acts or omissions in doing or being party to the killing.
>
> (Walker, 1968: 150)

It is clear from the parentheses that the intention was to restrict the scope of the defence to those suffering from states of mind recognized as diseases by psychiatrists, and to avoid any personal abnormality, like a short temper, from excusing. Dell (1982) argues the defence was introduced as a way of getting around the difficulties of the mandatory murder sentence (life or the death penalty). As Henry Maudsley had said in 1874: 'Abolish capital punishment and the dispute between lawyers and doctors ceases to be of practical importance' (Gunn, 1991: 30).

The notion of 'abnormality of mind' was defined in the trial of Patrick Byrne in 1959. He was a 27-year-old Irish labourer who burst into a girl's room in a Birmingham YMCA hostel, strangled her, sexually assaulting and mutilating her body. At his trial he pleaded DR, calling medical witnesses to testify he was a 'sexual psychopath', supposedly suffering from sexual impulses impossible to resist, and that this was an abnormality of mind under the Act. He was found guilty, appealed, and at the appeal Lord Parker defined abnormality of mind as:

> a state of mind so different from that of ordinary human beings that the reasonable man would term it abnormal. It appears to us to be wide enough to cover the mind's activities in all its aspects, not only the perception of physical

24

acts and matters, and the ability to form a rational judgment as to whether the act was right or wrong, but also the
ability to exercise will-power to control physical acts in
accordance with that rational judgment.

(Walker, 1968: 155)

The courts thereby accepted the admissibility of the Irresistible
Impulse Test (a volitional test). Byrne was found not guilty of
murder because he was judged unable to control his impulses,
but was sentenced to life imprisonment. This made the English
version of DR more liberal than the Scottish, as Lord Cooper
observed in a Scottish case: '[I]t will not suffice in law, for the
purpose of this defence of diminished responsibility merely to
show that an accused person has a very short temper, or is
unusually excitable and lacking in self-control. The world would
be a very convenient place for criminals and a very dangerous
place for other people, if that were the law' (Gordon, 1978: 394).
This ruling prevented Scottish law from excusing offenders on
the basis of 'irresistible impulses'.

Once again, the medical concept of mental illness was differentiated from the legal concepts of abnormality of mind and
mental responsibility – the one does not imply the other. As Lord
Cooper argued, the latter are for the law and not for psychiatrists
to decide:

Whether the accused was at the time of the killing suffering
from 'any abnormality of mind' is a question for the jury.
On this question medical evidence is, no doubt, important,
but the jury are entitled to take into consideration all the
evidence including the acts or statements of the accused
and his demeanour.

(Hamilton, 1990: 208)

Psychiatrists might be best placed to apply medical concepts, but
insanity and DR are matters for the jury.

EXCULPATORY CAUSES

Much of the nineteenth century was spent with lawyers and
psychiatrists speaking different languages and operating with
different concepts (Smith, 1983). Lawyers spoke a 'voluntarist'
discourse, assuming behaviour was voluntary and explicable in

terms of Folk Psychology concepts: intentions, desires, beliefs, and character flaws. On the other hand, psychiatrists spoke a 'determinist' discourse, assuming that the presence of physical illness undermined the voluntariness of everyday action and amounted to insanity. Smith (1983: 10) writes:

> It was normal to accept determinism and voluntarism as mutually exclusive statements of whether a person was or was not free to choose one course of ideas or movements rather than another. Maudsley wrote, 'medicine deals with matter, force, and necessity; law deals with mind, duty, and responsibility'.

Nineteenth-century psychiatrists assumed that if a disease was causally responsible for an action, the person was not responsible. Lawyers agreed with this assumption. Dr Winslow wrote in 1854: 'No mind can properly be considered to be "unsound" or "insane" which is not subject to actual disease, the "insanity" or "unsoundness" being invariably the products – the effects – the consequences, of some deviation from the healthy condition of the brain' (Smith, 1983: 15). In spite of the emerging distinction between a medical and a legal concept of insanity, most psychiatrists argued that the former implied the latter.

Five years after M'Naghten's trial, Isaac Ray published *A Treatise on the Medical Jurisprudence of Insanity* in America. It became the most influential work on forensic psychiatry in the nineteenth century. In it he criticized the English judges for their exclusively cognitive test of insanity which he felt was too narrow a test of criminal responsibility. While he had a point, he too confused medical insanity with legal insanity, claiming that in every hospital for the mentally ill, 'there are patients capable of distinguishing between right and wrong, knowing well enough how to appreciate the nature and legal consequences of their acts, acknowledging the sanctions of religion, and never acting from irresistible impulses, but deliberately and shrewdly. Is all this to be utterly ignored in courts of justice?' (Moore, 1984: 224). Such patients were medically insane, Ray argued, but assumed this meant they were also legally insane.

His book greatly influenced a New Hampshire lawyer, Charles Doe, who later became Associate Justice of the New Hampshire Supreme Court. Disturbed by current American views of insanity (which had adopted the M'Naghten Rules), he came to accept a causal defence: 'If the homicide was offspring or product of mental disease in the defendant he was not guilty by reason of insanity.' In a landmark New Hampshire murder trial in 1869, Doe, now a judge, said:

> [I]f the alleged act of a defendant was the act of a mental disease, it was not, in law, his act, and he is no more responsible for it than if it had been the act of his involuntary intoxication, or of another person using the defendant's hand against his utmost resistance . . . If his mental, moral, and bodily strength are subjugated and pressed to an involuntary service, it is immaterial whether it is done by his disease, or by another man . . . The whole difficulty is that the courts have undertaken to declare that to be a matter of law which is a matter of fact. All tests of mental disease are purely matters of fact, and that if the homicide was the offspring or product of mental disease in the defendant, he was not guilty by reason of insanity.
>
> (Quen, 1981: 18)

Although Doe introduced the idea that being caused by a mental illness was sufficient to excuse, he justified this by a tacit appeal to a volitional test, assuming acts caused by mental illness are involuntary.

It took a hundred years for a similar test to be adopted in another State. In 1954 a case reached the Court of Appeal for the District of Columbia. Monte Durham, who had a history of prior convictions and hospitalizations, appealed against his conviction for house-breaking. Psychiatrists testified that he was a psychopath with a psychosis – he suffered from hallucinations, and thought his fellow employees were spying on him. But, they testified, he could tell right from wrong. The Court of Appeal reversed his conviction, stating that: 'The rule we now hold is simply that an accused is not criminally responsible if his unlawful act was the product of mental disease or defect' (Moore, 1984: 226). In this reversal, Judge Bazelon stated what become known as the Durham Rule – another causal test.

This decision was welcomed by psychiatrists, but almost every state asked to adopt it refused. The ruling collapsed the legal concept into the medical one, excusing a defendant if he had a mental illness causing his behaviour. Because Doe and Ray believed that insanity depended solely on the presence of mental illness, and that deciding this was a scientific matter, they argued that psychiatrists were best placed to judge who should be excused. As Doe argued in an early dissent:

> Insanity . . . is the result of a certain pathological condition of the brain . . . and the tests and symptoms of this disease are no more matters of law than the tests or symptoms of any other disease in animal or vegetable life . . . What is a diseased condition of mind is to be settled by science and not by law.

> (Moore, 1984: 227)

Bazelon later recognized that responsibility was a legal matter for the courts and not a scientific matter for psychiatrists.

With the M'Naghten Rules being too narrow, and the Durham Rule too broad, most American states turned to a new insanity test proposed by the American Law Institute (ALI) in 1962:

> A person is not responsible for criminal conduct if at the time of such conduct as the result of mental disease or defect he lacks substantial capacity either to appreciate the criminality of his conduct or to conform his conduct to the requirements of the law. The terms 'mental disease or defect' do not include an abnormality manifested only by repeated criminal or otherwise antisocial conduct.

> (Moore, 1984: 30)

This ALI test combines a cognitive and volitional test. While it was adopted by many states, the outcry after the Hinckley trial led Congress to pass the Insanity Defense Reform Act of 1984 which reverted to a purely cognitive test for federal jurisdictions. The rationale was centred on the belief that the volitional test was difficult to substantiate while the cognitive one was more objective. After a hundred and fifty years the M'Naghten Rules were back!

There was a significant pragmatic difference, however. With the growth of liberalism, the indefinite detention of mentally ill offenders was declared unconstitutional. It was regarded as unacceptable that a healthy murderer should get 15 years, but a mentally ill killer found NGRI should get life. In America, legislation ensured that someone found NGRI could only be detained insofar as he remained ill and dangerous. If he recovered, he could not be detained. The insanity defence had begun by enabling a defendant to escape the death penalty, but when this had been abolished, it carried a harsher sentence than a guilty verdict. With this liberal legislation, it once again became an advantage to be found NGRI. As Stone (1982: 639) comments:

> For the last two hundred years, the insanity defence was a profound hypocrisy. The courts found defendants not guilty by reason of insanity and then relied on psychiatry to confine them for the rest of their lives. Thus there was no loss of protection to society. But beginning 20 years ago this hypocrisy was confronted. Perhaps for the first time in history, a successful plea of insanity has real bite.

In New York between 1965 and 1975, 31 defendants found NGRI on murder charges were discharged within a year (Appelbaum, 1994).

Matters changed again following the Hinckley verdict, with many States voting to remove the volitional prong from their insanity tests. While this did not affect the acquittal rate, there were some changes instituted that did make a difference. The trend started in the 1960s of adopting similar procedures for the release of insanity acquittees as for civilly committed patients was reversed. New reforms ensured that the State did not relinquish its coercive power over acquittees once released from hospital. Some States were given the power to monitor an acquittee's status, ensure continued treatment, and reconfine if necessary. The nightmare of a prematurely released acquittee committing further acts of violence was largely prevented. For example, Oregon created a Psychiatric Security Review Board (PSRB) to which insanity acquittees were committed for a period that could extend up to the maximum length of time they might have been confined had they been found guilty. The PSRB is empowered to decide when acquittees can be released or reconfined. Bloom and Williams (1994) found that this produced a significant reduction in re-offending. Whatever the effect, the 'real bite' of the insanity defence had now been diminished – if an acquittee is judged dangerous, he is better off being found guilty.

AUTOMATISM

When a person performs purposeful actions without conscious control of his behaviour, this is called an 'automatism'. The defence of automatism was first used in a British court when Simon Fraser was charged with battering his baby son to death in 1878. He claimed he was asleep at the time, dreaming that a wild beast had jumped into his bed. His father and sister both testified he had been prone to sleepwalking since childhood, and that he had once tried to strike his father, strangle his sister, pull his wife from a 'burning house', and rescue his sister from 'drowning' while he had been asleep. At the Lord Justice General's suggestion, the jury concluded that Fraser was unconscious at the time he had killed his son, and that he was not responsible. As part of the DR tradition in Scottish law, Fraser was not convicted of murder but was allowed to go free after giving an undertaking that he would henceforth sleep alone.

In 1955 Charlson, a devoted husband and father, suddenly and inexplicably attacked his 10-year-old son. He called him to the window to ostensibly look at a rat, and then picked up a mallet and struck him on the head, throwing him out of the window. He regained consciousness while driving away in his car, and sensing something dreadful had happened, he returned to be arrested by the police. At his trial, his defence argued that a brain tumour had caused an automatism and that he was not responsible. Summing up, Justice Barry said: 'If he did not know what he was doing, if his actions were purely automatic, and his mind had no control over the movement of his limbs, if he was in the same position as a person in an epileptic fit, then no responsibility rests upon him at all, and the proper verdict is, not guilty' (Fenwick, 1990: 273). Charlson was acquitted because he lacked *mens rea*, but was not found NGRI. Automatism was accepted as an excuse in its own right.

A year later this decision was reversed. Kemp was an elderly man of blameless reputation. One night in 1956 he made a motiveless attack on his wife with a hammer and was charged with causing her grievous bodily harm. In his trial, his counsel argued that he suffered from arteriosclerosis, and that this had interfered with the blood supply to the brain, depriving him temporarily of consciousness. But Lord Devlin, who was presiding, decided that arteriosclerosis was a disease of the mind and hence fell under the M'Naghten Rules:

The broad submission that was made to me on behalf of the accused was that this is a physical disease and not a mental disease ... The distinction between the two categories is quite irrelevant for the purposes of the law, which is not concerned with the origin of the disease, or the cause of it, but simply with the mental condition which has brought about the act ... Hardening of the arteries is a disease which is shown on the evidence to be capable of affecting the mind in such a way as to cause a defect, temporarily or permanently, of its reasoning, understanding and so on, and so is in my judgment a disease of the mind which comes within the meaning of the Rules.

(Fenwick, 1990: 274)

With this ruling, any automatism caused by a disease, mental or physical, became known as an insane automatism and fell under the M'Naghten Rules. If automatic behaviour is not the consequence of a disease of the mind, as in sleepwalking, this is a sane automatism and the defendant is free to walk.

In 1961, George Bratty was charged with killing a girl whom he had taken for a ride in his car. He claimed that he had lost consciousness, and medical evidence at his trial suggested that he might be suffering from psychomotor epilepsy. The trial judge dismissed the plea of automatism, and the case went to Appeal over the question whether the trial judge was right to do so. At Appeal, Lord Denning argued: 'All the doctors agreed that psychomotor epilepsy, if it exists, is a defect of reason due to disease of the mind and the judge accepted this view' (Fenwick, 1990: 274). Denning also discussed Barry's decision that Charlson's epilepsy did not fall under the M'Naghten Rules: 'Any mental disorder which has manifested itself in violence and is prone to recur is a disease of the mind. At any rate, it is the sort of disease for which a person should be detained in hospital rather than being given an unqualified acquittal' (Fenwick, 1990: 274). This was a significant ruling, illustrating how distinct the legal concept of insanity had become from the medical one. Those with arteriosclerosis or epilepsy are not medically insane, but according to this ruling, they are legally insane.

Quick, a diabetic nurse, was charged with assaulting a patient. His defence was that he was hypoglycaemic and suffering from the effects of an overdose of insulin. The trial judge followed Lord Denning's ruling – because Quick suffered from a disease (diabetes) affecting his reason and leading to violence, he was insane! This decision was reversed at Appeal:

> He may have been, at the material time, in a condition of mental disorder manifesting itself in violence. Such manifestations had occurred before and might recur. The difficulty arises as soon as the question is asked, whether he should be detained in a mental hospital. No mental hospital would admit a diabetic merely because he had a low blood sugar reaction ... Applied without qualification of any kind, Devlin J's statement of the law would have some surprising consequences. Take the not uncommon case of the rugby player who gets a kick on the head early in the game and plays on to the end in a state of automatism. If, while he was in that state, he assaulted the referee, it is difficult to envisage any court adjudging that he was not guilty by reason of insanity ... In this case Quick's alleged mental condition, if it ever existed, was not caused by his diabetes but by his use of the insulin prescribed by his doctor. Such malfunctioning of his mind as there was was caused by an external factor and not by a bodily disorder in the nature of a disease which disturbed the working of his mind.
>
> (Fenwick, 1990: 275)

Quick should have had the defence of sane automatism open to him. This restored some sanity to the law, but the whole idea of insane automatism shows how far apart the notions of legal and medical insanity have moved.

INTOXICATION

Intoxication raises interesting problems for the doctrine of *mens rea*: If someone is extremely drunk, he may not know what he is doing, and seems to deserve an excuse. However, being intoxicated to this degree is itself a voluntary act, something for which the person should be culpable, thereby creating the dilemma. There are three approaches the law can take to offences committed while intoxicated (Mitchell, 1988). First, it can excuse the drunken offender if he lacks *mens rea*. Second, it can hold him culpable of the offence because his drunkenness is voluntary. This view contradicts the doctrine of *mens rea*. And third, it can

regard the offender as guilty of a lesser offence – being criminally negligent or reckless, or guilty of a new offence of 'being
drunk and dangerous'. This latter defence is available in German
law: If the defendant did not realize what he was doing because
of drunkenness, he is not acquitted but found guilty for the
crime of putting himself intentionally or negligently into a state
of intoxication. This is what the Butler Committee (Home Office,
1975: 236) recommends: 'If evidence of intoxication were given at
the trial for the purpose of negativing the intention or other
mental element required for the offence, the jury would be
directed that they may return a verdict of not guilty of that
offence but guilty of the offence of dangerous intoxication.' Let
us see how Anglo-American law has handled this.

During the nineteenth century there was a move to allow
partial exculpation of the inebriated offender. In 1838 a drunken
man called Cruse seized a neighbour's child and battered its
head against a beam. When Cruse and his wife were tried for
attempted murder, the judge told the jury:

> Although Drunkenness is no excuse for any crime what-
> ever, yet it is often of very great importance if it is a
> question of intention. A person may be so drunk as to be
> utterly unable to form any intention at all, and yet he may
> be guilty of great violence. If you are not satisfied that the
> prisoners, or either of them, had formed a positive inten-
> tion of murdering this child, you may still find them guilty
> of an assault.
>
> (Walker, 1968: 178)

This is exactly what the jury did. It concluded Cruse was so
drunk that he lacked the *mens rea* for murder, and therefore could
not be found guilty of attempted murder. He was found guilty of
assault, and the doctrine was established that intoxication could
undermine the *mens rea* required for some crimes.

Beard was a night-watchman who drunkenly raped a 13-year-
old girl in his factory in 1920, and in placing his hand over her
mouth to stifle her screams, killed her. Beard had not intended to
kill her – being so drunk he had not understood what he was
doing, and so lacked the *mens rea* for murder. In the House of
Lords, Lord Birkenhead argued that Beard's drunkenness
rendered him incapable of forming the specific intent essential
for the crime of murder. He did not explain what he meant by

'specific', but he used the phrase 'the intent necessary to constitute the crime' interchangeably. He seemed to mean *mens rea*, for
he explained that 'speaking generally (and apart from certain
special offences), a person cannot be convicted of crime unless
the *mens* was *rea*' (Williams, 1983: 471). This left the distinction
between crimes of specific intent and of basic intent unclear until
the next case.

Majewski was involved in a public house brawl in 1976. He
had taken over a hundred Dexedrine ('speed') tablets the
previous day, and on the day in question took eight barbiturate
tablets. Then he went to the pub, got drunk, and was involved in
a brawl causing actual bodily harm. His defence was that he was
under the influence of drink and drugs and did not know what
he was doing. The judge at the trial told the jury that this was
immaterial: Assault was not an offence which required specific
intent, and therefore intoxication was not a defence. Majewski
appealed, but it was held that since assault was a crime of basic
intent, drunkenness provided no defence. No basis was given for
distinguishing crimes of basic intent and specific intent. The
Lord Chancellor rejected the idea that drunken offenders were
like patients acting unconsciously, and should be freed from
fault: 'If a man of his own volition took a substance which
caused him to cast off the restraints of reason and conscience no
wrong was done to him by holding him answerable criminally
for any injury he might do while in that condition' (Kenny, 1978:
65). But the crime of assault requires the offender to *intend* harm
to another person. If intoxication prevents the accused from
forming such intent, he cannot be guilty of assault because he
also lacks *mens rea*. The distinction between basic intent and
specific intent remained arbitrary and unjustified.

The majority of courts have chosen to see drug intoxication as
analogous to alcohol intoxication and hence allow that drugs may
prevent a person from forming the *mens rea* necessary for some
offences. But drug intoxication is different from alcohol intoxication in that hallucinatory drugs can frequently cause delusions
and hallucinations – states that may appropriately be classified as
'temporary insanity'. For example, Lipman killed his bed mate
while on LSD which made him hallucinate that he was fighting
snakes in the centre of the earth. He was found not guilty of
murder but sentenced to six years imprisonment. However, most
courts that have considered the insanity defence in relation to the

drug-intoxicated offender have rejected it because of the element of voluntary intoxication. As one judge ruled:

> His subsequent condition after taking amphetamines for several days, leading to his bizarre actions, was a result of an artificially produced state of mind brought on by his own hand at his own choice. The voluntary actions of the defendant do not provide an excuse in law for his subsequent, irrational conduct.
>
> (Fingarette and Hasse, 1979: 112)

If we adhered strictly to the doctrine of *mens rea*, we would have to accept that those intoxicated and unable to form the intent necessary for a crime, or temporarily insane according to any particular test, should be excused. But the fact that the person voluntarily assumes such a state is regarded as sufficient reason to overrule the doctrine.

In cases where the person unknowingly takes a drug, or does not know the effects of a drug, he does have a defence. In 1985 Hardie took five of his girlfriend's Valium tablets to relieve his depression, and subsequently set fire to her flat. He was charged with arson and reckless endangerment, and his defence was that he was unable to form the necessary *mens rea*. The judge directed that this was not a defence as Hardie had taken the drug voluntarily. The case went to Appeal where the judge ruled that in cases where the effect of the drugs was not known, the defendant is not reckless in taking the drug:

> There was no evidence that it was known to the appellant or even generally known that the taking of valium in the quantity taken would be liable to render a person aggressive or incapable of appreciating risks to others or have other side effects such that its self administration would itself have an element of recklessness.
>
> (Leng, 1990: 248)

As Hardie did not voluntarily assume any risk, he was not found guilty. In this way, involuntary intoxication is like mental illness, and excuses like insanity does (although the disposition is different).

INFANTICIDE

The last execution of a mother for murdering her baby was in 1849. After that the Home Office routinely commuted the crime. But judges still had to pronounce the death penalty knowing full well it would not be carried out. To avoid this hypocrisy, the Capital Punishment Commission (1864–6) was urged by jurists like Stephen to introduce a lesser category of crime: '[W]omen in that condition do get the strongest symptoms of what amounts almost to temporary madness, and ... often hardly know what they are about, and will do things which they have no settled or deliberate intention whatever of doing' (Walker, 1968: 128). The tough-minded judge, Baron Bramwell, was moved to recount:

> A young woman had an illegitimate child a year old: she was very fond of it and behaved well to it ... On a Sunday morning she cut its throat, and rushed out into the street and said that she had done so ... I cannot in my own mind believe that woman was as mad as the law would require her to be ... but it was an act of such a character that the only address to the jury was 'This woman may have had a sudden condition of mind come upon her, in which she really did not know what she was doing.' She was a very decent-looking young woman; everybody in the court wept ... she was acquitted.
>
> (Walker, 1968: 129)

Changes to the law had to wait until 1922 when Henderson, secretary of the Labour Party, introduced a Bill into Parliament allowing the jury to bring in a verdict of manslaughter instead of murder in such cases of infanticide. The Lord Chancellor moved to restrict the scope of the Bill to cases where a woman has 'not fully recovered from the effect of giving birth to such child, and by reason thereof the balance of her mind was disturbed'. This meant that a mother need not satisfy any cognitive or volitional standard, or even the causal test, but still be found not guilty of murder. She need not be ignorant of what she was doing, nor overwhelmed by her impulses, in order to be found not guilty. This opens the way to argue that a different category of excuse is being used – the excuse of character change. If a mother of 'decent' character is made by illness to do something out of character, we are inclined to excuse her on the basis that she was not

36

herself. This is why sympathy is so important in deciding who has an excuse – we are most sympathetic when illness makes a good person do something bad (Chiswick, 1985).

Over the last hundred and fifty years, the concept of legal insanity emerged from the medical concept. Except for a brief chapter when the causal test collapsed the legal concept into the medical, the two have been kept distinct. The medical concept only implies a person is either deluded or is hallucinating, but the legal concept implies the person deserves to be excused. The former is a factual and scientific matter best diagnosed by psychiatrists, and the latter is a moral or evaluative matter best left to the courts. The M'Naghten Rules established a cognitive test that has dominated our consciousness, but diminished responsibility introduced a volitional test and the idea that mental illness may provide a partial excuse. Some defences like the Infanticide Act provided no rationale for the excuse, but instead implicitly relied on the idea that we should excuse those who act out of character, paving the way for a new excuse.

2

A TAXONOMY OF DEFENCES

A PARADOX

Understanding if mental illness excuses helps us understand excuses in general. This sounds paradoxical: unless we first fully understand the notion of excuses, we cannot decide whether insanity is an excuse. But if the concept of excuses is already fully understood, how can understanding whether insanity is an excuse throw any further light on it? The answer is that we do not have to *fully* understand the concept of excuses before we tackle the question of whether insanity excuses. The final meaning of the concept remains open until we have answered this latter question. Take the example of numerical equality: to decide when one class has the same number of members as another, we need to count the members. However, answering the question of whether there are as many even numbers as whole numbers may change the way we think about numerical equality. A more basic way to decide whether two classes are equal in size is to put the members in a one-to-one correspondence: if every member of one class can be related to one (and only one) member of the other class (with no remainder), then the classes are numerically equal. But this can be done for all the even numbers and whole numbers – for any even number, there is a whole number to which it can be placed in one-to-one correspondence with no remainder. Therefore, the two classes are equal in size (both have an infinite number of members)! Having to answer this question requires some prior understanding of numerical equality, but this understanding is not fully settled until we examine this question. Similarly, I hope to show that answering the question of whether insanity is an excuse throws light on the notion of excuses itself.

METHODOLOGICAL MATTERS

To discover whether insanity is an excuse, we start off with excuses, arrive at their essence, and then judge whether insanity has this essence. But how do we select the examples with which we start? If we start off with a liberal group of excuses, we arrive at a liberal account of excuses, and will conclude that insanity is an excuse. If we start off with a conservative group of excuses, we arrive at a conservative account of excuses, and will conclude the opposite. How can we avoid begging the question here? Take Jed and Jess who are arguing whether to excuse someone who finds his spouse in bed with his best friend and murders that person in a fit of jealous rage. Jed thinks we should because he was overwhelmed by emotion, while Jess disagrees because he ought to have controlled his emotions. On the basis of his views, Jed develops a liberal concept of excuse, concluding that 'temporary insanity' excuses. Jess, starting with a different moral point of view, develops a conservative concept of excuse, and concludes that 'temporary insanity' does not excuse. How can we avoid understanding the concept of excuse without building in some moral point of view, and concluding that those who disagree (because they have an alternative moral point of view) do not understand the notion of an excuse?

The same problem applies to deciding what insanity defences are valid. We start with moral intuitions about whom we should excuse. If these suggest that Dahmer is not responsible even though he does not satisfy the M'Naghten Rules, we conclude that the Rules are too narrow. Conversely, if our moral intuitions suggest that Dahmer is responsible, we conclude that the Rules are adequate. It seems that substantive moral issues have to be settled before we can understand whether insanity excuses. But we do not want to say that someone with a different moral view does not understand the concept of excuse. We cannot avoid this problem by starting with uncontroversial cases of excuses because disagreement can arise here too. Even if Jed and Jess agree that someone should be excused for behaviour during a seizure, a radical moralist can argue that someone is responsible for this behaviour because seizures are preventable. He is not being incoherent simply because he takes a different moral point of view. As Glover (1970: 10) remarks: 'One would surely be unimpressed by any attempt to rule out one view or the other by any allegation that the word "excuse" was being misused.' The way out of this dilemma is to make a distinction between the form and the content of the concept.

FORM AND CONTENT

Can anything count as an excuse? Can a conceptual system count voluntary rather than involuntary behaviour as an excuse, and blame people for things that happened to them, rewarding them for things that are out of their control? Butler describes such a world in *Erewhon*:

> [I]f a man falls into ill health, or catches any disorder, he is tried before a jury of his countrymen, and if convicted is held up to public scorn and sentenced more or less severely as the case may be . . . But if a man forges a cheque, or sets his house on fire, or robs with violence from the person, or does any other such things as are criminal in our own country, he is either taken to a hospital and most carefully tended at the public expense, or, if he is in good circumstances, he lets it be known to all his friends that he is suffering from a severe fit of immorality, just as we do when we are ill, and they come to visit him with great solicitude, and inquire with interest how it all came about, what symptoms first showed themselves, and so forth.
>
> (Butler, 1970: 45)

Is this coherent?

There is nothing self-contradictory about being blamed for being ill or being excused for committing a crime. If criminal behaviour is seen as the result of a disorder, which is how it is described in *Erewhon* ('he is suffering from a severe fit of immorality'), it is coherent to excuse it. We already excuse criminal acts caused by seizures. Conversely, if illnesses are seen as things we do to ourselves, it is not incoherent to hold us responsible. We know we are responsible for many illnesses like lung cancer that afflict us because of our bad habits. So the world of *Erewhon* is not incoherent. Does this mean anything can count as an excuse? No. The reason why *Erewhon is* coherent is because Butler has changed the facts. In our world, avoiding illness is not (by and large) in our control, while avoiding criminal behaviour is. A person cannot choose (by a simple act of will) to stop being ill, but he can choose to stop committing a crime. For this reason, we hold someone responsible for criminal behaviour but not illness. *Erewhon* is coherent only because it reverses these facts. We can coherently regard a person as responsible for his illness only if we assume he has some control over it. Conversely, we can coherently excuse someone from his criminal behaviour only if we assume he lacks control over it. Far from painting a dramatically different conceptual system, Butler has not broken the simple rule that governs our concept of excuse: Someone is responsible for something only if it is within his control.

Like us, Erewhonians blame people for things they believe are within their control, and excuse others for things they believe are not within their control. If Erewhonians excused criminal behaviour because it was within their control, and blamed patients for illness that was not in their control, the story *would* be incoherent. Praising and blaming is governed by the principle that praise and blame must be fair, and we cannot be fair if we morally condemn someone for something not within his control. If we argue that praising and blaming must satisfy this constraint, then we can show it is incoherent to praise or blame an agent for behaviour that is not within his control. This means there are logical limits to what can coherently be viewed as an excuse – if something is within the control of the agent, it cannot be an excuse.

There is a second logical feature of the concept: it is relational in that someone is always excused *from* some degree of blame or punishment. Having an excuse implies that a person deserves less moral condemnation or punishment, and it is incoherent to argue that someone has an excuse but is *more* blameworthy or deserves *more* punishment. It is incoherent to suppose that an excuse makes a person *more* evil. These two logical features, together with the one described in the section below, define the concept of excuse independently of moral content. They constitute the logical form of the concept and enable us to speak the same language as someone with a different moral point of view. Disagreement without misunderstanding *is* possible.

JUSTIFICATION VERSUS EXCUSE

Both justifications and excuses are legal defences in that an agent can raise either of them in an attempt to avoid punishment.

Austin (1970: 176) writes: 'In the one defence [justifications], we accept responsibility but deny that it was bad: in the other [excuses], we admit that it was bad but don't accept full, or even any, responsibility.' Justifications show that the action was not evil, and excuses show that the agent doing the harmful act was not evil. Jane kills her neighbour. When she says she did this to prevent him killing others, she provides a justification. Because the harm done is balanced by a greater good, we do not consider the act to be evil. A justification, then, balances the harm done with a greater good, showing that, contrary to appearances, the act was not evil, and so the issue of blame does not arise. If Jane killed him because she thought (erroneously) that he was about to kill others, she gives an excuse. No greater good is cited to balance the harm done. The person offering the excuse concedes that the act was evil, but resists the natural inference that she is an evil person worthy of moral condemnation.

In both justifications and excuses, further information is provided which shows that the person doing the harmful act is not evil. In justifications, the circumstances are more fully described, showing the act is not evil, and in excuses, the person's mental state is more fully described, showing she is not evil. This suggests two tests that will enable us to decide whether a defence is a justification or an excuse. The first I call the *Mental Test*: If the mental state of the defendant is critical in determining whether the defence succeeds, it is an excuse. This is because the judgement as to whether someone is responsible depends on features of his mental state. If citing a feature of the person's mental state reverses the judgement that she is evil, then this feature is an excuse. The second is the *Moral Test*: If the moral circumstances surrounding the offence are critical in determining whether the defence succeeds, it is a justification. Justifications depend on producing beneficial consequences that outweigh the harms. If these moral facts are critical in showing the harmful act was really a good one, these facts provide a justification.

Understanding what justifications are helps us understand excuses: They are both ways we can identify evil men. They both provide rules for showing that harmful acts were not committed by evil men. Evil men cannot be identified from harmful acts alone because some men have excuses, others justifications. By examining excuses and justifications together, we can see that what is central to morality and law is the attempt to identify evil men in order to punish them and protect society from them. It is the concept of an evil man that is able to make sense of the nature of excuses and justifications.

Before we leave this section, I must mention the concept of mitigation. If we use the Mental Test, mitigating factors turn out to be partial excuses: they do not completely exempt the person from blame, but reduce his blameworthiness. As Dershowitz (1994: 10) puts it: 'A mitigating factor does not constitute a legal defence, though it may reduce the degree of legal (and moral) responsibility.' I will treat them as partial excuses. To summarize, something is a (complete) excuse if it is some fact about the person's mental state making the person cease to be evil or blameworthy, and a partial excuse if it is some fact about the person's mental state making the person less evil or blame-worthy than he would have been had he committed the act without that mental state. Something is a justification if it is some fact about the action such that it makes the action right. Partial justifications are facts that make the act less wrong. This feature of excuses (that something is only an excuse if it is a feature of the person's mental state) is the third property defining the logical form of the concept.

ARISTOTELIAN ORIGINS

Alfred North Whitehead once said that the history of Western philosophy was but a footnote to Plato. When it comes to our concept of responsibility, our understanding is a footnote to Aristotle. Although *The Nichomachean Ethics* was written over two thousand years ago, it is surprisingly modern, enlightening, and commonsensical. Central to Aristotle's notion of responsibility is his idea of voluntary action: 'It is only to [voluntary actions] that we assign praise or blame . . . Actions are commonly regarded as involuntary when they are performed (a) under compulsion, (b) as the result of ignorance' (Aristotle, 1955: 77).

Aristotle's view of compulsion is ambiguous – at one place, he seems to be talking about automatism, at another duress. 'An act is done under compulsion when it originates in some external cause of such a nature that the agent or person subject to the compulsion contributes nothing to it' (Aristotle, 1955: 77). This seems to describe automatism – when an agent kicks someone in the middle of a seizure, he 'contributes nothing to it'. The cause of his behaviour is not external in that it originates outside his body, but is external in the sense that it originates 'outside' his agency (his will). Such cases might include cases of emotional arousal when the person loses control of his behaviour. Since the behaviour is not within the agent's control, it is involuntary in Aristotle's sense. When discussing cases of duress like the man blackmailed by a tyrant who threatens his family, Aristotle is unsure whether such actions are involuntary. They seem

> more like voluntary than involuntary ones; because at the time that they are performed they are matters of choice . . . [I]n cases like the above the agent acts voluntarily; because the movement of the limbs that are the instruments of action has its origin in the agent himself, and where this is so it is in his power either to act or not. Therefore such actions are voluntary; but considered absolutely they are presumably involuntary, because nobody would choose to do anything of this sort in itself.
>
> (Aristotle, 1955: 77–8)

Aristotle admits the behaviour is voluntary and the agent is responsible, but believes such individuals should not be blamed.

What sounds foreign to our ears is identifying an action performed under ignorance as involuntary. If I swallow rat poison thinking it is medicine, my action is voluntary in that it is unlike a reflex action. But Aristotle makes this identification because he sees a voluntary action as implying that the person has the ability and opportunity to do otherwise. If I am ignorant that the medicine is in fact rat poison, I lack the opportunity to avoid it. I need to know what I am doing to have this opportunity. Voluntary actions are those I choose to perform. When I take rat poison because I think it is my medicine, I cannot be said to choose to take it.

> Virtue lies in our power, and similarly so does vice; because where it is in our power to act, it is also in our power not to act . . . [W]ickedness is voluntary. Otherwise we must dispute what we have just been saying, and assert that man is *not* the originator or begetter of his own actions as he is of his children. But if it is manifestly true that he *is*, and we cannot refer our actions to any other sources than those that

44

are in ourselves, then the actions whose sources are in us are themselves in our power, i.e. voluntary. This view seems to be supported by the practice ... of the legislators themselves; for they impose punishments upon malefactors (except where the offence is committed under duress or in unavoidable ignorance), and bestow honours on those who do fine actions; which implies that their object is to encourage the latter and restrain the former. But nobody is encouraged to do an act which is neither in our power nor voluntary; it is assumed that there is no point in our being persuaded not to get hot or feel pain or hunger or anything else of that sort, because we shall feel them just the same.

(Aristotle, 1955: 90)

If voluntary actions are those 'in our power' to avoid, we can understand why he sees ignorance and compulsion as undermining voluntariness.

This interpretation is supported by his view that where the agent has the power to remove his ignorance, his action is not involuntary:

Indeed they punish the offender for his very ignorance, if he is thought to be responsible for it. E.g. penalties are doubled for committing an offence in a state of drunkenness, because the source of the action lay in the agent himself: he was capable of not getting drunk, and his drunkenness was the cause of his ignorance. They also punish ignorance of any point of law that ought to be known and is not difficult to ascertain. Similarly too in all other cases where the offenders' ignorance is considered to be due to negligence, on the ground that it was in their power not to be ignorant, because they were capable of taking care.

(Aristotle, 1955: 90)

The notion of control is central to Aristotle's notion of responsibility. Interestingly, Aristotle holds an agent responsible for his character. He sees character as the collection of habitual responses. He thinks that while fully formed characters are unable to do other than they do, because acquiring different habits is originally in our power, we are responsible for our characters and our later actions. If we choose to develop bad habits,

45

our characters degenerate to the point that we are unable to act rightly.

> It does not follow that he can stop being unjust, and be just if he wants to – no more than a sick man can become healthy, even though (it may be) his sickness is voluntary, being the result of incontinent living and disobeying his doctors. There was a time when it was open to him not to be ill; but when he had once thrown away his chance, it was gone; just as when one has let go of a stone, it is too late to get it back – but the agent was responsible for throwing it, because the origin of the action was in himself. So too it was at first open to the unjust and licentious persons not to become such and therefore they are voluntarily what they are; but now that they have become what they are, it is no longer open to them not to be such.
>
> (Aristotle, 1955: 92)

Once our characters are formed, we are not free to do otherwise, but we are still responsible because we were in control of our character formation.

In summary, Aristotle identifies the two central excuses of ignorance and compulsion. Compulsion occurs when an agent's actions are not within the control of his will, as in automatism or loss of control, and ignorance occurs when he is not aware he is doing wrong. He also sees duress as a defence, but is unsure whether this is an excuse because the agent is responsible for his actions.

THE DEFENCES

Ignorance

Ngok Keir heard a noise outside his house in Sudan and assumed it was a marauding monkey. He went outside and threw his fish spear at the noise. Unfortunately, it had come from a village woman cutting durra heads on her husband's field. The spear pierced her chest and she died. The court declared there was no murder: 'The evidence shows that monkeys do frequent the durra cultivation in that locality, and that the spearing of such animals is not illegal, and that, when the accused threw his spear at the deceased, he assumed she was a marauding monkey, and did not know that she was a human being' (Katz, 1987: 165). Is Keir's ignorance an excuse or a justification? The Moral Test shows that there is nothing that offsets the evil done. On the other hand, the Mental Test shows that a feature of Keir's mental state (ignorance) undermines the judgement that he is an evil man. This means that ignorance is an excuse that shields him from the moral condemnation reserved for murderers. In a similar case, Abdullah Nur was out searching for a missing cow when he saw a figure walking towards him dressed in black. He had been warned a ghost was about, and when he got no answer from the figure, he became convinced it was a ghost and clubbed the man to death. The court found that

> the accused had grounds for believing that he was dealing with a ghost. After the fright his behaviour was so simple that he went to the village and proudly broke the news of his victory. From this we infer that the accused acted in good faith and in the honest belief that he killed the ghost without any intention of killing a human being ... Accordingly, we are satisfied that the act of the accused is not an offence and he should be set at liberty.
>
> (Katz, 1987: 168)

Ignorance can be a complete or a partial excuse. If Jill shoots an intruder mistakenly believing he plans to kill her, she has a complete excuse. This is because her ignorance shows her to be a good person – it is not evil to defend yourself against such an attack. If Jack shoots an intruder erroneously believing the man plans to box his ears, he only has a partial excuse. This is because his ignorance shows he is not such a good person – killing to prevent such an attack is not a good thing to do. Jack does not have a complete excuse, but he has a partial excuse because he is still less evil and deserves less punishment than a cold-blooded murderer.

Self-defence and defence-of-others

Pam is attacked by a serial killer while walking home, and defends herself, killing her assailant. She pleads self-defence. Is this a justification or an excuse? Harming a person appears wrong, but using the Moral Test here, there is something that offsets the harm done. Preventing rape and murder offsets the death of the aggressor, so that the act is no longer wrong. If it was an excuse, we would be conceding that the act was an evil thing to have done, and that she was not responsible for what she did. Neither is true.

Acting in defence of self (or another innocent person) is a defence. But not all acts of self-defence qualify. If Pam's assailant had only threatened to tickle her, killing him would not be justified. One is only entitled to use a degree of force that is warranted. Jane may dislike being tickled – to her it may be a form of torture. But however much she dislikes it, she is not justified in killing to avoid it. This is known as the *Proportionality Rule*:

> The proportionality rule is based on the view that there are some insults and hurts that one must suffer rather than use extreme force, if the choice is between suffering the hurt and using the extreme force. The rule involves a community standard of reasonableness, and is left to the consideration of the jury.
>
> (Williams, 1983: 506)

This rule fits in with the Moral Test – if the harm avoided does not outweigh the harm committed, there is no justification. Some might argue that tickling a person against her wishes *is* a greater harm than the death of someone prepared to violate another's rights in this way. If that is the person's moral point of view, he will argue that killing in 'self-defence' here *is* justified. This further illustrates that self-defence is a justification: whether it succeeds depends on whether the act is seen as wrong, and since this depends on a person's moral point of view, we expect some disagreement about when an act is justified. Notice too that self-defence can be a partial rather than a complete justification. If I kill someone who only plans to beat me up, I have only a partial justification, but I still deserve less punishment than a cold-blooded killer.

If Pam could have called out loudly and alerted a nearby policeman, she would not have been justified in killing her assailant. She is entitled to use a proportional amount of force only if it is the only way she can avoid the assault. This is the *Necessity Rule*. The English Court of Appeal has ruled: 'It is not, as we understand it, the law that a person threatened must take to his heels and run in the dramatic way suggested by counsel for the appellant; but what is necessary is that he should demonstrate by his actions that he does not want to fight. He must demonstrate that he is prepared to temporize and disengage and perhaps to make some physical withdrawal' (Williams, 1983: 505). If a person can avoid death by retreating, he can no longer justify his assailant's death by self-defence.

Is it necessary to wait until the attack actually happens before a person is entitled to use the plea of self-defence? If Jen is away with her husband in a remote cottage, without help, with no opportunity to escape, but possessed with the certain knowledge that her husband is planning to kill her that evening, she would be entitled to a pre-emptive strike. Why is this, since she can hardly claim to be defending herself against a (present) attack? The answer is that she is defending herself against a future attack, and that the only way she is able to do this is to strike pre-emptively when he is not on his guard. The Necessity Rule is satisfied here, and her act of self-defence is justified.

Is the honest belief that one's life is in danger a defence, or must that belief be reasonable? Shannon, a man with no history of aggression, was attacked by a man with previous convictions for violence. The man had made threats against Shannon for 'grassing' on him. Shannon defended himself with a pair of scissors, inflicting a fatal blow. Did the defendant use more force than was necessary in the circumstances? The case went to Appeal, where the conviction was quashed by this dictum from Lord Morris:

> A person defending himself cannot weigh to a nicety the exact measure of his necessary defensive action. If a jury thought that in a moment of unexpected anguish a person attacked had only done what he honestly and instinctively thought was necessary that would be the most potent evidence that only reasonable defensive action had been taken.
>
> (Williams, 1983: 506)

To have a defence, it is not necessary that the belief that one's life is in danger be reasonable – it need only be honest. But when the belief is unreasonable, the plea of self-defence cannot be a justification – there is no evil avoided to offset the harm done. Instead, Shannon has an excuse – his honest belief is a feature of his mental state that allows us to show that he is not an evil person in spite of the fact that he did something evil. While self-defence is a justification, in some cases where the defence succeeds, it is really an excuse!

Provocation

Sam is goaded by a group of white youths with racial taunts till he loses his self-control and strikes one of them in a fit of anger, killing him. When charged with murder, he pleads provocation. Is this a justification or a defence? The Moral Test tells us that if it was a justification, then killing the youth would not be wrong, and avoiding further humiliation is a benefit outweighing the harm done the youth. But while we might think that the youth deserved to be taught a lesson, we do not think he deserved to die – such retaliation was not justified. The Mental Test tells us that provocation is an excuse. What Sam did was evil and not justified, but he is not responsible because he lost control. We do not think of him as evil (unlike the cold-blooded killer).

Duffy killed her husband with a hatchet while he was in bed after being brutalized by him for years. Lord Goddard argued:

> Provocation is some act, or series of acts, done by the dead man to the accused which would cause in any reasonable person, and actually causes in the accused, a sudden and temporary loss of self-control, rendering the accused so subject to passion as to make him or her for the moment not master of his mind ... Circumstances which induce a desire for revenge are inconsistent with provocation, since the conscious formulation of a desire for revenge means that a person has had time to think, to reflect, and that would negate a sudden, temporary loss of self-control which is of the essence of provocation.
>
> (Williams, 1983: 529)

In British courts a jury must answer two questions: (1) Did the defendant as the result of provocation lose his self-control? (2) Was the provocation enough to make a reasonable man lose self-control? To be excused, a defendant must not only lose control. It must also be true that a reasonable person would also have lost control. This makes the law unfair – if someone has less ability than the reasonable person to resist the law, he will not have an excuse.

The defence of provocation is the ordinary man's insanity

defence – it allows someone *not* suffering from a mental illness to plead 'temporary insanity'. Instead of saying a mental illness undermined his ability to resist his impulses, he argues that emotion undermined it. If losing self-control is an excuse in the one situation, it will be difficult to resist the conclusion that it excuses in the other.

Necessity

Pete sees a man having a heart attack. Realizing the man needs a hospital, he breaks into the nearby house to call for an ambulance and the man is saved. When he is charged with breaking and entering, he pleads necessity – breaking the law was necessary to save the man's life. Is this a justification or an excuse? If it were an excuse, we would be conceding that he was wrong to have acted that way, and that he was not responsible for what he did. However, neither is true. The Moral Test shows that necessity is a justification – the greater good arising from breaking the law outweighs the harm done, and this shows that Pete was not an evil person.

> The solution is found not by considering the mental state of the agent, but by considering the objective situation, and deciding whether the objective action in this situation is to be regarded as something wrong at all. The agent is regarded as having a free choice, and his duty is to choose the lesser of the two evils before him, and so to preserve the greater value. There may be opposing values involved and the agent must then make a rough calculation and choose that course of action which preserves the greater value – the standard and measure of value being taken as that employed by the person to whom the agent is accountable. The question is not 'Was the agent responsible for what he did?' but 'Was what he did wrong?'.
>
> (Gordon, 1978: 417)

The Model Penal Code, an illustrative penal code on which most states in America draw in drafting their criminal statutes, puts it thus: 'Conduct that the actor believes to be necessary to avoid a harm or evil to himself or to another is justifiable, provided that the harm or evil sought to be avoided by such conduct is greater than that sought to be prevented by the law defining the offence charged' (Katz, 1987: 35). For example, Samuel Jackson kept his seriously ill daughter away from school before getting permission from the school board. The court ruled: 'A parent cannot be required to imperil the life of his child by delays incident to an application to the school board, before he can lawfully do what is apparently reasonably necessary for its protection' (Katz, 1987: 12).

While necessity is a defence in Anglo-American law, English law does not allow necessity as a defence for murder. In 1884 Dudley and Stephens were sailing the *Mignonette* to Sydney with another sailor and a 17-year-old cabin boy when the ship hit bad weather and was sunk by a large wave. The crew managed to get into a lifeboat with virtually no provisions. On the nineteenth day, a thousand miles from land, with no food and water for twenty days and near death, Dudley proposed that one of them, to be chosen by lots, be killed for the rest to feed on. The other sailor would hear none of it and the idea was temporarily abandoned. On the twentieth day, Dudley talked to Stephens about killing the cabin boy. He was the weakest of the four, seemed close to death, and had no wife or children. Finally Stephens agreed and Dudley stabbed the boy in the neck, killing him. The remaining three fed on him. Four days later they were rescued by a passing vessel in a state of prostration. The two men were charged with murder, but pleaded necessity as a defence. The jury refused to convict them, declaring 'whether the prisoners were and are guilty of murder, the jury are ignorant, and refer to the Court'. The court decided it was murder, but they were only given a six-month prison sentence.

On the other side of the Atlantic, necessity was accepted as a defence for murder. Holmes was charged with murder after the *William Brown* was wrecked. One lifeboat was overloaded, and Holmes put sixteen men overboard, letting them drown. The defence of necessity which he pleaded was not rejected out of hand – the court accepted the principle but held that the choice of victims should have been settled by lottery. As Williams (1983: 605) remarks:

> The decision in *United States v Holmes* does recognize that, in extreme emergency, and subject to reasonable conditions, a deliberate killing can be justified by the necessity of saving lives. If the choice is between doing nothing, when the whole boat will founder, and throwing out half the

people, with the chance of saving the rest, it is useless for the law to continue its usual prohibition of murder.

The judge, James Baldwin, acknowledged to the jury that necessity was like self-defence, and that 'the law overlooks the taking of life under circumstances of imperious necessity'. Holmes was convicted of manslaughter and sentenced only to six months in prison and a $20 fine.

Even when the defence of necessity fails, the person committing the offence does not deserve the same condemnation as those committing similar offences without 'necessity'. Dudley and Stephens do not deserve the same punishment and condemnation as a man who kills for money. How do we explain this? A failed defence of necessity may offer a partial justification for the action. Dudley and Stephens had some justification for their action – if they hadn't killed the cabin boy, they would all have died. Necessity does not completely justify the act here to the point that it makes it right, but it partially justifies it in that the act was not as evil as cold-blooded murder. Because there is some justification for the action, those committing it are not worthy of extreme condemnation. Therefore, we feel inclined to punish them less, which is exactly what happened. How much we feel inclined to condemn them will depend on the completeness of the justification. A person stealing a car to avoid a freezing walk home and possible frostbite has less justification than a person stealing a car to rush his sick wife to hospital. But the former has some justification in that we are inclined to condemn him less than a person stealing the car simply to sell it for personal advantage.

However, such situations of necessity also provide partial excuses. Kant's (1959) drowning swimmer ousts another man from the only plank in the sea. He does not have any justification. Ousting the man on the plank does not produce any greater benefit – either way, one person will drown. But when doing the right thing requires a person to be extremely heroic, we are not inclined to condemn him for not doing it. When the right thing to do requires extreme heroism, the person failing to do it cannot be described as evil (although he did the wrong thing), and therefore cannot be condemned. In these dire circumstances, it is difficult to resist doing what is wrong. Using the Mental Test, we can conclude that the swimmer was in a mental state such that he is less blameworthy than a cold-blooded killer. So we should partially excuse him. Similarly, we can argue that Dudley and Stephens had partial excuses – their dire circumstances put them in a mental state making it difficult for them to resist what was wrong. Their resultant mental states provide them with a partial excuse, because it is in virtue of them that they are to be condemned less.

Duress

In 1975 Lynch was charged as an accomplice in the killing of a Belfast constable. Meehan, a notoriously ruthless member of the IRA called on Lynch and ordered him to accompany IRA gunmen on a 'car theft'. Lynch drove them to a garage where the IRA shot the policeman. Lynch's defence was that he was forced to do it as the lives of his family and his life were threatened. He was convicted in the lower courts but the case went to Appeal. Lord Kilbrandon argued against acquittal: 'He has decided to do a wrong thing, having balanced in his mind, perhaps unconsciously, the consequences to himself of refusal against the consequences to another of acquiescence' (Gordon, 1978: 430). Lord Salmon warned:

> I spoke of the social evils which might be attendant on the recognition of a general defence of duress. Would it not enable a gang leader of notorious violence to confer on his organization by terrorism immunity from the criminal law? Every member of his gang might well be able to say with truth, 'It was as much as my life was worth to disobey'. In my respectful submission your Lordships should hesitate long lest you may be inscribing a charter for terrorist gang leaders and kidnappers.
>
> (Gordon, 1978: 432)

But Lord Morris argued persuasively:

> [I]t is proper that any rational system of law should take fully into account the standards of honest and reasonable men . . . In the calm of the court-room measures of fortitude or of heroic behaviour are surely not to be demanded when they could not in moments for decision reasonably have been expected even of the resolute and the well-disposed.

The law must, I think, take a common sense view. If someone is forced at gun-point either to be inactive or to do something positive – must the law not remember that the instinct and perhaps the duty of self-preservation is powerful and natural? I think it must. A man who is attacked is allowed within reason to take necessary steps to defend himself. The law would be censorious and inhumane which did not recognise the appalling plight of a person who perhaps suddenly finds his life in jeopardy unless he submits and obeys.

(Gordon, 1978: 431)

The House of Lords allowed the acquittal by a majority of three to two, establishing the rule that duress can be a defence to murder where the accused was not the actual killer.

Is duress a justification or an excuse? If it was an excuse, we would be saying that the act was wrong and that he was not responsible for what he did. Neither is true. The Moral Test tells us that because a greater evil was averted, it was not wrong to submit to the terrorists, and therefore duress is a justification. As Gordon (1978: 417) comments:

Coercion where the choice is forced on the agent by someone whose interests are not involved in the value calculation is essentially the same as necessity occasioned by natural events. When a man has, for example, to choose between his own life and that of others, the situation is governed by the same principles whether it is the result of a natural disaster such as a shipwreck caused by storm, or of the coercive action of a human being.

We can see that duress is a justification by changing the moral facts. If Lynch had been coerced to rob a bank on the pain of his whole village being killed, the defence succeeds more easily because the evil done here is clearly outweighed by the evil avoided. On the other hand, if the terrorists had threatened to throw mud on his newly shined car, duress would not succeed.

In 1976 Malik threatened to kill Abbott's mother unless Abbott helped kill a woman living in their commune. He ordered Abbott to dig a grave and throw her in. Once in the hole, Abbott held her while another of Malik's men stabbed her. When charged with murder, Abbott claimed duress. The court agonized. While the case was like Lynch, Lynch had not actually helped to kill the policeman. Speaking for the majority, Lord Salmon argued:

> In the trials of those responsible for wartime atrocities such as mass killings of men, women or children ... it was invariably argued for the defence that these atrocities should be excused on the ground that they resulted from superior orders and duress: if the accused had refused to do these dreadful things, they would have been shot and therefore they should be acquitted and allowed to go free. This argument has always been universally rejected. Their Lordships would be sorry indeed to see it accepted by the common law of England.
>
> (Gordon, 1978: 432)

He went on to argue an acquittal would provide a charter for people to do whatever terrorists coerced them into, concluding: 'Is there any limit to the number of people you may kill to save your own life and that of your family?'

Duress is like necessity. It makes no difference if a person is put into an awful dilemma by another person or by nature. John's family are crossing the railway and a runaway truck is hurtling towards them. He has a choice of sending the truck towards an empty house, destroying private property, or leaving it to kill his family. James is captured by a criminal wanting to destroy a house as part of an insurance scam. He is told that if he does not divert a truck towards the house, his family will be killed. Both divert a truck. John acts under necessity, James under duress. Is there any moral difference between them? They both have to make difficult choices. They both choose to destroy private property to save their families. In both cases they choose the lesser evil. The only difference is that nature creates the dilemma for John, and the criminal creates it for James.

It may seem that a person coerced to do something does not choose to do it, and if he does not choose it, he acts involuntarily, and hence has an excuse rather than a justification. This is not correct. Someone who is coerced is not deprived of choice. He is only given a difficult choice:

> We may feel inclined to excuse on the ground that the agent had, in the circumstances, no real choice. But although this

is a colloquially natural way of speaking, it would be more accurate to say that he did have a choice but to spell out what that choice was – for example, between doing what some tyrant demanded and having his relatives safe, and defying the tyrant and having them tortured or killed. Though his being confined to just these alternatives was not voluntary, the agent's choosing one of these complex alternatives rather than the other was wholly voluntary and intentional. And to hold him responsible for his intentional act, adequately described, is appropriate and has no undesirable implications. Instead of taking duress or necessity as negating responsibility because it deprives the agent of any real choice, we should see each of these as helping to determine the precise act for which he is responsible, as adding justifying circumstances to the description of what he intentionally did.

(Mackie, 1977: 182)

On the other hand, if someone is coerced, and is so overwhelmed by fear that he cannot resist doing what he is ordered, then he *will* act 'involuntarily'. In this situation, he will have an excuse, but not because his act is justified, but because he has lost control and is not responsible for his action (Schopp, 1991).

Someone who acts under duress but whose action is not justified is less blameworthy than someone doing the same thing without coercion. How do we explain this? As before, we accept that there can be a partial justification. The more the harm threatened exceeds the harm done, the more the act is justified, and the less blameworthy the defendant. The fact that the blameworthiness of the defendant varies with the moral circumstances shows once more that the defence is a justification. As the majority said in Abbot:

> Any murderer who kills under duress would be less, in many cases far less, blameworthy than another who has killed of his own freewill. [O]n a charge of murder, duress, like provocation, should not entitle the accused to a clean acquittal but should reduce murder to manslaughter and thus give the court power to pass whatever sentence might be appropriate.
>
> (Gordon, 1978: 440)

If I assist in a murder because I am threatened with bodily harm, I have less justification than if I am threatened with death. But I still deserve less punishment than a cold-blooded killer.

Someone who acts under duress but whose action is not justified also has a partial excuse. If only a hero would have done the right thing, then we exempt someone from punishment for doing the wrong thing. When it is unreasonable to expect anyone to have done otherwise, the inference from the wrong deed to the evil nature of the agent breaks down. If a man's family is threatened if he does not help some terrorist to plant a bomb, he is not justified in killing other people. But if only a hero would have done otherwise, he is not an evil man. The circumstances do not provide a complete justification – the act is still wrong. If the same number of people are threatened as the number of people killed, there can be no justification for the action. But the dire circumstances make it difficult for the ordinary person to resist doing the wrong thing. He is in a mental state that makes us condemn him less. Therefore he has a partial excuse.

Involuntary intoxication

Will is slipped a Mickey Finn. He becomes intoxicated, and thinking someone is trying to attack him, defends himself, killing an innocent person. When charged with murder, he pleads involuntary intoxication. Is this an excuse or a justification? He is not saying that it was a good thing to have done, so the Moral Test does not apply. Rather, he is saying that he should not be seen as evil because he was intoxicated and did not know what he was doing. Some feature of his mental state makes him less evil, making it an excuse. Note that Will might also have argued that the drink (or drugs) had weakened his self-control so that he lost control of his actions. This too would be an excuse. As Justice Martin (1981: 23) remarks: 'Automatism produced by *involuntary* intoxication is a complete "defence".'

While involuntary intoxication is an excuse, most legal systems do not admit voluntary intoxication as a defence. It is easy to see why: Someone who takes a drink knowing it will make him liable to commit a crime (because it makes him less aware and more disinhibited) knowingly takes a risk that he will offend. He is like a man who takes a dangerous weapon into a park and shoots it into the bushes around him, knowing there might be someone there but not bothering to check. He knowingly takes a risk that someone will be injured and would be guilty of murder (in English law) if he killed someone. So too with voluntary intoxication. But the law does allow intoxication to count as a partial excuse. Beard was only convicted of assault when he murdered a girl unintentionally while raping her in a state of drunkenness. If a person did not know what he was doing when he was drunk, he seems less blameworthy than a cold-blooded killer.

What if the person who takes a drink is an alcoholic and cannot stop himself getting drunk? Is his drunkenness not involuntary? He did not voluntarily assume any risk of harming others, and should not be held culpable. Those like Jellinek (1960) who argue that alcoholism is a disease argue that it causes a craving for alcohol the alcoholic cannot resist. If this is correct, the voluntary intoxication of alcoholics is actually 'involuntary' in that the alcoholic cannot help it, and would constitute a complete defence. We will discuss whether this view of alcoholism is correct in Chapter 10.

Automatism

Kemp made a motiveless and irrational attack on his wife in a state of unconsciousness. When he claimed automatism as a defence, was he offering a justification or an excuse? The Moral Test tells us it is not a justification – he is not appealing to some greater benefit produced by the act that shows it was not wrong. Instead, he appeals to his mental state, arguing he was not responsible for what happened and should not be judged an evil man. The Mental Test confirms he is offering an excuse.

Spike knows he drives his car when he sleepwalks. But not caring whether he hurts anyone, he takes no precautions to prevent driving while asleep. As a result, he runs over and kills his neighbour. Here we are inclined to think that he does not have an excuse. As with voluntary intoxication, his knowledge of what happens when he is sleepwalking and his ability to prevent this makes him responsible for what happens. Because we think of him as evil as the person who recklessly shoots his gun into the bushes without checking whether there is anyone there, and kills someone, we do not excuse him.

TAXONOMIES

There are many different taxonomies for actions not deserving blame. Aristotle (1955) cites ignorance and compulsion, where the latter includes automatism, loss of control, and duress. Hart (1968) enumerates acting accidentally, inadvertently, in ignorance, in self-defence, under provocation, under duress, and during madness as reasons not to blame someone. Glover (1970) mentions three sorts of excuses: if the behaviour was not an action, if it was an unintentional act, and if it was an excusable intentional act (which includes justifications such as necessity and excuses such as provocation and insanity). Robinson (1984) lists four socially accepted types of excusing conditions: where the conduct was involuntary, where the person acted in ignorance of the facts, where he acted in ignorance of the law, and where he lost control. While we do not need another taxonomy, for what it is worth, I divide defences into Justifications (which includes self-defence and defence of others, necessity, and duress) and Excuses (which include automatism, involuntary intoxication, insanity, ignorance, and loss of self-control – which I will call 'Compulsion'). I also accept that there can be partial justifications and partial excuses (as in some cases of necessity and duress).

Something is an excuse if it is some fact about the person's mental state making the person cease to be evil or blameworthy. Something is a justification if it is some fact about the moral circumstances of the act that shows that the act is not wrong. Ignorance and compulsion (loss of self-control) are the principal excuses in that we will show that other excuses like automatism excuse because of either ignorance or loss of self-control. Our central question is whether insanity is an excuse distinct from these two.

3

IGNORANCE AS AN EXCUSE

LEGAL EXCUSES AND MORAL EXCUSES

We must distinguish between excuses from moral blame and excuses from legal punishment. This book addresses the question of why mental illness counts as excusing someone from moral blame and why it *ought* to excuse from legal punishment. I will call these two different excuses moral and legal excuses. Let me illustrate the distinction. In 1975 Morgan invited three friends home to have sex with his wife. He told them to expect some show of resistance but that this was his wife's way of enhancing her sexual enjoyment and so they were to ignore it! They went home and forcibly overcame her genuine resistence believing she was consenting. The men were convicted of rape because the judge ruled that their mistaken belief that she was consenting was not based on reasonable grounds and so did not excuse them. However, the case went to Appeal and the House of Lords rejected this argument by a 3:2 majority, holding that someone who has sex in the honest (though unreasonable) belief that a woman is consenting is not guilty of rape. In the eyes of British law, having an honest belief that a woman is consenting is an excuse even if that belief is unreasonable. But from the moral point of view, their ignorance does not excuse them from moral condemnation because they did not take sufficient care to discover whether she was indeed consenting. Ignorance counts as a legal excuse here but not a moral excuse – they were exempted from punishment but not moral condemnation (Duff, 1990).

The converse obtains too. In the eyes of the law, having sex with a minor is an offence even if the accused is not aware she is a minor. In Canadian law, sexual assault on a girl under 14 is

61

committed by a man 'whether or not he believes that she is four-teen years of age or more' (Dickens, 1986: 42). This is a crime of strict liability. These crimes, like selling contaminated food, are an exception to the doctrine of *mens rea* – the person is guilty if he simply performs the bad act, and *mens rea* is not required for guilt. These are cases where the person is not permitted to make the legal excuse of ignorance because reference to any mental state is irrelevant to establish that the crime was committed. However, a person may have a legitimate moral excuse in these cases. Suppose a girl looks mature, is at university, and produces a birth certificate indicating she is 18. A man who has sex with her has every reason to believe she is not a minor, and has a moral excuse exempting him from moral condemnation even though he has no legal excuse. Ignorance is not a legal excuse here but is a moral excuse.

DEGREES OF EVIL

Something is an excuse if it is some fact about the person's mental state such that it makes him less evil or blameworthy. Fred kills his mother by giving her cyanide, thinking it is peni-cillin, for her pneumonia. His ignorance counts as an excuse because it is a fact about his mental state that makes him less evil or blameworthy. It shows that he does not have the evil character suggested by the act of killing somebody. This implies that evil comes in degrees, and that we can make sense of this notion independently of the notion of excuses. I will first define an evil character in terms of his evil will, and then show how this admits of degrees.

An evil person cannot be identified by his acts alone because he may have an excuse or a justification. In order to identify him from his acts, he must have the intention to commit unjustifiable harm (a wrong). We identify evil characters by their evil wills. This idea is encapsulated in the law in the notion of *mens rea*:

> Mens rea, or dole [the Scottish equivalent], in our criminal law is the wicked and felonious intention which impels the criminal to commit a crime. It is a state of mind which results in a criminal act, and I fail to see how there can be a distinc-tion between the wickedness resulting in murder, and the wickedness resulting in an attempt to murder. Hume, in

his book on Crimes, describes dole as 'that corrupt and evil intention, which is essential (so the light of nature teaches, and so all authorities have said) to the guilt of any crime'.

(Gordon, 1978: 213)

We identify an evil character by the evil he intends. Horai and Bartek (1978) confirmed this by studying what influences our attribution of blameworthiness, showing that intended harm influenced whether people saw others as evil.

Doing evil deeds is not necessary for being an evil character either. Someone might be a wimpish evil person – he may wish harm on others, this being his only pleasure, but he may never act on his desires for fear of being punished. As Benn (1992: 192) argues:

[S]omeone who was fully conscious and rational but also completely paralyzed and aphasic, who spent his life hating everyone about him, rejoicing in their misfortune, wishing them ill, and reveling in malignant fantasies, would be a wicked person who did no wrong at all. Indispensable, however, to the notion of a wicked person is a cognitive capacity, or at the least a capacity to envisage states of affairs in the imagination, conjoined with a set of attitudes towards such states of affairs.

Or someone might be an incompetent evil person – he may wish harm on others and take steps to harm them, but be too stupid or weak to get the job done. Or someone might be an unlucky evil person – he may have the intelligence and the strength to carry out his evil deeds, but his best-laid plans come to grief. What makes someone evil is his evil will – his preparedness to harm others without justification.

An evil character is someone who does not care sufficiently about others and is therefore willing to embark on unjustified actions that harm them. We need the clause 'sufficiently' here because someone may choose in an emergency to save his own neck rather than risk it to save someone else. If he cared more about others, he would rescue others. However, because we judge such heroism is not necessary for someone to qualify as a good person, we do not judge those who care less than our hero as evil. We set a particular standard for caring that defines what it is to be a good person. When a man saves his own skin rather than attempt a heroic rescue, this degree of 'indifference' to others does not mean he is evil. Only when he falls below our standard will he be evil. This definition also does not imply that anyone who has an evil thought is evil. We all wish to harm others at one time or another. But there is a difference between a simple wish to do something and a willingness to do it. The first is idle, and is entertained with the knowledge one will not act on it. The other is a true engagement with the prospect of doing harm, and this qualitative difference marks off the evil person from the daydreamer.

Obviously, there are evil characters and evil characters. The serial killer does not care sufficiently about the others (his victims), killing them in the pursuit of his own gratification. The shoplifter also does not care sufficiently about the needs of others (the shop owners), stealing from them in the pursuit of his own advantage. We tell how evil a person is by the sorts of harms he intends – the greater the harm intended, the more evil he is. A person prepared to kill another without justification cares less about others than someone only prepared to unjustifiably wound another person, and he less than someone only prepared to steal money without justification. Evil characters, like many other things, come in degrees.

When we compare a cold-blooded killer like Rick, who poisons his mother to inherit the family fortune, and Fred, who killed his mother by accident, we judge Rick is more evil than Fred even though both do the same amount of harm. We cannot explain this by saying Fred has an excuse because we wish to understand the notion of an excuse in terms of degrees of evil. Because Fred does not intend to harm his mother, he is not an evil character – he did not intend to do evil – and therefore deserves to be excused. The feature of his mental state that explains why he is not an evil character – ignorance – is therefore an excuse. Excuses, then, are mental features that show a person not to be evil, and not being evil is a matter of not being predisposed to intend to do unjustifiable harm to others.

IGNORANCE OF THE FACTS

Ignorance of the facts provides a person with a moral excuse. But do all instances of ignorance count as excuses? Dick wishes to kill his mother to inherit the family fortune. He thinks that cutting the gas pipes in the house will lead to dangerous carbon monoxide fumes infiltrating the house and poisoning her. However, unbeknown to him, there is no carbon monoxide in the gas mains. But when his mother switches on the light, a spark ignites the gas and the explosion kills her. Does Dick's ignorance provide him with an excuse?

The *If-only Rule* states: Ignorance is an excuse if the person would have abstained from his action had he not been ignorant. Had Fred known that the bottle of penicillin contained cyanide, he would have abstained from the action while Dick would have gone ahead knowing he would achieve the result in another way. However, this will not help in this case: Mario is considering mugging an old lady and stealing her purse. He figures that the odds on getting caught are low if he mugs her in the alley. But, unbeknown to him, the police have stepped up their surveillance of the alley and Mario is caught. Mario mugged the old lady only because he believed that there was a low chance of being caught. But he was mistaken. Had he not been ignorant, he would not have mugged her. But this sort of ignorance does not excuse Mario even though it satisfies the If-only Rule.

The *As-if Rule* states: Ignorance is an excuse if in the event that the belief is true, the person does not perform an evil deed. The As-if Rule asks us to assume that Fred was not ignorant and that the bottle contained penicillin. Then it asks whether the deed was wrong. Since the answer is no, he has an excuse. This rule neatly explains our intuitions about the second case. We do not believe Dick has an excuse because if he had not been ignorant – had the gas contained carbon monoxide – Dick would have done an evil deed. The As-if Rule correctly predicts that we should not excuse him. However, the principle will not do as it stands. Suppose Fred gives his mother cyanide thinking it is penicillin. Unbeknown to him, his mother is allergic to penicillin and would have died had it been penicillin. We have to amend the rule: Someone is excused on the basis of ignorance if, in the event that *all* his beliefs about the action are true, he does not perform an evil deed. It is because Fred also thinks that the penicillin will do her good that he gives her the tablets (containing cyanide). If he believed that his mother also had an allergy to penicillin, and wanted her dead (in order to inherit her fortune), we would not consider his ignorance exculpating. This is explained by the modified As-if Rule.

Ignorance can be a partial and a complete excuse. Steve wants to scare off his neighbour so he can buy his house. He gives him a scare, but unbeknown to Steve his neighbour has a weak heart and dies. Should we excuse Steve? He did not foresee the neighbour's death, and so cannot be blamed for this. But we still think he should not be completely excused – while he cares more than a cold-blooded killer, he did not care whether his neighbour became miserable. Therefore, he deserves *some* moral condemnation and we should not completely excuse him. His ignorance counts as a partial excuse (because it makes him less blameworthy than a cold-blooded killer) but not a complete excuse.

The As-if Rule is necessary for ignorance to count as an excuse, but not sufficient. Harry is a physician. He gives one of his patients penicillin not enquiring about allergies. Had he asked, he would have discovered the patient is allergic to penicillin. The patient dies. Harry believed she had no allergies, and thus the As-if Rule tells us to excuse him – supposing his belief to be true, he does not do an evil thing. However, he ought to have known better. He has a duty to meet certain standards of care – a duty to enquire about allergies. Ignorance is only a complete excuse if it also satisfies the *Duty Rule*: Ignorance is an excuse only if there is no duty to be free of that ignorance. Similarly, Ted finds a gun. He thinks it is unloaded and shoots it at his friend. Unfortunately it is loaded and his friend is killed. The As-if Rule tells us that Ted's ignorance counts as an excuse. But Ted ought to have taken reasonable steps to discover whether the gun was loaded – we all have this duty when handling deadly weapons. His ignorance does not satisfy the Duty Rule and does not excuse.

Nevertheless, negligent killing is less blameworthy than intentional killing. Dick is more evil than Harry and Ted and therefore deserves more moral condemnation. In most legal systems, this moral distinction is reflected in a distinction between murder and manslaughter. While Harry's (and Ted's) ignorance is not a complete excuse, it is a partial excuse – they are not worthy of the moral condemnation deserved by a cold-blooded killer. Similarly for reckless murder. James tries out his shotgun by shooting it in the woods where he knows children play. He does not know that there are two children behind the bushes and unintentionally kills them. Should we excuse him? The As-if Rule suggests we should not. Belief is not an all-or-none affair – he believed there was (say) a 50 per cent chance he would kill the children, but still went ahead. Because it is wrong to take such risks, the As-if Rule tells us that he is blameworthy, but not as blameworthy as a person taking a 100 per cent chance of killing someone.

To show why Harry has some excuse but not a complete excuse, we need to grade the evil of premeditated murder, reckless homicide, negligent homicide and accidental death. In premeditated murder, the person cares so little about others in the pursuit of his own desires that he is prepared to take 100 per cent chance that another person will die. In reckless homicide, the person cares more, but is still prepared to take a 50 per cent chance that someone will die. In negligent homicide, the person cares more, but still little enough to take reasonable steps to eliminate (say) a 5 per cent risk that a person will die. In accidental death, the person cares about others to the extent that he tries to reduce the chance of killing another person to 0 per cent, but in spite of this another person still dies. If we rank how little each of these people care about others – their willingness to unjustifiably harm others – the murderer cares the least and the accidental killer the most. By assessing the degrees of evil independently of excuses, we can use it to analyse the concept of excuses. (This same logic can be used to create a category of negligent rape. Morgan's friends have a partial excuse – by not taking sufficient care to ascertain consent, they took (say) a 50 per cent risk of rape compared to the cold-blooded rapist who takes a 100 per cent risk.)

There is a caveat here. The person who, in a fit of anger, intends to kill someone without adequate justification is less evil than a person who displays utter indifference to others, not caring whether he kills anyone in the pursuit of his own ends. This is in spite of the fact that the one takes a 100 per cent chance that another will die, and the other only a 50 per cent chance that others will die. Why is this? There appear to be two reasons. First, the person utterly indifferent to others takes a 50 per cent chance that many people will die, so that in effect he takes virtually a 100 per cent chance that many will die (over time), making him more evil than the man who kills in a fit of anger. And second, the man who kills in a fit of anger is not someone who does not care about others. He does care about others, but has lost control of his behaviour. His loss of control blocks the inference from his intention to harm another person to his being an evil character. Another way of looking at this sort of case is that his anger supplants his normal caring attitudes, but more of this later. Either way, we judge the person has an excuse because we judge he is not an evil character.

A surgeon often takes a 10 per cent risk that his patient will die, but is not evil. How does he differ from James who sprays the woods with his shot gun? The difference does not lie in a difference in intentions, as neither intends to do anyone any harm, or both intend to do something with a 10 per cent chance of harm. The difference lies in how much they care about others – in their willingness to harm others without justification. The surgeon takes the risk of killing the patient because if he does not act, there is a 50 per cent chance the patient will die anyway. It is not so much that he cares so little but that he cares so much. This is not true of the reckless killer. He takes the risk because he cares so little. (There is of course another important difference between the reckless killer and the surgeon whose patient dies on the operating table. In the case of the surgeon, it is the patient who agrees to and takes the risk.)

Ernie is dim-witted and gullable. He is told a man against a wall is a dummy, and when he is encouraged to shoot at it, he kills a man. Is Ernie's ignorance an excuse? It fails to satisfy the Duty Rule in that he did not take reasonable steps to ascertain the figure was not a man. But we feel inclined to excuse Ernie because he lacked the ability to think critically. It is only if we think someone is able to take reasonable steps to remove his ignorance that we take him to be responsible. Annie is distraught because she has lost her 2-year-old son. When she sees a man walking out of the store with a child, she assumes her son is being kidnapped and assaults an innocent man walking out with his son. Because she fails in her duty to take reasonable steps to discover the man was not a kidnapper, she lacks an excuse. But in her state of emotional distress, she was unable to think clearly and remove her ignorance. Both Ernie and Annie have an excuse according to the *Disability Rule*: If a person is not able to remove his ignorance, then even if the ignorance does not satisfy the Duty Rule, he has an excuse.

Are these three rules necessary and sufficient for ignorance to be a complete excuse? Gus gets drunk, mistakes a real knife for a theatrical knife, and stabs and kills a drinking companion. According to the Disability Rule, he has an excuse – in his drunken state, he was not able to discover whether the knife was real. However, unlike Ernie, we think Gus is responsible for his disability. He voluntarily put himself into a state where he had an impaired ability to take reasonable steps to remove ignorance. Thus we do not think that Gus has a complete excuse. Such men are blameworthy because 'it is in their power not to be ignorant' (Aristotle, 1955: 90). Of course, if Gus had not been responsible for his ignorance – if he had been slipped a Mickey Finn, we would excuse him because he satisfies the *Responsibility Rule*: If a person is not responsible for his inability to remove his ignorance, he has an excuse.

We now face a vicious circle. In order to understand what an excuse is, we need to understand what it is to be responsible. But being responsible for some action means not having an excuse. Ignorance is an excuse if one is not responsible for one's inability to reverse that ignorance, and one is not responsible for one's inability to reverse ignorance if one has an excuse for that inability. If we wish to avoid this circle, we are launched on an infinite regress. Whenever we find an inability leading to ignorance, to discover whether it is an excuse, we need to see whether the person is responsible for the inability. To see this, we need to see whether ignorance led to that inability. Then the question arises once again whether the person was responsible for that ignorance. And so on *ad infinitum*. But the regress is not infinite, and ends in one of a number of ways. Gus's inability to remove his ignorance (because of his drunkenness) is the result of an action – getting drunk. Because ignorance did not lead to it, he lacks an excuse. Suppose he was ignorant (because he was slipped a Mickey Finn). Is he responsible for this? Being slipped a Mickey Finn was not something he did, and therefore the issue of his responsibility here does not arise. One can only be responsible for an action. Therefore he has an excuse. The regress is far from malignant and the analysis is not threatened.

IGNORANCE OF THE LAW

Does ignorance of the law count as a moral excuse? Ron goes to the Middle East mistakenly believing that raping women is not

69

against the law there. He rapes someone and is charged. In his defence he pleads ignorance of the law. Is this an excuse? It does not excuse him from moral condemnation because, using the As-if Rule, even if it was the case that raping women is not against the law, he would still have done an evil thing deserving of our moral condemnation. On the other hand, ignorance of the law might constitute a moral excuse where we do not believe that act is an evil thing to have done. In Canada it is not illegal to have anal intercourse with another consenting adult, while it is in Britain. If a Canadian mistakenly thinks it is not illegal, and has anal intercourse with a consenting adult in Britain, he has a moral excuse because we do not consider anal intercourse between consenting adults to be an evil thing.

Ignorance of the law does not constitute a legal excuse for criminal offences either. This is because every citizen has a duty to know the law. Whenever there is a duty to know, and someone fails to meet that duty, their ignorance is not exculpating. In Scotland, Clark was charged with killing a sheep and pleaded that he thought it was his legal right to kill the sheep because it was trespassing on his land. The Lord Justice-General said: 'The accused in this case acted deliberately. He knew what he was doing. The mere fact that his criminal act was performed under a misconception of what legal remedies he might otherwise have had does not make it any the less criminal' (Gordon, 1978: 334). However, ignorance of the civil law can be a defence in offences requiring *mens rea*. As Williams (1983: 457) argues:

> On a charge of bigamy, the defendant will not be heard to say that he did not know that bigamy was a crime, but it will be a defence that he (mistakenly but reasonably) thought that his first marriage was dissolved by divorce at the time of the bigamous ceremony, when as a matter of civil law the supposed divorce was invalid because it was pronounced by a court not having jurisdiction. The law of divorce is not part of the criminal code, so a mistake as to it can be a defence.

However, a person has a stronger duty to know the criminal code than the civil code because most of the criminal code is underpinned by our moral code, which we are all expected to know. If a person comes from a culture where it is not illegal for a husband to beat his wife, but beats her, his ignorance does not count as a legal excuse. We expect him to know that such things are morally wrong. Where an offence violates our moral code, we are not inclined to see ignorance as a legal excuse. This is why ignorance of the law is not an excuse in criminal offences. This is also why the proposal for a 'Cultural Defence' in Canada has been appropriately condemned. According to this defence, someone might have a legal excuse for a criminal offence if such behaviour is not morally condemned by his culture. But because the law is there to protect us from what we judge as immoral behaviour, this cannot be allowed as a legal excuse.

MORAL IGNORANCE

Does moral ignorance count as an excuse? To answer this, we need to differentiate ignorance of the facts from ignorance of morality. Paedophiles argue that it is not evil to have sexual intercourse with children. They claim that sex with children does not cause such harms as depression. We think they are ignorant. This seems to be a factual disagreement. If we have good evidence that sex with children *does* cause depression, we can conclude that paedophiles are ignorant of the facts. But suppose we only have evidence that sex with children leads to their becoming paedophiles. The paedophile would use this to support his view that sex with children is a good thing while we do not. This is not a factual disagreement, but a disagreement over values. Should we conclude the paedophile is morally ignorant? Can we differentiate moral ignorance from moral disagreement?

If all cases of moral disagreement qualify as cases of moral ignorance, and moral ignorance counts as an excuse, then anyone who does something wrong because he does not share our values has an excuse! Aristotle differentiated ignorance of the facts from moral ignorance:

As a matter of fact, every bad man is ignorant of what he ought to do and refrain from doing, and it is just this sort of fault that makes people unjust and generally bad. An act is not properly called involuntary if the agent is ignorant of his own advantage; for what makes an act involuntary is not ignorance in the choice (this is a cause of wickedness), nor ignorance of the universal (for this people are blamed), but *particular* ignorance, i.e. of the circumstances and objects of the action; for it is on these that pity and pardon depend, because a man who acts in ignorance of any such detail is an involuntary agent.

(Aristotle, 1955: 78)

If we do not differentiate between moral disagreement and moral ignorance, somebody who kills Jews because he thinks that the purity of his race is more important than the lives of Jews has an excuse. But this is absurd. It makes the existence of an evil person impossible.

The whole notion of moral ignorance would only work if there were incontrovertible moral facts. But many do not accept there are such facts, and those who do disagree over what these moral facts are. Unfortunately there is no agreed upon method of establishing the existence of such moral facts. The only time we can say uncontroversially that someone is morally ignorant is when that person makes a mistake he himself can acknowledge. Moral ignorance occurs when someone is wrong in his own lights. For example, Jane is wondering whether to have an abortion. She accepts Thomson's (1986) argument justifying abortion. Thomson gives the example of someone waking up to discover he is being used as a dialysis machine for a patient with renal failure. He has the choice of unplugging himself and killing the patient, or enduring nine months of being disabled by the dialysis. Thomson concludes that since he has a right to stop the dialysis, so does a pregnant woman have the right to terminate her pregnancy. Jane assumes rights are inviolable, and concludes she is entitled to an abortion, which she has. She then realizes that rights are not inviolable. Her right not to have her car stolen can be overridden in an emergency if greater values (like human life) are at stake. Jane recognizes that her right not to be inconvenienced for nine months is overridden by the greater value of human life, and recognizes she made a mistake in her moral reasoning. She concludes it was wrong to have an abortion. If we judge abortion is wrong, we would find her less blameworthy because she was suffering from moral ignorance. She is basically a good person who has respect for living beings, but who was temporarily confused about what she believes is right, and therefore is not deserving of punishment.

Is there any difference in blameworthiness between someone doing evil out of conscience and someone cynically doing evil knowing it is wrong? Paul Hill killed an obstetrician in Pensacola in 1994 who was performing abortions because he wanted to protect unborn babies from being 'murdered'. He believed that what he was doing was right and that the act was one of justified defence of others. Is Hill less evil than Dahmer who knew that what he was doing was wrong? Hill seems less evil because he has some justification (but not a complete one). We agree that potential human beings have value, but we disagree that this justifies killing an abortionist. The more justification someone has (in our terms), even though we think he has done something wrong, the less we think we should blame him. But this is not because he has the excuse of moral ignorance, but because he has some justification. Eleanor kills her demented mother. She argues that a demented existence is a miserable one and not worth enduring. We might think she is wrong to do this because she has no consent, but Eleanor feels her mother is incapable of consenting, and would have consented had she been able. If we conclude Eleanor is wrong to have killed her mother, we feel she has more of a justification for what she does than Hill had – helping her mother avoid a miserable and meaningless life partly justifies her action, and justifies it more than Hill's action is justified by the avoidance of the death to the foetuses. When a Nazi justifies his mass murder by arguments of racial purity, because we think this offers no justification, we think he is in exactly the same situation as the cynical evil-doer. If we judge that the person acting on conscience has diminished blameworthiness in comparison to the cynical evil-doer, this arises from partial justification rather than moral ignorance. Moral ignorance *per se* does not excuse.

Complete excuses are psychological features that show a person is not evil, and partial excuses are psychological features that show a person to be less evil than a person doing the same act without those features. Not being evil, or being less evil, is a matter of not being predisposed to intend unjustifiable harm to others, or being predisposed to intend less unjustifiable harm to others. If a person is ignorant that he is doing something harmful, and is not the sort of person who wants to do others harm, if he does something bad we excuse him because of his ignorance. Ignorance excuses a person from moral responsibility by showing that he was not the evil person he seemed when he committed the offence, and that he does not deserve punishment. Ignorance excuses because it shows us the person committing the harmful deed was himself not evil.

4

COMPULSION AS AN EXCUSE

UNJUST LAWS

Self-control is necessary for responsibility. If a person is not in control of his actions, he could not have done otherwise (had he wanted to). If he could not have done otherwise, he is not responsible. This is the Principle of Alternative Possibilities (PAP): a person should not be held responsible unless he could have done otherwise (Schopp, 1991). According to this, if a person is overwhelmed by a powerful emotion and loses control of his behaviour, he should not be blamed for his actions. This is the excuse of compulsion (loss of control) – he has an excuse because he cannot do otherwise. If genetic engineers gave us the ability to remain in control of our powerful emotions and impulses, there would be no such excuse as compulsion. But there is another reason why we are not inclined to blame or punish those who lose control.

When we are in control of our actions, our actions will reflect our characters. Conversely, when we lose control, our actions do not reflect our characters. If we have no respect for other people's rights to property, we will steal. However, if we have respect for private property, but find ourselves destitute, starving and desperate for something to eat, we may have difficulty controlling our impulses to steal some food. The fact that we steal in these circumstances (when we lose control) does not accurately reflect our underlying characters. I might care for others and not be an abusive or violent man, but when I discover my wife in bed with another man, I may lose control and assault them both. This behaviour is not an accurate reflection of the fact that I am a gentle and caring person. For this reason, losing control provides a person with an excuse. When we learn that someone has lost control, it defeats the normal inference from harmful behaviour to evil character. Because we cannot assume that the person is a bad character deserving of punishment, we excuse him. This is the excuse of character change, and we will examine it later.

The circumstances that allow us to excuse someone on the basis of his losing control are all 'abnormal'. This is because it is true by definition that a person's character will reveal itself in normal circumstances. These are circumstances when he is not over-whelmed by extreme emotion, stress, or temptation, but instead experiences a normal range of feelings and temptations. A person is regarded as strong-willed when he resists an ordinary range of temptations. We do not conclude he is weak-willed when he fails to resist the most powerful of temptations. A person's character is revealed by his reactions to normal circumstances. Of course, many characteristics such as courage, cowardice, self-restraint, calmness, and so on, can only be revealed in such circumstances as danger, temptation, and stress. But even here, we consider someone brave when he faces a range of dangerous situations. But it would be a mistake to consider him a coward if he runs away in the face of the most terrible danger. Even here, we classify some circumstances as 'abnormal'. When the circumstances are abnormal, we cease to be confident that the person's behaviour reflects his character, and this is especially true in circumstances where the person loses control. Similarly, we describe someone as strong-willed if he is able to resist acting on a range of tempta-tions. But if he succumbs to the most irresistible of temptations, he does not cease to be strong-willed.

But losing control does not always provide a legal excuse. If a person makes a reasonable effort to restrain his actions, but finds he is overwhelmed, he has a moral excuse. It is not losing control that makes someone blameless – it is his not wanting to give in to his impulses, his exercising every effort to restrain his actions, and only then losing control, that excuses. The law, however, may not excuse someone who loses self-control even after he has exercised a reasonable effort to restrain himself. It sets a 'reasonable man' standard such that anyone who fails to meet this standard is not excused. A person is only excused if he loses control in a situation where a reasonable man would have lost control.

The law is mercifully flexible about this standard, making it relative to the individual. Camplin was a 15-year-old boy who had been forcibly sodomized and taunted by a middle-aged homosexual. He responded by assaulting the older man with a pan, killing him. Charged with murder, Camplin raised provocation. The judge directed the jury to ignore Camplin's age and apply the standard of a reasonable adult. On Appeal, Lord Diplock clarified 'that the reasonable man is a person having the power of self-control to be expected of an ordinary person of the sex and age of the accused, but in other respects sharing such of the accused's characteristics as they think would affect the gravity of the provocation to him' (Hamilton, 1990: 212). The 'characteristics' are taken to mean enduring traits such as physical or mental handicap but not bad temper:

> [T]he characteristic must be something definite and of sufficient significance to make the offender a different person from the ordinary run of mankind and also of a sufficient degree of permanence to warrant its being regarded as something constituting part of the individual's character or personality. A disposition to be unduly suspicious or to lose one's temper readily will not suffice, nor will a temporary or transitory state of mind such as a mood of depression, excitability or irascibility.
>
> (Hamilton, 1990: 212)

This was designed to make the law more just. It is significant that evil character traits are not allowed as excuses, which is what we would expect if the whole notion of excuses was designed to identify evil characters. If the act of retaliation *does* reflect the person's bad character, then we are not inclined to excuse him, as this account entails.

But the reference to any reasonable standard makes the law unjust. If a certain amount of provocation would cause a reasonable man to lose self-control, then anything less does not entitle a person to be excused. Anyone with less self-control than the reasonable man would be punished for losing control. But why should those who happen to have less self-control than the reasonable man standard be penalized here? As Gordon (1978: 783) puts it:

> Instead of being used as a way of testing the truth of the accused's statement that he lost self-control, the reasonable

man has been turned into an objective standard of self-control. Even if the jury believe that the accused, in fact, lost control to an extreme degree, and that he killed because of this, they must convict him of murder unless they think that the reasonable man would have lost control to that degree, a result which, it is submitted, is clearly unjust.

The man who is less cool-headed than the standard will be unfairly punished.

The law sets this standard because it wishes to deter bad-tempered men from indulging themselves and using bad temper as an excuse. But Gordon (1978: 783) objects that there are other ways to avoid this:

The principle of deterrence is sufficiently satisfied, it is submitted, by asking if the accused made reasonable efforts to control himself. He would have to satisfy the jury that he did not just 'fly off the handle' and indulge his temper because that was the easiest way of reacting to the situation: he would have to show that he was provoked beyond his endurance. It seems unfair to ask. that he should go further and show that he was provoked beyond the endurance of a reasonable man.

If this standard makes the law unjust, why does the law set it? The law has a choice between setting a subjective standard or an objective one. A subjective standard allows any person to say that he should be excused because he lacked the ability to restrain his impulses. An objective standard, on the other hand, sets a level of restraint expected of everyone. The danger of a subjective standard is that it is tempting for criminals to do whatever they want but claim that they lacked self-control. The danger of an objective standard is that someone who is less able than the standard will be unfairly punished. The law has to choose between putting society at risk by adopting the subjective standard or convicting the occasional innocent man by using the objective standard.

This applies to any reasonable man standard. Choosing a standard of a reasonable belief creates a demand that others take care in discovering the facts (as in whether a woman is consenting to intercourse), but may convict the occasional innocent man (who is less able to discover such things). However, some courts take individual traits into account. Nelson, a 60-year-old man from Ohio who was not robust mentally or physically, shot a neighbour with whom he was quarrelling over damage to property when the neighbour approached him with a hammer. The court ruled:

> The conduct of any individual is to be measured by that individual's equipment mentally and physically. He may act in self-defence, not only when a reasonable person would so act, but when one with the particular qualities that the individual himself has would do so. A nervous, timid, easily frightened individual is not measured by the same standard that a stronger, calmer, and braver man might be.
>
> (Goldstein, 1967: 205)

The more individual characteristics that are taken into account, the more the 'objective standard' of the reasonable man ('objective' in the sense of being independent of the individual's abilities) approaches the subjective standard (dependent on individual's abilities). As Goldstein (1967: 205) comments, 'the "reasonable man" has often been endowed with so many of the defendant's characteristics as to make this standard almost indistinguishable from a completely subjective one'.

These arguments apply not only to being overwhelmed by anger (as in provocation) but also to being overwhelmed by fear (as in some cases of duress). If a person threatened by torture if he does not help rob a bank becomes so fearful that he cannot control his actions, he should be excused. As Tam (1990: 68) puts it: '[I]n some cases a person who is faced with a deadly threat or some grave danger may in some sense be said to "lose control over himself".' Note again the presence of a standard here. If a person is less able than the reasonable man to withstand anxiety, he will lose control of his behaviour in situations where the reasonable man will not. And therefore the law will not excuse him. Once again the law becomes unjust in pursuit of encouraging people to withstand terror.

If having a moral excuse depends on exercising whatever power of restraint a person has but failing to control himself, then it is irrelevant whether he has fallen below some standard. If the law says that a person only has a legal excuse if he loses control in a situation where a reasonable man would have lost control, then the law is unjust. It penalizes those who make every effort to control their actions but who are less able to restrain themselves than a reasonable man. The law has decided to tolerate this injustice because it hopes to encourage everyone to exercise as much restraint as they can.

CAPACITY FOR RESTRAINT

Someone has a moral excuse if he made every effort to restrain himself but failed – if his capacity for restraint was over-whelmed. But how do we decide when someone lacks the ability to restrain himself? How do we differentiate between someone who chooses not to restrain himself and someone who is unable to? Let us start with the concept of ability in general. Here failure to do something does not imply incapacity, as Glover (1970: 65) notes:

> The fact that a man failed in his attempt to climb the mountain is not by itself sufficient to establish that he could not do so. One needs the assumption that he still wanted to, and consequently, that he was trying to, and that his failure was not attributable to lack of will. Granted this assumption, and only granted this, and given that the normal background conditions presupposed are not suddenly changed, it does indeed follow from the fact that the performance was in fact a failure that the power was at that moment lacking.

We should adopt a naturalistic reading of the concept of ability. We talk of things and persons as having abilities, and there is no reason to think the concepts are different. Wood can burn and glass can break, and this is true even if they are not currently burning or breaking. We have a simple way of determining the truth of such claims. If a substance is raised to a particular temperature and does not burn, it is not inflammable. If a substance is subjected to stress and does not fracture, it is not brittle. Similarly for human abilities. When we say that Linford Christie has the ability to run 100 meters under 10 seconds, we imply that if he is placed in certain circumstances, he will achieve the feat more often than not – if he is provided with the opportunity and adequate incentive, he will usually run under 10 seconds. We can only conclude someone is unable to do something if he is given the opportunity and adequate incentives, and fails (more often than not). Michael Jordan has the ability to score from free throws even though he does so less than 100 per cent of the time. On the other hand, I lack this ability even though I get lucky and score in 10 per cent of throws.

Our task is to decide the circumstances in which a failure to behave differently represents a person's incapacity to restrain himself. This requires us to know the circumstances that will induce a desire sufficient to lead to successful restraint. Consider Matt who has been provoked into assaulting his tormentor. Can he restrain himself? He may not want to stop himself at the time he commits the offence, but this does not tell us whether he is able to restrain himself. Let us change the circumstances, introducing his friend who bets him £1,000 he will not restrain himself. Matt wants to win the bet, but in spite of his wanting to restrain himself for this reason, he fails to do so. Does this mean he cannot? What if we changed the circumstances by introducing the proverbial policeman at his elbow? Matt wants even more to avoid going to jail, and this time he successfully restrains himself. Does this mean he is able to control himself?

How do we decide which circumstances test whether Matt has the ability to restrain himself? We decide this by reminding ourselves of the *purpose* our concept of ability is designed to serve. Take the example of athletic ability again. Linford Christie is able to run 100 metres in under 10 seconds. Even though he is not at this moment achieving this feat, if we change his circumstances providing him with the opportunity and sufficient incentive, he will do it. On the other hand, I am not able to achieve this feat because if given the same conditions and incentives, I could not do it. However, there are circumstances and incentives where I *would* achieve the feat. If the conditions include a gale-force wind, and the incentives include a threat to the life of my family, I may achieve the feat (much like the parent who lifts a car off her child in an emergency). But the fact that I run 100 metres in under 10 seconds in such extraordinary circumstances in no way shows that I have this capacity. We are not interested in knowing whether I can achieve this feat with such 'assistance', but only if I am able to do it in 'normal' circumstances. Similarly, we conclude Ben Johnson is unable to run the 100 metres in 9.79 seconds because he only did this in extraordinary circumstances (with drugs). If someone achieves a feat in non-standard circumstances, we do not take this as evidence of their having the ability. Similarly for physical objects, natural and artifactual. It would be misleading to say that a Volkswagen Beetle is able to reach 300 mph. But if we replaced the engine with a racing car's engine, and tested the car on a steep incline, then no doubt it would reach that speed. But this would not convey the information we want. We want to know whether the Beetle will reach 300 m.p.h. in ordinary circumstances. Similarly, it is misleading to say that metal is brittle. But if we super-cooled it, it would be brittle. When we ask for a metal's properties, we are asking whether it manifests a particular disposition in *standard circumstances*.

The purpose of the concept of restraint is to allow us to make a moral distinction between the cold-blooded killer and the man acting under provocation, between the professional thief and the kleptomaniac. What the former possess that the latter lack is the ability to be influenced by factors that constitute a reason to act otherwise. If the latter agents are presented with a reason to act otherwise, and they choose to act on them, they do not change their behaviour. Thus for the concept of our ability to do otherwise, standard circumstances are those that constitute reasons to do otherwise. Exactly what reasons we allow as standard depends on our moral point of view. We can be strict and say that a policeman hanging a noose in front of a person is a standard circumstance, and if this makes a person inhibit his impulse most of the time, he has the ability to restrain himself. This would enable us to judge that Dahmer had the capacity of restraint because he was able to control his beastly activities when interrupted by the police. Note that this is not an 'objective test' because it does not use a 'reasonable man' standard. If Dahmer had less ability to restrain himself than the reasonable man, he would not be found responsible on this test. If a person is unable to restrain himself, this holds irrespective of whether a reasonable man can or cannot.

This position has the awkward consequence that those provoked may turn out to possess the capacity to restrain themselves (because they would have behaved differently had a policeman appeared). Should we then hold such defendants responsible for their actions and blame them? On the other hand, if we are less strict and narrow the range of circumstances counting as standard, only allowing weak incentives, this will mean that those suffering from weakness of will have excuses. The fact that the person judges that he has sufficient reason not to act in a certain way does not mean that if he acts he has been unable to do otherwise. It only means he is irrational. Suppose I find myself wanting another slice of cake. Can I restrain myself? We introduce a weak incentive – we point out that my health will be adversely affected. I realize this, and want overall to preserve my health, but I choose to indulge myself and have the slice anyway. It would be absurd to say that I was overwhelmed by my desire for the cake, and am not responsible for my actions. But this is a consequence of only allowing weak incentives to count as standard circumstances. We really want to know whether I would have stopped myself having the slice knowing it contained arsenic. If I fail here, then I truly lack restraint. If we set standard circumstances too narrowly, it turns out we are not responsible for ordinary actions. We need to distinguish those who suffer from compulsion from those who are irrational. On the other hand, if we set standard circumstances too broadly, it turns out that most people who are provoked are responsible for their actions.

WHOSE INCENTIVES?

To decide whether a person has the ability to do X, we create the opportunity and desire to do X by varying his circumstances within a range of standard possibilities, and if he does X as a result, he has the ability to do X. The same applies to the ability to do otherwise. We need not assume that having the ability to do otherwise implies that determinism is false. Even within determinism, we make a distinction between the thief who can do otherwise and the kleptomaniac who cannot. As Nowell-Smith (1954: 60) puts it: 'Some basis must be found for that distinction, and I suggest that it is to be found in the fact that, while potential thieves will be deterred by the prospect of six months' hard labor, potential kleptomaniacs will not.' In other words, kleptomaniacs lack the ability to do otherwise because when faced with the prospect of being imprisoned (a standard change in circumstances), they do not desist. Glover (1970: 100) adopts a similar view, arguing that a person is unable to do otherwise if his intention is unalterable, and it is unalterable when the agent 'is not open to being persuaded by reasons to alter it':

One has some psychological incapacity whenever one is presented with reasons for changing one's course of action and yet does not do so. The reasons may not be good ones, or they may be outweighed by better ones. I only suffer from a psychological incapacity of this kind when I am not open to persuasion by reasons.

A person is unable to restrain himself if he is given sufficient reason to do otherwise (by standard changes in his circumstances), but still does not.

The notion of a reason or incentive is ambiguous between a formal and a substantive reading. It can refer to a (formal) reason or incentive the person has (because of some value of his), or to some (substantive) reason or incentive he ought to have (because of what we consider is good for him). Glover (1970: 100) thinks that someone can lack the ability to restrain himself because he fails to act on a reason which he (Glover) considers he ought to have:

> A drug addict who is in a state of appalling suffering, and certain to die as a result of his condition, may refuse to recognize that he would be better off if he were cured. But the avoidance of suffering and the saving of one's life are reasons such that in these circumstances we can only suppose they are ignored as the result of some delusion or inability to reason. It seems preposterous to deny that the addict is unable to give up the drug, on the grounds that he does not accept the reasons for doing so.

This view is problematic. Tam (1990) provides the counterexample of a zealous patriot. The patriot is happy as long as he is fighting for his beloved country, and genuinely does not mind being injured in pursuit of this end. We consider that he has a good reason to avoid almost certain death in the front line, and therefore when he does not do otherwise when faced with this reason, Glover will have to judge that he was overwhelmed by his patriotic impulses. However, this is wrong. Because the zealot has different values, *he* does not have a sufficient reason to run away from the enemy, and therefore his failure to do so does not mean he is overwhelmed by his patriotic impulses. If the notion of having the ability to restrain oneself is to do the work we want it to, it must employ the formal notion of a reason rather than the substantive one.

We might agree that the drug addict would be happier if he accepted he had a sufficient reason to avoid drugs, but if he has different values, we cannot argue that this makes him unable to restrain himself. Of course, if the addict did value happiness above everything, but thought erroneously that drugs were the best route to happiness, then he would have a reason to abstain. This means that if we can show him he was mistaken, and if he wanted to act in accordance with this new insight, but still failed to inhibit his impulse to abuse drugs, we could legitimately conclude that he was unable to do otherwise. But this is only because now he has a formal reason to do otherwise. What is objectionable about allowing substantive reasons to figure in our understanding of capacity for restraint is that anyone with radically different values (who does not recognize the sort of things we value as reasons for actions) becomes unable to restrain himself and not responsible. All criminals would cease to be responsible for their actions because they are not influenced by factors we judge are a sufficient reason for them to act otherwise! Someone who does not care about hurting others is uninfluenced by reasons we consider ought to be sufficient to get him to behave otherwise. But this does not mean he lacks the capacity to restrain himself.

Glover's account is ambiguous in another way. He describes the case of an alcoholic whose intention to drink cannot be altered by facts about his health. This could be interpreted to mean that the alcoholic recognizes he would be better off in the sense that his health would be better, but still chooses to drink, or it could be interpreted as meaning that he accepts he would be better off abstaining, wants to abstain, but finds he cannot act in accordance with this judgement (Holborow, 1971). Only in the second case does the alcoholic lack the capacity to do otherwise. This means that someone has the ability to do otherwise only if he does otherwise when a standard change in circumstances give him sufficient reason to do otherwise, *and* he wants overall to do otherwise. In the first case, the alcoholic does not want to stop drinking (in spite of the fact that he has reasons to stop), but his irrationality does not mean that he was incapable of stopping. He simply chooses not to.

This point is particularly relevant when we are dealing with people who are strong-minded and idealistic. They cannot be deterred from their course of action, even by the threat of the law. As Pritchard (1974: 635) puts it: 'Nothing seems to dissuade serious protestors such as Gandhi and Russell from violating laws in the name of various causes.' The fact that their intention is unalterable does not mean they are incapable of doing otherwise and not responsible for their actions. If they choose, even irrationally, to continue their protest, then even though they might have sufficient reason to do otherwise, as long as they do not want overall to do otherwise, we cannot say they are incapable if they do not do otherwise.

CHOOSING VERSUS WANTING

We have the capacity for restraint only if standard changes in our circumstances induce in us the desire to restrain ourselves and we do. But is this right? Simon, for instance, is a cautious person, always calculating carefully what to do, and trying to minimize the worst option, which he takes to be the standard of rationality. When faced with an airplane trip, he recognizes that he will enjoy being on the beach, but wants to minimize the worst option (of being killed in an airplane crash), and so chooses not to go. But one day Simon gets fed up with being constrained by this rationality and, realizing he might die on a rollercoaster, throws rationality to the wind and takes the ride, thoroughly enjoying it. By his own lights, he is failing to act on sufficient reasons. But it would be a mistake to say he was overwhelmed by the impulse to take the ride. Because Simon makes a choice (to be irrational), he is responsible.

Being responsible is not to be identified with being rational. Both Simon and the alcoholic who chooses to ignore his reasons to stop drinking are irrational (in their own lights), but because they choose to be irrational and decide to act in the way they do, they are responsible. We can see this also if we understand what it is to be rational. First, the rational agent looks at all the courses of action open to him. Second, he calculates all the consequences of each course. Third, he arranges his values in a consistent and decidable hierarchy of values. (By 'decidable', I mean that for every conflict of values, he has a higher-order value that resolves that conflict.) Fourth, he calculates for every course of action a total weighting which is a function of adding the values he assigns to every consequence of that course of action. Fifth, his beliefs about the options open to him and the consequences of each option are rational. Finally, he chooses the course of action that satisfies his most important values. If this degree of rationality is required for responsibility, none of us would be responsible!

Of course, on this sense of rationality, only an omniscient God could be rational. No human being can look at all the courses of action open to him, or calculate the consequences of each action. We need to recognize that we can be rational even though we do not meet the ideal. But my objection to identifying responsibility with rationality goes deeper. Responsibility has more to do with choice than with rational desires. In the paradigm case of making a choice, we examine (some of) the options, weigh up (some of) the pros and cons, and make a judgement as to which course of action minimizes the worst outcome, or maximizes the satisfaction of our desires. But this judgement does not plummet us willy-nilly into action – realizing what is best to do does not reflexly cause our bodies to move. The belief (that this is the most rational thing to do) and the desire (to do the most rational thing) do not automatically generate the action. I have to decide to act on the judgement – I have to make a *decision*. If I feel lazy, I may let things slide. It is my *choosing* to take a particular course of action that makes me responsible. And this choosing is something that I do.

The failure to recognize the importance of the element of will can be seen in accounts of our capacity to restrain ourselves in terms of free action. Such theories define loss of control in terms of unfree actions. There are two accounts of unfree actions. Frankfurt (1982) contends that a person exercises free will when he acts on his second-order desire as to which first-order he wants to act upon. Matt does not want to act on his desire to assault his tormentor, and only if he acts in accordance with this second-order desire will he be free and responsible for his actions. Watson (1982) contends that a person is free when he acts on his most important desire. A distinction is thus made between our motivational system and our evaluational system. If Matt thinks it is more important to avoid assaulting his tormentor, he only acts freely when he acts in accordance with this (most important) desire.

But this is wrong. Alan is extremely selfish. Although he has weak altruistic desires, he mostly does what serves his own interests. He would like to act on his altruistic desires rather than his selfish ones because he recognizes this will make him feel good about himself. But when he is faced with a choice of stealing a purse, he acts on his stronger selfish desires rather than his weak altruistic ones. Are we forced to say that he is overwhelmed by his selfish desires and not responsible for his actions? Similarly, Lawrie wants the good life – he likes skiing, driving expensive sports cars, owning original art, and so on. He would like to have an interest in a lucrative career such as medicine. But his interest in medicine is weak, and he has a stronger desire to study philosophy. He chooses a career in philosophy. Is he not responsible for his action?

Frankfurt argues that we act freely when we act on second-order desires because he assumes we are only free when we act on a desire with which we identify, and that we identify with our second-order desires rather than our first-order ones. The first assumption seems to makes sense in that if we do not identify with a desire, we see it as an alien force controlling us. But why assume that we identify with our second-order desires rather than our first-order ones? Alan identifies more strongly with his first-order desires, and because of this he does not see them as alien forces controlling him. Frankfurt forces us to say that he is not responsible when he acts on desires with which he identifies most. This is wrong.

What happens when there is a conflict in second-order desires? Frankfurt commits us to the view that if there is no resolution of this conflict, we are not responsible. I may want another piece of pecan pie. I want to indulge this desire as I am a hedonist. But I also have a desire to remain slim, and want to satisfy this desire because of my interest in longevity. These two second-order desires are in conflict. Unfortunately I have not resolved this conflict by acquiring a third-order desire telling me which second-order desire I want to act on in this situation. In the end, I decide to have the pecan pie. The fact that there was no third-order desire in accordance with which I acted does not show that I was not responsible. While the ideal of rationality requires that we put all desires into a neat hierarchy where every conflict of lower-order desires is resolved by higher-order desires, the ideal seldom occurs in reality. We are, in this sense, divided selves. But this does not mean that when we choose to act on one higher-order desire in an unresolved conflict with other higher-order desires, we are not responsible.

Watson argues that we have a reason for concluding that a person should be identified with the desires that he thinks are most important, and in this way avoids the problem of assuming an agent should be identified with his higher-order desires. He argues this is because a person cannot dissociate himself from his values without ceasing to be who he is:

> The important feature of one's evaluational system is that one cannot coherently dissociate oneself from it *in its entirety*. For to dissociate from the ends and principles which constitute one's evaluational system is to disclaim or repudiate them, and any ends and principles so disclaimed (self-deception aside) cease to be constitutive of one's evaluational system ... In short, one cannot dissociate oneself from all normative judgements without forfeiting all standpoints and therewith one's identity as an agent.
>
> (Tam, 1990: 72)

However Watson's view runs into the same problems. Lawrie values the jet-set life more than he does the rewards of philosophy. Finding he is not interested in any career that can give him this deeply saddens him. But he recognizes he cannot manufacture an interest in other careers and must make the most of the fact that he happens to be interested in philosophy. He chooses to become a philosopher. In spite of the fact that he is acting on a desire that he does not value as much as his abstract desire to go into medicine, he is still responsible.

What if a person has conflicting values and, unable to resolve the conflict, acts on one of his desires because he has to do something? Mary is 16 years old and becomes pregnant after a rape. She judges her life will be ruined if she does not terminate the pregnancy, and believes she is entitled to control over her life. On the other hand, she believes it is wrong to terminate the life of a potential person. She is not able to resolve this conflict. In the end, she decides to have the abortion. She chooses to act on one value not because she values her own autonomy more than the life of a potential person. She simply decides this is what she is going to do. Although she does not act in accordance with the desire she judges to be most important (because she cannot decide which is most important), she is still responsible for her action. It might be objected that by acting on one of these conflicting higher-order desires or values, a person has *created* a hierarchy – she has decided that one value is more important than the other, or she has identified a highest-order desire. When Mary decides to have the abortion, she is automatically affirming that her own autonomy is more important than the life of a potential person. But this solves the solution by fiat. By legislating that any action necessarily implies a unitary value system (resolved by the act itself), or a system of desires with a highest-order desire, it becomes logically impossible to act with a conflicting set of higher-order desires and values. However, we know this *is* possible – in fact, it is probably the rule rather than the exception. The problem cannot be resolved in this way.

The most important flaw shared by these two theories of free and responsible action is that they fail to take account of the fact that there is a decision involved in responsible action, and that someone should only be held responsible when he can act in accordance with his decisions. If Alan decides to steal the purse, even though he might have a higher-order desire to act on his weaker altruistic desires, he is responsible. Similarly, when Mary has an abortion, even though she has a conflict of values which she cannot resolve, she is responsible for what she does because she makes a decision. It is this choice that makes her responsible. While many of our actions are not fully rational, we are responsible for them because, after deliberating, we decide on one course rather than another. As Elliott (1991: 51) puts it: 'If we insist that whenever a person acts in opposition to what he has deemed best his intention to act was unalterable, then it becomes difficult to distinguish between actions which are irrational and those which are compelled.' This point is illustrated best in cases of weakness of will. In such situations, a person judges that some course of action is in his best interests, but chooses not to do it (Davidson, 1980). Don knows (because of the real risk to his good marriage) that his best interests are not served by having an extra-marital fling with his flirtatious secretary, but he goes ahead anyway. He knows he has more reason to do otherwise, but chooses to give in to the temptation. He is irrational, but because he is not overwhelmed by the temptation, he is responsible. He is responsible because if we gave him a sufficient reason and he decided to do otherwise, he would.

AN ALTERNATIVE VIEW

Someone has the capacity for restraint if standard changes in circumstance induce him to decide to do otherwise and he does do otherwise. While this view seems to give a coherent account of our concept, it fails to capture many cases of compulsion where we feel the person has an excuse. A black man may lose control when taunted mercilessly by a group of racist bullies. But if there had been a policeman at his elbow, he might not have assaulted them. If we believe he has an excuse, we must find some other reason why we should excuse him. But if we try to do this by setting the range of standard circumstances too narrowly, it turns out that we are all not responsible for many ordinary actions (as in weakness of will). On the other hand, if we set the range of standard circumstances too broadly, it turns out that those provoked are able to do otherwise, and are hence responsible. How do we avoid this problem?

The heart of the difficulty with this account is that it assumes that the person losing control is a divided self in the sense that he has a powerful desire, but also a (higher-order) desire not to act on the powerful desire. But is this correct? I think not. When someone is provoked, he does not necessarily feel a powerful desire to attack *as well as* a desire to stop himself acting on this desire. He may be so infuriated that the most important thing for him at that moment becomes his desire to retaliate. At the moment he acts, he is not a divided self. He may say afterwards: 'I know now that the most important thing was to walk away, that I was jeopardizing everything important to me. But in that state, those things ceased to be important. The most important thing was to hit back. I was so mad!' He does not necessarily desire not to act on his desire to retaliate at the time he acts. The truth is not that he wanted to act otherwise but could not, but that he did not want to act otherwise. Once the person provoked wants (undividedly) to retaliate, we have no way of distinguishing him from the agent who wants to act on his most important desire. Douglas wants more than anything to rescue his drowning daughter. No standard change in circumstances will provide him with the incentive to do otherwise. Does this mean that he has lost control and is not responsible for his act of heroism?

We are faced with the problem of trying to explain why

someone acting under provocation should be excused, if this is the correct account of the phenomenology. In Chapter 11, I will argue that the reason why we are inclined to excuse such people is that the abnormal circumstances (of the extreme duress or provocation) induces a temporary change in character. Because the person's bad behaviour does not reflect his underlying good character, we should excuse him. The issue is not so much a question whether the person was in control or not, as we have defined it, but whether he was his normal (good) self.

Compulsion, or losing control, excuses a person from moral responsibility by showing that he was not the evil person he seemed when he committed the offence. If someone wanted to do the good thing but lost control, doing the wrong thing is not a reflection of his good character and we should not punish him. Someone has the excuse of compulsion if he is provided with the incentive and opportunity to restrain himself (by standard changes in his circumstances), and decides to do otherwise, but still fails to restrain himself. But in many cases that we are inclined to excuse, we cannot show that the person 'could not have done otherwise' in this sense. In such cases, we need a different reason to excuse, and I will argue later that we excuse because in such cases, the bad act does not reflect an underlying bad character because of a temporary change in character brought about by the extreme circumstances.

5

AUTOMATISM AS AN EXCUSE

AN INSANE LAW

The legal definition of automatism was given by Viscount Kilmuir in Bratty's Appeal:

> [I]t means unconscious, involuntary action, and it is a defence because the mind does not go with what is being done . . . This is very like the words of the learned President of the Court of Appeal of New Zealand in Reg. v Cottle where he said: 'With respect, I would myself prefer to explain automatism simply as action without any knowledge of acting, or action with no consciousness of doing what was being done.'
>
> (Fenwick, 1990: 273)

This makes the excuse of automatism identical to the excuse of ignorance, which seems sane enough.

Of course, while the excuse of automatism amounts to the excuse of ignorance, this is not to say that automatism is simply a matter of acting in ignorance. In ordinary cases of ignorance the person is aware that he is performing some action, although not under the description he believes. For example, Fred believes he is administering penicillin, while in fact he is poisoning his mother. But the person with an automatism is unaware that he is acting at all, under any description. He is not just ignorant of what he is doing; he is unaware. Nevertheless, this is a sort of (more radical) ignorance, and nothing more is needed to enable it to qualify as an excuse.

English law distinguishes two types of automatism: sane and insane. Sane automatism occurs when the mind is disordered by an external factor like an injection of insulin or a blow to the head, and an insane automatism occurs when the cause is an intrinsic factor that is prone to recur and may lead to violence. This distinction is absurd, as Fenwick (1990: 275) points out:

> For a violent act committed while the mind is disordered owing to an excess of insulin is a sane automatism if the insulin is injected, but an insane automatism if the insulin comes from an insulinoma of the pancreas. The distinction between sane and insane automatism is a meaningless one, and if the legal profession could bring itself to do so, it is probably best abandoned altogether.

Sleepwalking has even been classified as an insane automatism. Burgess was accused of unlawful wounding – he had hit his girl-friend on the head with a bottle and a video machine, and was strangling her when she managed to stop him by saying: 'I love you, Bar.' He pleaded sane automatism, but the prosecution argued that sleepwalking had a genetic cause, arose from a specific stage of sleep, and that violence during sleepwalking tended to recur. It therefore fulfilled the criteria for an insane automatism, making sleepwalking a disease of the mind!

There is a more fundamental reason why the distinction will not work. From matches to people, everything they do is a function of both external and internal factors. A match will ignite if it is dry (internal factor) and heated (external factor). When people become ill, it is because of some external factor (such as a virus) and an internal factor (such as immune vulnerability). This applies even to those disorders we consider to be induced wholly by external factors (infections) as well as those we consider to be induced wholly by internal factors (metabolic disorders). So too for mental illness. Consider this case: In 1980 Rabey discovered a letter written by the woman he loved indicating she did not care for him. When he met her the next day, he struck her with a geological specimen after a short conversation and attempted to strangle her. A psychiatrist testified he was in a state of dissociation, and the jury acquitted him of attempted murder on the grounds of insanity. At the Appeal, the minority view in the High Court of Canada pointed out that Rabey 'exhibited no pathological symptoms indicative of a previously existing, or ongoing, psychiatric disorder', but the majority held that 'the dissociative state must be considered as having its source primarily in the respondent's psychological or emotional make-up' (Martin, 1981: 26). Rabey's behaviour had its origin both in the stress of rejection and his psychological make-up – dissociation was not caused by one factor to the exclusion of the other. This means any distinction based on this will be misleading.

The distinction is motivated by the desire of the courts to separate those defendants who are safe to release from those who are not. The former are excused on the grounds of sane automatism and released unconditionally and the latter are 'excused' on the grounds of insane automatism and detained in a mental hospital. Those whose automatisms are induced by external factors (such as blows to the head) run little risk of further violence, while those whose automatisms are induced by internal factors (such as tumours) do run such a risk. The verdict is determined by the court's opinion regarding the appropriate disposition rather than the disposition being determined by the verdict. Schopp (1991: 83) objects:

> Judges must justify their decisions by appeal to principles that are neutral as to outcome preference so that they can be applied to all other cases of this class. This requirement of principled decision-making protects the rule of law by preventing judges from merely pursuing their personal preferences. When British judges decide between the sane and insane variations of automatism on the basis of their evaluation of the proper disposition of this particular defendant, they endanger this fundamental principle of judicial decision-making.

A verdict must justify a particular disposition or punishment rather than the disposition require rationalization by a particular verdict.

WHAT IS INTENTIONAL ACTION?

Many conditions have allowed defendants to be excused on the basis of automatism – somnambulism, concussion, hypoglycaemia, dissociation, and epilepsy (Fenwick, 1990). The Mental Test tells us these are excuses – they make a person less blameworthy because they are features of his mental state showing he is not as evil as the person doing the same degree of harm intentionally. If a person only does something harmful because he is behaving automatically, we cannot infer that he is an evil character. But exactly what is this feature of his mental state? At first glance, it seems that those who commit a crime while concussed, or in the middle of a temporal lobe seizure, do not act intentionally. It is intentional action that most reveals a person's character, and hence when he is not acting intentionally and does something bad, we excuse him because this defeats the inference that his underlying character is bad. But what is intentional action?

Action that is directed towards some goal is intentional action. It is this understanding that made Freud (1975) suggest that many of our mistakes or accidents are in fact intentional. Saul has to invite a person he dislikes to a party, and gives his wife the wrong address. Freud would argue that Saul did not want to invite that person and unconsciously gave the wrong address to achieve that end. Far from making an error, his behaviour is goal-directed, and it is this goal-directedness that makes it intentional. But much automatic behaviour is like this. Schopp writes:

> The problematic cases of automatism are those in which the defendant acted in such a manner as to indicate that he not only knew what he was doing; he acted in that way for the purpose of performing the act constituting the objective elements of the offence ... Automatism can sometimes involve acts done in a skilled, coordinated manner, apparently for the purpose of achieving some specific end. For example, some defendants have drawn guns, pointed them at their victims and shot them repeatedly, or struck their victims repeatedly and then pushed them from the car in which both had been sitting and driven away. Such cases involve behaviour that was apparently done in a directed, effective manner to achieve a purpose ... These facts seem to indicate that the actors knew what they were doing and acted as they did precisely for the purpose of performing the act constituting the objective elements of the offence.
>
> (Schopp, 1991, 135–6)

Since such behaviour is goal-directed and therefore intentional, it cannot be the absence of this feature that allows automatism to excuse. Perhaps it is because of unconsciousness that it does so.

DOES CONSCIOUSNESS MATTER?

Let me tell you about the Quearthlings. They are like us except for their sleep. Whereas we have limited control of our behaviour during sleep – we can wake up at 6 o'clock sharp for that important interview – we cannot command ourselves to do more complicated things. Quearthlings, on the other hand, are able to tell themselves to do almost anything in their sleep. They do this by performing a ritual of repeating instructions aloud in a mantra before going to sleep. When they reach stage 4 sleep (the profound level of unconsciousness when sleepwalking occurs), they get up from their beds and perform the task. Apart from this, their sleepwalking is like ours.

Interesting cases have arisen in Quearthling law relating to offences committed during sleep, the landmark case being that of Quemp. Quemp had a long-standing quarrel with his neighbour over the boundary of their fence. The neighbour moved the fence and blocked Quemp's access to his garage. Quemp was enraged. One night, his wife observed him repeating the mantra: 'Kill your neighbour' before going to bed. She was bedridden and unable to prevent Quemp sleepwalking to his neighbour's house and killing him. At his defence, Quemp argued that he had been unconscious at the time, that he had neither known what he was doing nor been able to stop himself, and therefore that he lacked *mens rea*. The court was not impressed. They pointed out that he had *mens rea* at the time he had commanded himself to kill the neighbour and Quemp was convicted of murder. Quemp appealed to the House of Ladies, arguing a person cannot be guilty of a crime if at the time of the offence he does not know what he is doing or is unable to control his behaviour. Lady Quenning ruled:

> The standard we should use here is already in our law on offences committed under the influence of fermented drinks. The man who gets drunk knowing he will become violent is a man who satisfies all the requirements of *mens rea* even though when he acts he lacks awareness and self-control. He has control because he has control over whether he drinks. He is aware of what he is doing because when he drinks, he knows the consequences. So too the man who commands himself to break the law while in his sleep. As long as there is some time at which he knows what he is

doing and has control over his actions, he satisfies the *mens rea* requirement even though he may lack this at the time of the offence.

This ruling, known as the *Rule of Prior Mens Rea*, became Quearthling law. We agree – Quemp is no different from a cold-blooded killer. If a person knows he *will* commit the offence and is in control of what he *will* do, then he is guilty.

Another landmark case in Quearthling law is the case of Quimp. He developed a viral illness during which he did things in his sleep he had not commanded. On the day before the offence he was fired from his job. He went to sleep with murderous thoughts about his boss, and that night he killed his boss while sleepwalking. At the trial, he argued that he had not performed the mantra, and therefore had not intended to kill his boss. He had been unaware of the connection between simply thinking of something (without the mantra) before falling asleep and performing it while asleep. He was convicted, but this was quashed by Lady Quenning at Appeal:

> We can turn to the same law pertaining to offences committed under the influence of fermented drinks to decide this vexatious case. It is Quearthling law that if a person receives a fermented drink unknowingly, and goes on to break the law because of his drunkenness, he should be found not guilty. This is because he did not know what he would do. Similarly for Quimp. Because he did not know he would act in this way, he should be found not guilty.

Involuntary sleepwalking became an accepted excuse in Quearthling law.

What do these cases tell us about consciousness and its importance for responsibility? They tell us that unconsciousness is neither necessary nor sufficient for automatism to excuse. Morgan suffers from temporal lobe epilepsy and knows (from previous seizures) that he becomes violent during a fit. He wants to kill his wealthy uncle to inherit his money, and knows if he has a seizure in his uncle's presence, he will kill the uncle. He stops his medication, has a fit, and kills his uncle. Is he guilty of murder? Certainly. The fact that he lacked control and awareness at the time is not an excuse. Only if he lacked awareness and control of what he would do does he have an excuse. He has prior *mens rea* and is guilty. Fingarette and Hasse (1979) introduce a culpability requirement into their assessment of whether any mental state excuses. If a person is responsible for acquiring a mental state, it cannot excuse. Therefore, unconsciousness is not sufficient for automatism to count as an excuse.

It is not necessary either. Jake has partial epilepsy. It does not affect his consciousness but leads to his right arm convulsing uncontrollably. Suppose his arm convulses while eating and he accidentally stabs another patron. While Jake is aware of what he was doing, he is not in control of his actions and cannot stop his arm convulsing. His lacking responsibility has nothing to do with being unconscious as he was conscious throughout the seizure. Nevertheless his behaviour was involuntary because he lacked control over it. This suggests that automatism excuses because (in general) it implies that the person lacks control over his actions. It is because the action performed during automatism is involuntary that the person has an excuse. This leads us to the question: What is a voluntary action?

VOLUNTARINESS

How does someone who suffers from an automatism differ from someone who is overwhelmed by emotion? Both are unable to prevent themselves from acting. Are both actions involuntary? Does voluntariness consist in being in control, so that if overwhelming emotion causes loss of control, the behaviour is involuntary? Or does it consist in being the product of a desire and a belief? There are two different conceptions of voluntary action – a broad conception (Aristotle, 1955; Feinberg, 1986), and a more narrow conception (Hart, 1968). According to the broad conception, an act is voluntary when it is free from ignorance and compulsion. Voluntariness is sufficient for culpability, and having an excuse undermines the voluntariness of the action. This is not the ordinary sense of the word. When a man acts in ignorance, we still think of his action as voluntary. On Hart's view, voluntariness is a necessary condition for culpability (rather than sufficient). Some action can be voluntary but the agent can fail to be culpable if he has some excuse, but anything that negates voluntariness will negate culpability. According to Hart, involuntary conduct is behaviour not governed by the agent's will. The narrow conception is to be preferred – we would be speaking a different language if we said that a person acting in ignorance or under provocation was acting involuntarily. However, this does not mean that voluntariness is necessary for culpability. Quemp's behaviour when he killed his neighbour was involuntary but he is culpable. But this does not imply one is responsible for things outside one's control either. Quemp *did* have control over his behaviour – only it was remote-control.

What makes behaviour involuntary? When is a bodily movement an action? What differentiates an action from a reflex knee-jerk or a seizure? The most plausible approach is to differentiate these on the basis of their causes. A bodily movement is a knee jerk if it is caused by a stretched tendon stimulating a reflex arc via the spinal cord causing the contraction of the quadriceps muscle. It is not caused by the agent's desire to move his leg and the belief that some goal of his will be achieved by this movement. Bodily movements are a convulsion if they are caused by an epileptic focus in the brain producing rhythmic contraction of muscles. They are not caused by the agent's desires and beliefs in the characteristic way that intentional action is caused. What differentiates automatic behaviour from action is its being caused independently of the agent's desires and beliefs and decision-making processes. Hart (1968: 105) argues involuntary movements 'are "wild" or not "governed by the will" in the sense that they are not subordinated to the agent's conscious plans of actions: they do not occur as part of anything the agent takes himself to be doing'.

Someone may object that reasons for actions cannot be the causes for those actions. But why not? Reasons *must* be causes – if they are not, then it would follow that they do not influence our actions – we act because of reasons and yet the reasons will have no influence on our behaviour, which is absurd (Davidson, 1980). If we wish to differentiate reasons from rationalizations, we must assume that reasons are causes. If the reason I go next door is to flirt with the neighbour's wife, but rationalize that I need to discuss the car pool, how do we draw this distinction unless reasons causally influence my behaviour and rationalizations do not? Reasons are those desires and beliefs which are causally instrumental in bringing about our behaviour, while rationalizations are those desires and beliefs which we erroneously take to be the cause of our behaviour. Flirting with the neighbour's wife is the reason for my action because this desire causes me to act, and discussing the car pool is the rationalization because this desire does not bring about my behaviour.

However, the causal theory of action faces the problem of deviant causal chains. Jock wants to eliminate his rival. When driving home and encountering him crossing the street, he realizes he can kill him by running him over. This thought so unsettles him that he loses control of the car and kills the rival. He did not perform a voluntary action even though this behaviour was caused by a desire and a belief. For an action to be voluntary, it must cause the behaviour *in the right sort of way*. But voluntariness in this sense is not necessary for responsibility because agents can deliberately induce deviant causal chains:

> One may have caused oneself to be, or unreasonably risked being, in the position where one would commit a specific criminal harm by reason of D.O.M. [Disability of Mind]. Such a person would be one who, knowing he is unpredictably susceptible to syncope or coma from epilepsy or heart failure, nevertheless drives a car or operates highly dangerous machinery and in consequence of such coma causes the death of another . . . More gravely criminal, though still rare, is the case where the individual intentionally causes the D.O.M. with further intent or recklessness as to bringing about the harm. Here the typical example would be the person who drinks or uses a drug, either in order to build up 'Dutch courage' to carry out a specific criminally prohibited act, or in order to gird up 'nerve' to take action that risks eventuating a specific criminal harm.
>
> (Fingarette and Hasse, 1979: 213)

Morgan's behaviour during the fit he deliberately induced is not caused in the right sort of way. This might make it involuntary, but he is still responsible for it.

Voluntariness is not sufficient for responsibility because many automatisms (such as people acting purposively in a dissociated state) are voluntary in this sense. Schopp (1991) argues that while they are caused by desires and beliefs, they are not caused by the agent's deliberations, and this is part of being caused in the standard way. It is this deliberative process that distinguishes voluntary action from such automatisms. When an agent acts, he does not have a single desire (D) and a single belief (that by doing A he will get D) which cause his behaviour. He also realizes that there are other ways of achieving D, he has other desires, and evaluates the impact of each option on all his desires. After a deliberative process of weighing the pros and cons, he makes up his mind and chooses one course of action. It is only when actions are determined in this more complex way that they are voluntary.

> A person who acts in a state of impaired consciousness is acting in a state of distorted awareness and attention such that his acts may be caused by an action-plan, but the plan is selected with access to only a small and nonrepresentative portion of his wants and beliefs. The actor's wants and beliefs do not cause his acts, therefore, in the manner characteristic of ordinary human activity.
>
> (Schopp, 1991: 140)

If a somnambulist kills someone, he has not been able to allow other desires, like the desire to avoid prison, to influence his action. Therefore, it is involuntary in this sense. Is this view correct?

The problem is that there are many voluntary actions we perform which are not the result of a complex act of deliberation. I want to type the word 'deliberation' and I believe by moving my fingers in a certain order, I will achieve this, and I go right ahead. I have not deliberated one jot. Yet this is a voluntary action. The flaw arises because what is important is not the causal relationship that *actually* obtains between the reasons and the behaviour, but the causal relationship that *could* have obtained. The spontaneous actions of mine have a causal relationship much like the one that obtains in automatisms, but they are free and voluntary because I have the *ability* to deliberate in this situation even though I did not. This marks off the voluntary action from the automatic one. If something had arisen that had given me an overriding reason for not performing the spontaneous act, I would have inhibited it. However, if something had arisen in the middle of the automatic act that had given the individual an overriding reason to stop, he would not have been able to inhibit his response because he would not have been able to deliberate.

But even this is not good enough. In one interesting case of sleepwalking, a woman rose every night to binge on food in her fridge. All treatment had failed. However, she had a phobia for snakes, and when a toy snake was placed conspicuously in the kitchen, she no longer sleepwalked there for a binge. She *was* able to take into account other factors, because this made her abstain. If we are going to explain the difference between voluntary action and automatisms by reference to the ability to alter one's course of action when provided with other reasons, we will have to conclude her behaviour was voluntary. In addition, we face problems of weakness of will. I am tense and tired, and want a sherry. However, I have a deadline with the publisher, and know that if I have the sherry, the call of sleep will be irresistible and I will not meet my deadline. I know that the most important thing for me is to keep my publisher happy. But I really feel like that sherry and so I have it. Although my action was not amenable to alteration by an overriding reason, I am still responsible. Taking other factors into account is neither necessary nor sufficient for responsible action.

We are forced to conclude that voluntariness is a matter of degree. The nocturnal binger had the ability to take into account *some* but not all other factors. It is because she still has a limited access to all the relevant reasons that we say that the behaviour was relatively automatic. Some conscious actions are like this too. A woman escaping an assailant intent on raping her might not have access to all the reasons relevant to her actions. In her state of panic, she might be unaware of any injury she is causing to herself, and unaware that she is breaking the laws of property and trespass. But she still acts voluntarily. Consciousness allows us to review our reasons for acting, and let certain reasons override others. This executive function is absent in automatism, but it clearly comes in degrees. We could then argue that people whose behaviour does not exceed a certain threshold of voluntariness have an excuse.

However, there is another way out of this problem. We could argue that the sleepwalker undergoes a change in character, and it is on this basis that the person should be excused. When she acts automatically, her behaviour is not a reflection of her character, and therefore she deserves to be excused. I will argue for this in Chapter 11. Suffice it to say, there are difficulties with the traditional explanation of why lack of consciousness should excuse that are sufficient to force us to look elsewhere.

UNCONSCIOUS MOTIVATION

There is another form of acting unconsciously. In it the agent is fully conscious but acts on unconscious reasons. There are two sorts of cases – acting on unconscious desires and acting on unconscious beliefs. Let us start with unconscious desires. Francis Pollard was a Detroit police officer who attempted to rob several banks. He was singularly ineffective – he was nearly caught several times, and escaped with no loot. When he was apprehended, he confessed to fourteen attempted robberies. At his trial, psychiatrists testified that although he knew right from wrong, he

> may have been governed by unconscious drives which made it impossible for him to adhere to the right. It is our belief that this unconscious motivation might have been related to guilt feelings in connection with the death of his wife and child [who were murdered when he was out of the house], which compelled subsequent acts that would certainly lead to apprehension and punishment.
>
> (Moore, 1984: 350)

Because his behaviour was 'governed by unconscious' drives (to assuage his guilt), he was judged not guilty. But did he have an excuse?

Blumenfeld (1972: 430) argues that if we are unaware of the desires on which we act, we are not in control.

> I cannot bring to bear my powers of consideration, rational faculties, power of review or whatever we will to call the agency of conscious control, upon some aspect of my mental makeup that is unknown to me. And this seems to me a paradigm of the limitation of freedom. The desires I am unable to assess consciously continue to affect me without my having access to them or control over them.

We might want to excuse the unconsciously motivated person not because he lacks *mens rea* for the deed, but because his action was not fully voluntary. Bertrand, for instance, thinks he wants to study art because it is a soft option when in fact he wants to avoid medicine to irritate his father. He thinks he dislikes medicine because it will be a lot of work. When he deliberates about what to do, and sees that medicine requires a lot of study

104

and art only a little, he takes this to be enough to settle the issue. He is not aware that he does not wish to do medicine to anger his father. If he was aware of this, he might decide to express his anger in some other way, and elect to medicine (because the issue of avoiding work is not overriding). If he would have decided differently had he been aware of his unconscious desires, we might think he lacks control over his actions.

But this is wrong. To have control over our behaviour, we need only be aware of what we are doing and be able to refrain from doing what is impermissible to do, and these conditions are satisfied in the case of someone unaware of his motives. Bertrand was not able to optimally satisfy his desires, but being irrational in this sense is different from being out of control. Similarly, even though Pollard thought he was robbing for money, he was still aware that he was robbing banks. He might not have known *why* he was robbing, but it could not have escaped his notice *that* he was robbing. The fact that he was acting because of a reason unknown to him does not mean he lacked control. If his action would have been deterred by standard circumstances, and it often was interrupted by police, he was in control.

Radden (1985: 36) thinks ignorance of our real motives excuses an agent. Such agents 'may believe that they act without ignorance . . . because they are aware of what they (falsely) take to be the reasons for their action . . . They do not act without ignorance, for all that, for they do not know why they act.' But not all ignorance is exculpatory. If a hit man kills for pleasure while thinking he is killing for monetary gain, he does not have an excuse. He is not any the less evil for being mistaken in this way. If a father abuses his son, it does not matter that he thinks he is doing it for the good of his child when it is really because he is venting his anger at his own abusive father. The important thing is that he was aware of what he was doing and could have stopped himself. If a (good) father found himself being unnecessarily harsh with his son, he might fail to understand why, but he has a choice: he can rationalize his action, saying that discipline is good for the boy, or he can stop if he finds what he is doing is morally unacceptable. We do not have to understand where our desires are coming from to be responsible. The important thing is that we be aware of and in control of our behaviour. Someone acting on an unconscious desire might not be aware of *why* he is acting, but he is aware *that* he is doing certain things, and since there is no reason to think that unconscious desires are uncontrollable, there is no reason why, if he finds what he is doing is unacceptable, he cannot stop himself. Moreover, most of us are unaware of the reasons why we act. When I pursued an academic life, was it because I found philosophy more exciting than anything else, or because I wanted the approval of my brilliant mother? Did I combine medicine with philosophy because I wanted to earn a living, or because I wanted the approval of my GP father? If a person cannot be held responsible for actions performed because of unconscious desires, most of us will not be responsible for many of our actions.

So much for desires that are hidden from consciousness. What of unconscious beliefs? Damion invites his rival to dinner. He unconsciously knows his rival is allergic to crab meat, and prepares sea-food soup with crab in it. He is aware of his desire to have his rival's job, but unaware of the allergy to soup. As a result, he kills his rival. Is Damion responsible? He was not conscious of the fact that the soup would kill his rival. He was not aware of the moral significance of what he was doing, and so deserves to be excused. As Moore (1984: 342) comments about the composer unconsciously copying a tune he has already heard:

> Whatever else the principle of responsibility might include, it should include the power or ability to appraise the moral worth of one's proposed actions. A person who lacks this ability cannot fairly be blamed because, although he is acting intentionally, he does not know that what he is doing is wrong . . . When factual knowledge is unconscious, the ability to perceive the moral nature of one's actions is lacking.

But anyone who knows unconsciously what he is doing is not ignorant (at some level). What influences us in determining whether he has an excuse is ultimately his underlying character. Compare these two variations: Suppose Damion is a ruthless person, and does not hesitate to override the needs of others to get what he wants. But his need to appear perfect in his own eyes makes him repress the awareness of certain crucial facts which would tell him he is a bad man. Damion is an evil character, and even though he is unaware of giving his guest an allergic reaction, we have little inclination to excuse him. Now suppose Damion is a good person who would never hurt a fly.

He has a phobia for allergies, and deals with this by repressing any facts about allergies from awareness. This leads to his being unaware of his rival's allergy. Here he has an excuse, and the reason is that he is a good character. We are only inclined to see unconscious beliefs as an excuse when the resulting act does not reflect the underlying good character of the agent.

HYPNOSIS

The Model Penal Code explicitly lists hypnosis as a condition that can cause automatism. There are many examples where hypnosis has induced people to break the law. In the 1930s a con artist hypnotized a young German woman and induced her to have intercourse with him and his friends. When her husband grew suspicious, he ordered her to kill him, and she actually made six unsuccessful attempts! The woman was never charged, but the con man was convicted to 10 years' imprisonment. In another case, an unscrupulous neighbour hypnotized a young school teacher who had recently inherited a house and store from his father, and induced him to give him gifts, and even shoot himself in the left arm. The teacher rationalized this last act by saying that cramp had caused him to pull the trigger. The neighbour then induced him to commit an insurance swindle, and he was caught. He could not convince the police he was not an accomplice and was convicted (Katz, 1987).

There are two aspects of the behaviour we must consider – whether hypnosis deprives the agent of his awareness of what he is doing, and whether it deprives him of his control. If subjects are hypnotized into opening a window, they rationalize their actions, saying that the room was 'stuffy' (Hilgard, 1965). The fact that they are able to rationalize what they did shows they are aware of opening the window. The only thing they were unaware of was *why* they did it. Hypnotists have been aware for a long time that it is impossible to get subjects to do what they would not ordinarily do. If their moral views proscribe killing, they cannot be induced to commit murder. But a hypnotist can persuade a person to view what he is doing in a different way. Fred might have a moral prohibition against killing, but if a hypnotist convinces him that he is giving his mother penicillin (when it is in fact arsenic), he is capable of killing her. In such a situation, he is not responsible for his actions. As Schopp (1991: 154) argues:

The hypnotic process is essentially one that alters the focus of the subject's attention ... As the subject's attention is directed toward those selected matters, other information and considerations that usually matter may fade from awareness, depriving the subject of the perspective of a broad reality orientation.

By depriving the subject of his awareness of the moral implications of what he is doing, hypnosis can provide an excuse.

But not in all cases. John has been hypnotized to want the only glass of water available when there is someone dying of thirst. Tam argues that if John is the sort of person who cares about the needs of others, finding this desire in himself will not sway him from offering the glass to the dying man. On the other hand, if he is someone who puts his own needs first, he will ignore the fact that someone else needs the water more.

It would not be inappropriate to adopt a blaming attitude towards John for drinking the water because his drinking the water does reflect a morally objectionable quality of his, namely, a readiness to ignore the interests of others in order to satisfy his own desires. In fact, the causal origin of his desires does not make any difference to his responsibility; if instead of a post-hypnotic suggestion he has just suddenly felt like drinking some water, not because he has thought about it or has chosen it out of a set of options he has been considering, but simply because at that moment he happens to feel like drinking some water, it is still true that he is prepared to satisfy his own desire rather than leave the water to the person who needs it more than he.

(Tam, 1990: 178)

If the person is aware of what he is doing, he is able to exercise his moral views. If he behaves badly, he is responsible for what he does. Of course, if the subject is so focused (because of the post-hypnotic suggestion) that he is unaware of the moral significance of his actions, he will have an excuse.

Does hypnosis deprive the agent of control over his actions? A post-hypnotic suggestion is not the same as an overwhelming desire. Finding oneself acting on a post-hypnotic suggestion is not like witnessing oneself having an epileptic seizure. However, hypnotists can prevent subjects from doing things by telling them that they cannot stand up, or lift up their hand. Here the post-hypnotic suggestion does seem to undermine the subject's ability to control himself. Can it undermine his ability to control his impulses too? There is some reason to suspect so. If a hypnotist tells a life-guard that when he hears a call for help, he will be unable to get up, the life-guard would have an excuse if a swimmer drowned. This is because the hypnosis made him unable to do otherwise. Hence, there will be some circumstances where hypnosis can excuse on the basis of compulsion too.

DISSOCIATIVE STATES

Patients with hysteria may, under stress, experience fugue-like states where they act in a purposive and goal-directed way, but appear to have reduced awareness, and afterwards have no recollection of what they did. Such states are called dissociative states in that the person becomes dissociated from her body which behaves in an 'automatic' way (Kaplan and Sadock, 1991). This mental state has been recognized by Anglo-American law as providing grounds for the excuse of automatism.

> A 45-year-old man who killed his wife's lover following escalating depression gave a previous history of recurrent hysterical episodes. In such a hysterical, dissociative state he wandered out in his underpants in the middle of the night when his wife threatened to leave the matrimonial home. Later, again when she threatened to leave him for another man, he went shoplifting and took some goods which he did not really need. It was accepted that he had no intent and was in a dissociative, hysterical state and was found not guilty.
>
> (Enoch, 1990: 806)

Although the defendant behaved purposively and carried out a murder, he was excused because he lacked *mens rea*.

Why should we excuse such cases? We can argue that the agent lacks control because of his narrowing of consciousness. But while lacking full awareness may mean the person is less able to take other factors into consideration when he acts, I may be so determined to kill my rival that I cease to be aware of what is going on around me, just as a boxer ceases to be aware of pain while concentrating on the job. But this does not make me less responsible. However we resolve this, the main reason we excuse such cases lies in the fact that during dissociation the person is not herself – she changes character. While a person with a dissociative state is able to deliberate and act intentionally, we might not hold her responsible because hysteria makes her act out of character. It is because the action does not reflect her underlying (good) character that she has an excuse. We will explore this argument in Chapter 11.

MULTIPLE PERSONALITY DISORDER

The most dramatic cases of dissociation occur in multiple personality disorder (MPD). There is considerable controversy whether this entity exists, or whether it is an artefact of over-zealous psychiatrists training needy patients to organize their symptoms in an exotic way (Merskey, 1995). This controversy aside, we still need to explore the question whether MPD would excuse if it was a bona fide entity. In MPD, a person supposedly develops a number of autonomous selves each with their own personalities and memories, each dissociated from the next. Childhood trauma supposedly forces the child to create autonomous selves to deal with the trauma while the central personality distances herself as a defence. These selves operate in isolation, but may be reintegrated with therapy (Kaplan and Sadock, 1991). It is possible for one self to operate without the knowledge and control of the principal self. 'Sometimes, despite the often inhibited and prudish character of the individual before the onset of the disorder, at least one of the personalities is sexually disinhibited, wildly extravagant and overtly criminal in a psychopathic way' (Sims, 1990: 374). The possibility is set for an alter ego to commit an offence.

Kenneth Bianchi, known as the 'Hillside Strangler', was responsible for abducting, torturing, sexually assaulting, and killing ten young women in Los Angeles and leaving their naked bodies on the hillside to taunt the police. Under hypnosis, Watkins (1984: 78) discovered an alter ego calling himself 'Steve' who claimed to have committed the murders that Bianchi denied, and argued Bianchi was not responsible:

> He vividly described how he (Steve) had strangled and killed 'all these girls,' reiterating that 'I fixed him [Ken] up

good. He doesn't even have any idea' ... When Steve wanted to kill, he 'made him [Ken] go away.' He described how he and Angelo took turns killing the girls in Los Angeles. Ken could not 'appreciate' the actions of Steve, and he did not have the ability to control them. Accordingly, I considered him insane.

Because the central self was considered ignorant and out of control, he was excused. Orne (1984) argued for the prosecution that Bianchi was a psychopathic sadist who was simulating MPD. At the time when Bianchi was exhibiting two personalities, Orne suggested to him that 'real' sufferers of MPD had at least three personalities. 'It had been predicted that if Mr. Bianchi was feigning multiple personality, a third "personality" would emerge in response to the social cue given in the wake state, and thus the appearance of "Billy" further brings into question the validity of Mr. Bianchi's behaviour' (Orne, 1984: 118). Orne concluded Bianchi had only one personality and was responsible for the killings.

Bianchi agreed to plea bargain (to avoid the death penalty), and in 1979 he was sentenced to two consecutive life terms. Let us suppose he had really suffered from MPD. Does this provide an excuse? Why should we excuse Ken when he committed the offences? We can adopt one of three approaches here. First, a person is responsible if there is at least one self who knew what he was doing and was in control. This is the position the law takes. Second, the person is responsible if all selves knew what he was doing and were in control. This implies those with MPD lack responsibility:

> Multiple-personality persons should be regarded as but a special case of suspended personhood. There was but one person originally, and (if therapy is successful) there will be but one person again. During the time that intervenes, the only answer to the question, How many persons? may be none.
>
> (Moore, 1984: 406)

Third, the person is responsible if the central self knew what he was doing and was in control. Let us discuss each in turn.

The law adopts the first theory. Grimsley was arrested for drunken driving, and in her defence claimed that she (Robin) had not done it but that one of her alter egos (Jennifer) had. The court ruled: 'There was only one person driving the car and only one person accused of drunken driving. It is immaterial whether she was in one state of consciousness or another, so long as in the personality then controlling her behaviour, she was conscious and her actions were a product of her volition' (Lewis and Bard, 1991: 744). The decision implied that 'the law adjudges criminal liability of the person according to the person's state of mind at the time of the act; we will not begin to parcel criminal account-ability out among the various inhabitants of the mind' (Lewis and Bard, 1991: 746). This position is flawed. If we already have reason to excuse someone in a dissociative state, we cannot without inconsistency blame an MPD sufferer who dissociates into an alter ego. Halleck (1990: 306) argues MPD patients are responsible because they can control 'switching' personalities: 'The case for ascribing responsibility to the total patient is strengthened when the clinician infers that the patient has influ-ence over the appearance of the various personalities.' While some MPD sufferers can switch personalities at will, dissociating in general is not within a person's control. But the real problem with this position is why we should not embrace the contrary theory that a person is *not* responsible as long as there is one self who did not know what he was doing or was not in control? We have as much reason to excuse the person (because one self was ignorant and lacked control) as to punish the person (because another self was aware and in control).

The second position has problems too. If we deny that an MPD sufferer is a person and can be responsible, we have to conclude she is never responsible for anything that she does as her principal self. If she seeks treatment or tells the police of what she has done as an alter ego, is she not responsible? When the central self is not dissociating, why not consider her responsible? Suppose Sybil, without dissociating, commits an offence as her principal self, stealing some clothing she has always wanted. Moore would have us conclude that she is not responsible simply because she has other (quiescent) selves. Moreover, as Halleck (1990: 303) argues: 'The strongest argument for excusing the undesirable conduct of the multiple personality disorder patient is that such conduct occurs at a time when the patient does not have the full resources of his/her integrated personality available to him/her.' But when the principal self acts, she has enough resources of her personality available to her to count as responsible. Only when she is an alter ego, do we suspect that she does not.

The third position seems correct. It is consistent with our view that dissociative states can excuse. If Bianchi were really suffering from MPD, and knew nothing of what he did as his alter ego, he would have an excuse. This theory can also resolve the paradox generated by the first position which suggests we have as much reason to punish as to excuse the person. By identifying the person with her principal self, we can give some reason for holding her responsible for some acts and excusing her from others. But even if this position is correct, it still leaves us the problem of trying to explain why those in a dissociative state *per se* should be excused. As we have seen, the dissociated person still acts intentionally, consciously, and with the ability to do otherwise with a change in circumstances. Why then should we excuse him?

It is only when the person acts out of character that we are inclined to excuse him. Only if he is basically a good person do we consider him worthy of excusing. If Ken was as evil as Steve, the one as ruthless and callous as the other, and Steve committed the murders in a dissociative state, there would be little inclination to excuse Ken. If Ken is the sort of character that would love to kill other women, is too timid to do so, but more than happy to have himself dissociate and commit these offences, there would be little inclination to excuse him from the offences Steve commits. This is because one suspects his evil character *is* responsible for what he does as Steve. It is also because the best evidence for Ken's dissociation is if he acted out of character as Steve, and if he did not, this suggests there was no dissociation in the first place. If this is right, then we are forced to rely on a different rationale for excusing those with MPD. If an MPD sufferer of good character uncharacteristically kills her abuser, we are inclined to excuse her because she is not the sort of person who would normally have acted in this way. It is only because she is a good person that we excuse her. The justice of excusing her has more to do with her acting out of character than with the fact that this was as an alter ego, or that she was in a dissociative state.

Automatism excuses for the same reason that ignorance and compulsion excuse – someone does not deserve moral

113

condemnation for behaviour over which he lacks control, and for behaviour he does not know is wrong. However, we have seen that knowledge and control come in degrees, and that in many cases of automatism, the agent does have significant knowledge and control, and yet still has an excuse. In these cases, we are inclined to excuse the offender because he acted out of character. This suggests we will have to develop the novel excuse of character change.

6

THE JUSTIFICATION OF EXCUSES

TWO THEORIES

Punishment needs justification because it consists of the infliction of harms such as pain or the deprivation of goods such as freedom (Culver and Gert, 1982), and we cannot inflict these without good reason. But if punishment is justified in certain circumstances, we will need to justify withholding it in others. We also need a justification for excuses. There are two theories that justify punishment and excuses – Retributivism and Utilitarianism, and they have to answer three questions: (1) Why should we punish? (2) Who should be punished? (3) How much should we punish? The first question asks for the Justifying Aim of punishment, while the second and third enquire about its Distribution (Hart, 1968).

According to Retributivism, the aim of punishment is to ensure that justice is done. Kenny (1978: 70) writes:

> Justice demands – so the theory runs – that he who has done harm shall suffer harm. Independently of any deterrent or remedial effect which the criminal's suffering may have on himself or others, justice is better served if the criminal is made to suffer than if he is allowed to go scot free. Each man must be done by as he has done.

Retributivism answers the second question by stating that we should punish those who deserve it. Fletcher (1978: 800) expands:

> A fuller statement of the argument goes like this: (1) punishing wrongful conduct is just only if punishment is measured by the desert of the offender, (2) the desert of an offender is gauged by his character – i.e., the kind of person

115

he is, (3) and therefore, a judgement about character is essential to the just distribution of punishment.

This is like the version of Retributivism I defend which holds that someone deserves punishment if he (1) freely (2) does wrong (3) because of his evil character. Let me expand on these elements: someone acts freely when he could have done otherwise: 'One necessary condition of the just application of a punishment is normally expressed by saying that the agent "could have helped" doing what he did' (Hart, 1968: 124). A wrongdoer is someone who harms another person without justification – if a person has a justification for harming another (as in self-defence), it is unjust to punish him. Someone has an evil character if he has a willingness to wrong another person in the pursuit of his own selfish interests, and when a person's intention to do wrong is an expression of his enduring propensity and willingness to do wrong, he has acted *because* of his evil character. Retributivism answers the third question by requiring the punishment to fit the crime. We should give more punishment to those who are more evil. We measure the degree of evil by assessing the amount and probability of the harm that is intended. The more harm a person intends, and the more certain that harm will result, the more evil the person.

Utilitarianism justifies punishment by its beneficial consequences – its deterrent, rehabilitative, and incapacitating effects reduce the amount of harm done by further crime, thereby enhancing our welfare (Smart and Williams, 1973). It deters the person who is punished from further crimes (Special Deterrence) as well as potential offenders (General Deterrence). It rehabilitates the offender who is encouraged to turn away from crime, and it incapacitates the offender by imprisoning him and taking him out of circulation. Utilitarianism answers the second question by stating that we should punish all and only those when it will produce a beneficial overall effect (outweighing the harm of the punishment). Finally, a person should be punished just as much as is needed to achieve the optimal benefit.

WHY PUNISH?

Assume human behaviour is governed by two laws: the Self-Fulfilling Law and the Forbidden Fruit Law. According to the first, when a person is labelled as a criminal, he embraces this identity and embarks on a life of crime. According to the second, the prohibition of crime glamorizes and encourages it. If these two laws were true, then punishing offenders would neither deter nor rehabilitate – punishing a murderer would encourage further murders. If we knew this would happen, we would be forced to choose between giving a criminal his just deserts and avoiding an innocent person being murdered. There is little doubt we would choose to avoid the suffering of innocent people over giving criminals their just deserts. For similar reasons we set high standards of proof for determining guilt – it is a greater evil to have an innocent man suffer than an evil man not get his just deserts. Retributivism here condemns innocent people to suffering.

This seems to imply that Utilitarianism is correct – having beneficial consequences is necessary to justify punishment. Retributivism replies that the reason why the consequences of punishment are so unpalatable here is that innocent people – that is, people who do not *deserve* to be harmed – get hurt. Only by sneaking in a Retributivist principle does the example succeed. Suppose in addition to the two laws, our behaviour is governed by the Law of Retribution: whenever a further crime is encouraged (by punishment), the crime is perpetrated on those who themselves have committed the same crime. Punishing a murderer will encourage someone else to murder another murderer, and so on. No *innocent* person gets harmed – only those who deserve it. Punishment would be justified here – it is only when the consequences of punishment violate Retributivist principles of justice that punishment is unpalatable. This shows that it is fair consequences of punishment that justify it. We end up with a Hybrid theory.

WHOM TO PUNISH?

Is having beneficial consequences sufficient to justify punishment? McCloskey (1968) gives us a damning case against Utilitarianism, showing that it is not. He describes the problem of scapegoating. A black man rapes a white woman in a small town. Because of existing racial tensions, unless the man is apprehended, race riots will result in the injury and death of many innocent people. The sheriff can prevent this violence by framing an innocent man who will be accepted by the community as the rapist, and harm to fewer innocent people will result if he is punished. But punishing him is unjust. If Utilitarianism tells us to do this, it must be wrong.

Utilitarianism replies that we must distinguish Act-Utilitarianism (AU) from Rule-Utilitarianism (RU). AU tells us to choose the *act* that has the best consequences relative to alternative acts. RU tells us to choose the *rule* that has the best consequences relative to alternative rules. In the sheriff case, while the act that produces the best consequences is punishing the innocent man, the rule with the best consequences does not endorse this. This is because if punishing innocent men becomes a rule, there will be some cases where the innocence of the person will be publicly known, and this will produce such a loss in confidence in the law that anarchy and considerable suffering will result. Because this rule would produce disaster in some cases, it does not have the best consequences overall. RU suggests we should not punish the innocent man.

There are problems with RU. If justification ultimately consists in beneficial consequences, why should we follow a *rule* that in one case does not produce the best consequences? If the sheriff knows that his deception will not be discovered, why should he not break the best rule and punish the innocent man? When justification derives from the consequences, we have no reason for not departing from the rule and ensuring that in each and every case, good consequences result. Moreover, why not accept a more complex rule that we should punish an innocent man only if the deception will not be discovered? This rule has better consequences than the one outlawing the punishment of innocents because in situations where the deception will not be discovered, greater benefits follow from punishment. RU would have to endorce it, which seems wrong.

What of Retributivism? Suppose we have conclusive evidence that a mafia boss has committed murder. If we convict him, he will command widespread killings, whereas if we release him, fewer murders will result overall. Retributivism dictates that we should punish the mafia boss in spite of the massive harm that results to innocent people, which is wrong. Deserving punishment is not a sufficient justification for giving it. Is it necessary? Moore (1984) raises the problem of preventative detention. He asks us to imagine a judge discovering that a person accused of a crime he did not commit is dangerous (about to become a serial killer). Should the judge violate the principles of justice and punish him, preventing him from becoming a serial killer? Unlike Moore, I think he should. Quinton (1971) argues that if it is certain that a much greater evil (death) will befall many innocent people, we are justified in inflicting a lesser evil (incarceration) on a single innocent man (the potential serial killer).

This suggests that punishing an innocent person is justified provided the harm done to him is minor in comparison to the harm avoided to many innocent people. Are we ever justified in punishing an evil person when no good comes of it? Kleinig (1973) gives the example of a Nazi war criminal who escapes to a desert island after the war and is found 30 years later living an idyllic existence. He is unrepentant, but will do no further harm. Suppose too that, by punishing him, we do not add further to the deterrent effect of the Nuremberg trials, and we will not rehabilitate him. Should we punish him? None of the Utilitarian functions of punishment applies here, but we feel he should not escape unpunished.

If these arguments are correct, we should again accept a Hybrid theory: Punishment is justified if (1) someone deserves it provided punishing him does not harm innocent people, or (2) it produces an overall benefit by reducing harm to innocent people, provided that where an innocent person is punished, his punishment is minor compared to the total harm avoided. As Ten (1987: 80) puts it:

> Punishing a person is justified if and only if (i) he is an offender who has voluntarily violated a legitimate law, or an innocent person whose punishment will inflict much less suffering on him than the suffering that at least one other innocent person would have experienced as an additional victim of crime had there been no punishment; and (ii) punishing him does not have serious adverse effects on others.

Hart (1968) also holds a Hybrid theory – a person's voluntary commission of the offence is a necessary condition for punishment, but we are entitled to punish him only if it produces beneficial effects.

How does the Hybrid theory handle evil people who fail for

various reasons to perform any wrongful deed? Evil people matter to us because of the harm that they do – if evil intentions could be satisfied by fantasy alone and never led to harmful actions, we would not be so concerned about detecting evil people. Because wimpish and incompetent evil people are no danger to us, we are not inclined to punish them. On the other hand, the unlucky evil person may get lucky next time and we are inclined to punish him on Utilitarian grounds. We punish the unlucky assassin who misses his target unlike the voodoo follower who tries to kill by sticking pins into a doll, or the cowardly killer who just dreams of killing. While they are all equally evil, only the first is dangerous and needs deterring.

THE TROUBLE WITH RETRIBUTIVISM

Why it is just to inflict suffering on someone who has inflicted suffering on others, especially if no good will come of it? One explanation is that it is unfair that he remains happy while his victims suffered. But

> the claim that one person has an unfair share of happiness or suffering compared to another cannot be based on the effects of a single act, but must take account of the total span of their respective lives. But if that is done, then there will be many cases in which offenders have obtained less than their fair share of happiness and their victims more than their fair share. Consider the case of a particularly deprived offender who, through no fault of his own, but as the result of social and economic circumstances beyond his control, led a very unhappy life. On the other hand, his victim is someone who, through the happy circumstances of her birth and not through any special effort on her part, had a very pleasant life until she became the victim of crime. It cannot be said that the distribution of happiness and suffering across their respective lives has been unfairly favourable to the offender and unfavourable to the victim.
>
> (Ten, 1987: 50)

Retributivism cannot justify punishing criminals by saying they had an unfair share of happiness.

Retributivism may justify punishment as payment for the wrong done. Morris (1973) argues that the wrongdoer owes a debt to society. Criminal law confers benefits to all by protecting an area of everyone's life from non-interference from others. These benefits are only possible if a burden of self-restraint is accepted such that people do not satisfy their desires by interfering with the protected area of the lives of others. When a criminal violates the law, he not only enjoys the benefits of the law but also renounces the burden of restraint. In short, he takes an unfair advantage of law-abiding citizens. On this view, punishment is justified because it restores the just equilibrium of benefits and burdens that was upset by the criminal's act. But this is a strange theory. First, it seems to misplace the debt that is owed – the murderer owes a debt to his victim rather than to society in general. Second, the theory is inapplicable in societies where there are vast inequalities of wealth and opportunities. Here criminals come from socially disadvantaged groups which cannot be said to derive much benefit from the operation of the rules of society. Only if there is a just equilibrium of benefits and burdens does a criminal take an unfair advantage, and would it be just to punish him. But if the distribution of benefits and burdens is in the first place unfair, punishment would not restore fairness (Ten, 1987).

Kenny (1978: 73) argues that this leaves Retributivism in a hole: it is forced to argue that punishment

> is sought directly as an end in itself, and not as a means to deter or correct. But to seek the harm of another as an end in itself is the paradigm case of an unjust action. Retribution of this kind would not restore any balance of justice or square any accounts. It would increase, instead of diminishing, the amount of injustice in the world. Popular wisdom, which has many adages which seem to favour the retributive theory, has one which is conclusive against it: two wrongs don't make a right.

But this objection is misplaced. First, the harm is not sought as an end in itself but to serve the (Retributive) principle of justice. Second, if we ask of Retributivism why justice requires inflicting harm on an evil wrongdoer, we must also ask of Utilitarianism why justice requires producing beneficial consequences. Any theory must start from certain principles and cannot be called upon to justify these principles. If it must, it will either be launched on an infinite regress or become circular. If a theory can justify a principle, this must either be because there is some more basic principle which itself cannot be justified, or because the justification is circular and therefore suspect. This means that any theory will have to start off with some basic principles that cannot themselves be justified. Retributivism cannot be blamed for this.

THE AMOUNT OF PUNISHMENT

How much should we punish? It is accepted that those who inflict greater harm on their victims should be punished more severely than those who inflict less. How can we justify this? According to Utilitarianism, more punishment for murder is justified because the greater the evil, the more the benefit in avoiding it, and this justifies more deterrence. Utilitarianism can also explain why we punish the deliberate killer more than the reckless killer, and him more than the negligent killer. While the harm done is the same, the penalty must be different. We need less punishment to deter an action that may be dangerous than an action that is likely to be dangerous, and this, in turn, less than an action certain to be dangerous:

> Actions which, for all one knows, may be dangerous are less dangerous than actions which one positively knows to be a risk to life. Hence the more severe threat of punishment is held out to the citizen contemplating the more dangerous action. Just as actions known to be likely to cause death are in general more dangerous than those not known not to be so likely, so actions done with the intention of causing death are in general more dangerous than those merely foreseen as likely to cause death.
>
> (Kenny, 1978: 89)

If we wish to deter people from using more reliable methods of getting what they want, we need to deter intentional murder more than reckless killing; otherwise we will give reason to criminals to use the more certain method of achieving their ends.

However, deterrence is not the only consequence Utilitarianism considers. Suppose people do not obey parking laws. No matter how much we fine them, they park anywhere. Suppose that the only efficient way to deter them is to meet out a 10-year prison sentence. Utilitarianism is not committed to such punishments. As Ten (1987: 142) points out: 'The utilitarian, who regards punishment as something that is in itself bad, will only justify a particular punishment if the suffering inflicted by that punishment is less than the harm caused by the crime which would have occurred had there been no punishment.' But suppose petty thefts are widespread in society, and that thieves are clever enough to elude the law. While the harm done by each theft is small, the total harm done to society over time is great. If a particularly harsh sentence (10 years in prison) would deter all other thieves, the suffering to one petty thief will be outbalanced by the avoidance of harm to society over time. But this does not make the amount of punishment just. Conversely, suppose that sentencing murderers to more than one year in prison does nothing to lower the murder rate. Does this mean that we should only imprison them for one year? Utilitarianism gives us the wrong answers here (Ten, 1987).

Retributivism, on the other hand, seems equally unpalatable because it commits us to *lex talionis*: an eye for an eye, a tooth for a tooth, and a life for a life. This principle has a number of defects. First, it is inhumane. If someone has tortured an innocent child to death, should we take him (or, even worse, his child) and torture him to death? Second, there are many offences where the appropriate punishment is not available. As Ten (1987: 151) argues, 'what penalty would you inflict on a rapist, a blackmailer, a forger, a dope peddler, a multiple murderer, a smuggler, or a toothless fiend who has knocked somebody else's teeth out?' Third, if we calculate the amount of punishment according to the amount of harm done, then we arrive at some strange results. For example, compare someone killing an elderly woman dying of cancer to someone killing a woman in her prime. One robs a person of six months of a miserable existence while the other robs the youth of her whole life. The harm done to the elderly woman is much less than that done to the young woman. Should we punish them differently? If a thief steals £100 from a billionaire, he does less harm than if he steals £100 from a pensioner living on the bread-line. If justice requires greater punishments for greater harms, should we punish them differently?

To be fair, this third problem arises for Utilitarianism too: the action that will deter or reform one (more sensitive) offender may not deter or reform another (more hard-hearted) offender. Should we then punish people differently when they commit the same offence? Unlike Retributivism, Utilitarianism has an answer to this, but it is one of which Retributivism would approve. If we punished people differently for the same crime, our sense of justice would be outraged, and our moral allegiance to the law would be seriously threatened. As a result, people would be less inclined to obey the law, and widespread lawlessness and harm would result. Once again, we see how a Hybrid theory works best.

To answer these objections to Retributivism, we must distinguish Quantitative Retributivism (QR) from Ordinal Retributivism (OR). QR specifies the *absolute* amount of punishment for any crime, and OR only the *relative* amount. Most contemporary Retributivists adopt a proportionality principle making the amount of punishment proportional to the moral seriousness of the offence (Cross, 1975; von Hirsh, 1985). This principle demands that we construct two ordinal scales, one of punishments and the other of crimes. Punishments are ranked in order of severity and crimes in order of moral seriousness. OR requires only that the most severe punishment on the scale be reserved for the most serious offence, and so on. This answers the first two objections to Retributivism. To answer the third, we need a Utilitarian argument. If we made the punishment of a theft proportionate to the relative loss to the person, there would be no disincentive to steal from millionaires. If millionaires could not hang onto their money, no one would ever work hard and society would suffer. Similarly, the elderly or terminally ill would become easy prey, and would have to take extraordinary steps to protect themselves, fending off potential attackers whenever they felt at risk, and chaos would result. To justify the amount of punishment, we need a Hybrid theory too.

JUSTIFYING EXCUSES

Justifying excuses and justifying *mens rea* involve the same issues. If we justify excuses, we justify the excusing power of mental states, and this amounts to justifying *mens rea*. By making *mens rea* necessary for guilt we accept the idea that a person only deserves punishment if he is in a certain mental state. Once we have done this, we allow that someone should not be punished if he is in a different mental state, that is, if he has an excuse. We cannot justify the one without automatically justifying the other.

Bentham (1982) gives a Utilitarian justification for excuses – when an offender has an excuse, punishment has no good effect on his conduct, and therefore is not justified. Let us see how it works, starting with ignorance. If Fred is ignorant that the pills he gives his mother contain cyanide, the knowledge that murder is a punishable offence will not deter him (because he does not think he is murdering her). Since he has a good character, he needs no reform either. This also explains the As-if Rule: Dick was also ignorant, gassing the house because he wanted to poison his aunt. He does not have an excuse, and there is a point to punishing him – he is an evil character needing deterrence and reform. In provocation the agent loses control. With his behaviour no longer under his control, the knowledge that he will be punished can have no effect on his conduct. The threat of punishment only has a beneficial effect on someone who knows what he is doing and whose conduct is under his rational control. Voluntary intoxication is not an excuse even though punishment will not influence the behaviour of a drunk (because he does not know what he is doing or has lost control). The threat of punishment can influence someone from taking a drink, but this is not true of involuntary intoxication, which is why it is an excuse. Finally, automatism is an excuse because the threat of punishment cannot affect an unconscious agent. Is this Utilitarian account correct?

There are problems. First, Utilitarianism is wrong to suppose that punishing those with excuses cannot be a Special Deterrent. A person who is unaware that he is breaking the law *can* be influenced by the threat of punishment. He can be influenced to acquire more knowledge. A person who knows that he will be punished for an offence even if he does not know he is doing it will be motivated to take more care to avoid ignorance. Fred would have been encouraged to make doubly sure that he was not poisoning his mother. Similarly, if we disallow the excuse of provocation, we would encourage people to avoid situations that could potentially escalate, and encourage them to stay in control of their emotions. Even in the case of automatisms, punishment will encourage people to take special care to avoid hypoglycaemia, concussion, et cetera. Punishment might be ineffective on those acting with excuses, but this is not the point at which it is designed to influence people. It encourages potential re-offenders to be aware of what they are doing and to stay in control.

125

Second, punishing those with excuses would be a General Deterrent, encouraging others to take care to avoid ignorance, loss of control, and automatisms. By giving an incentive to avoid ignorance by punishing those with the excuse of ignorance, more crime is reduced, creating a greater benefit than the harm of punishing the ignorant. Similarly, by closing the loophole of provocation, the law encourages self-control. If it turns out that laws not permitting excuses (strict liability laws) are more effective at deterring criminals, then Utilitarianism is committed to the elimination of the *mens rea* requirement and the prohibition of excuses. Since not allowing excuses will force people to take more care and reduce the likelihood of further crime, Utilitarianism seems committed to it.

But Utilitarianism has an answer to this. Laws not only enhance our welfare by reducing the harm caused by crime, they also inhibit our liberty. If we punished those who make a causal contribution to anyone's death, it would be imprudent of me to do many things, like drive a car, in case I killed someone accidentally (Brandt, 1992). If we punished anyone who harmed others unknowingly, I would have to spend too much time checking everything before acting in case I inadvertently harmed another. Taking every precaution to prevent situations that might lead to loss of control would also constrain our lives. Life would become unbearable. Because the cost of strict liability laws is so high – because it has such a negative impact on our lives – Utilitarianism can justify excuses after all. Hart explains the consequences of criminal law that operated without excusing conditions:

> First, our power of predicting what will happen to us will be immeasurably diminished; the likelihood that I shall choose to do the forbidden act (e.g. strike someone) and so incur the sanctions of the criminal law may not be very easy to calculate even under our system; as a basis for this prediction we have indeed only the knowledge of our own character and some estimate of the temptations life is likely to offer us. But if we are also to be liable if we strike someone by accident, by mistake, under coercion, etc., the chances that we shall incur the sanctions are immeasurably increased.
>
> (Hart, 1968: 48)

126

It is the detrimental effect of strict liability laws (disallowing excuses) on our liberty that allows Utilitarianism to justify excuses. There is an optimal amount of care we can take to avoid offending. Knowing we might be passing a counterfeit bill might make us look for the watermark, but beyond this the effort required to ascertain this outweighs the benefits of not passing the counterfeit bill. Similarly for avoiding committing offences accidentally. Do I try to keep everyone at a distance just in case I am pushed into (and 'assault') someone else? The effort to do this will not be balanced by avoiding such harms. Since we cannot achieve total control of our environment, excessive vigilance becomes too costly.

But Utilitarianism is not out of the woods. Suppose a black man has a fit while driving his car, crashes into and kills a white child. Suppose too that if the authorities excuse him, other whites (who believe the black man crashed deliberately) will cause a riot and many innocent people will be killed. Utilitarianism directs the authorities not to excuse him, which is clearly unjust. But Retributivism is not right either. If not excusing innocent people does them minor harm in comparison to the harm avoided to others, then this is justified. If not excusing a black person of a minor offence (like shoplifting) would avert a major riot and many deaths, it would be justified. The Hybrid theory allows Utilitarian considerations to override Retributive ones in certain circumstances.

Can Retributivism alone justify the existence of excuses? It holds that we should punish those who freely do wrong.

> I can be justly convicted of homicide only if I had a fair opportunity to avoid committing the *actus reus* of homicide – to avoid causing death. This makes *knowledge* and *control* the two basic conditions of criminal liability: I have a fair opportunity to obey the law against homicide if I know (or could easily realize) that my conduct will or might cause death, and only if I control that conduct – only if I could avoid acting thus. This argument would justify the principle that criminal liability should normally depend on a 'voluntary act', since it is unjust to hold a person liable for an involuntary act which she could not control.
>
> (Duff, 1990: 107–8)

127

I have added the requirement that the person freely do wrong *because of his evil character*. An evil person is identified by his willingness to do others unjustifiable harm. This willingness can be measured not only in terms of the degree of harm the person is willing to cause, but also the certainty with which that harm is inflicted. Someone who has a mental state that reduces the degree to which he is an evil character has an excuse and deserves less punishment. In short, we excuse a person who does something bad when this is not a reflection of his good character.

When Fred gives his mother cyanide thinking it is penicillin, his ignorance shows he has no willingness to inflict unjustifiable harm. He has a good character and deserves no punishment. Therefore ignorance is an excuse. Conversely, Dick should not be excused because his ignorance does not show he has no willingness to do wrong. Because he has an evil character, he deserves punishment. If a good person is provoked and loses control, harming in spite of his wishes, he is not evil and therefore should not be punished. If he is a good character, and only in extreme circumstances does something bad, we should excuse him because of his fundamentally good character. The Retributivist can explain why intoxication does not excuse. While the drunken offender might be ignorant and out of control, when he takes a drink he demonstrates a willingness to harm others because he knows he may become violent. Because he knowingly takes a risk of becoming a lethal weapon, he is an evil person and deserves some punishment. Someone who behaves automatically and harms another does not deserve punishment because he too has no willingness to do wrong and is not evil. A person with a good character who only does something bad when he is sleepwalking, or concussed, deserves no punishment.

> The distinguishing feature of excusing conditions is that they preclude an inference from the act to the actor's character. Typically, if a bank teller opens a safe and turns money over to a stranger, we can infer that he is dishonest. But if he does all this at gunpoint, we cannot infer anything one way or the other about his honesty. Typically, if a driver knowingly runs over someone in a roadway, we might infer something about the driver's indifference to human life. But we cannot make that inference if the choice open to the driver was going over a cliff or continuing down the

incline and running over someone lying in the roadway ... The same breakdown in the reasoning from conduct to character occurs in cases of insanity, for it is implicit in the medical conception of insanity that the actor's true character is distorted by his mental illness.

(Fletcher, 1978: 800)

Factors that show a person to be of good character usually excuse.

Retributivism can also explain why a cold-blooded killer, the reckless killer, and the negligent killer deserve varying degrees of punishment. The deliberate killer does something that he knows has a 100 per cent chance of causing death, and the reckless killer does something that he knows has a 25 per cent chance (or thereabouts) of causing death. The negligent killer intends to do something knowing that he has not taken steps to ensure that no one dies. In this way, he does something that he knows has a 1 per cent chance of resulting in a death. If we measure how evil a person is by his preparedness to do harm, the deliberate murderer is more evil than the reckless killer, and he more than the negligent killer. Therefore they deserve varying amounts of punishment.

The Hybrid theory wins out. The Retributivist element explains why ignorance, compulsion, and automatism are excuses. The Utilitarian element explains why we might excuse someone deserving punishment if this avoids considerable suffering, and conversely why we might not excuse an innocent person – where the punishment is minor and the harm avoided is massive, we are justified in disallowing a valid excuse. On this theory, an excuse is justified (1) if someone deserves it provided that exempting him from punishment does not result in much more harm to other innocent people, or (2) if someone does not deserve it, but excusing him leads to the avoidance of much harm to innocent people.

CHARACTER OR INTENT?

Those who freely do wrong because of their evil characters deserve to be punished. Let us call this Character Retributivism (CR). Why not adopt an Action Retributivism (AR) that holds that a person deserves punishment if he freely does wrong? Why is the reference to evil character necessary? A similar question arises for Utilitarianism. Should we punish people for their evil acts, or only when these acts arise from their evil characters?

CR holds that an agent deserves punishment only if he has an evil character, while in AR it is only if he does evil. Which is correct? Bill is a thug extorting protection money with threats of violence. He is not averse to assaulting others, but has never killed anyone. One day he meets Hannah, a philanthropic soul working for the homeless at the food depot. Bill has never seen someone so beautiful and instantly falls in love. He comes daily to see her at the food bank, and joins in to help with distributing food to gain her affection. He enjoys helping because it gains her approval, but eventually he enjoys it for its own sake, turning away completely from a life of crime. He uses his knowledge of street people to reach them, marries Hannah, and leads an exemplary life. While Bill remains the same person, he has undergone a change of character. Suppose someone now brings charges against him for assault while he was a thug. Should we punish him? According to AR, we should because he is the same person who did wrong. CR tells us we should only punish Bill if he did wrong because of his evil character. This has two interpretations: (1) because of the evil character he possessed at that time, and (2) because of the evil character he had *and* continues to possess. Bill does not have the same character he had when he performed those actions. It seems unjust to punish him now for what he did as a different character – he is not evil now and does not deserve punishment. Bill is now not the sort of person we want to punish.

If this is correct, then factors aggravating an offence and warranting more punishment will be ones that show the person to have a 'worse' character. Factors that aggravate offences are premeditation, unnecessary violence, sadism, abuse of positions of authority or trust, harm done to someone to whom the offender owed gratitude, the helpless state of the victim, and previous offending (Walker, 1991). According to CR,

> an offender is blamed for being a person of the sort which is normally capable of doing whatever he did. Previous good behaviour, on the other hand, undermines this inference, and makes us wonder whether the act was perhaps 'out of character'. Conversely, repeated offending of the

same kind not only confirms that he is *capable* of turning thought into action but suggests that he is *likely* to. This view not only makes sense of taking character evidence into account: it also fits the other mitigating, excusing, and aggravating factors which courts take into account. Mitigations and excuses tell us that what the actor did should not be regarded as an indication that he is normally capable of it, because the circumstances were exceptional, or at least such that most people would have done likewise. Aggravations tell us that his moral character is even worse than the act itself suggests.

(Walker, 1991: 71)

The same point applies to a person who experiences genuine remorse for what he has done. If we are punishing people with evil characters, then remorse will indicate an improved character, determined not to act in such a way again, and will count as a mitigating factor. In short, Retributivism holds that it is only just to punish Bill if he is (continues to be and not just was) an evil character.

Utilitarianism supports this conclusion. Punishing Bill has little benefit – it hurts him and those he is helping. The only benefit is a General Deterrent effect on others contemplating a life of crime and hoping to plead reform to avoid punishment. Utilitarian arguments favour Character Utilitarianism over Action Utilitarianism. A person should be excused if his action does not arise from a 'defect of character', where this is construed dispositionally as an insufficient degree of some desire or aversion. For example, callousness is the possession of an insufficient degree of concern for others, and dishonesty is the possession of an insufficient aversion to deception, and so on.

If we construe 'defect of character' as suggested, our present thesis is that a utility-maximizing moral system would not condemn a certain action – that agent would be trained not to feel guilty about it, and others would be trained not to feel disapproval of it – unless it manifested insufficient motivation of a kind of importance for the moral system ... If a person's level of motivation to do certain sorts of things is adequate, the 'moral system' has done its job. The 'adequate' level of motivation is what we want, in general, neither more nor less; this level, we have

131

seen, is the one that maximizes utility . . . If a person damages through inadvertence (not negligence), or through mistake of fact (not culpable mistake of fact), through defect of memory (when the failure to remember does not show inadequate interest in remembering), through the effect of drugs or fatigue (since these leave open the possibility of adequate motivation in the dispositional sense), there was no failure of motivation.

(Brandt, 1992: 231)

We have to persuade people to behave in a moral way even if this does not serve their own interests. To do this we have to create the motivation, and the law does this by threatening to punish those who break it. By these threats, the law hopes to create in those who are tempted to break the law a motivation to abstain from doing so. Those who are already motivated to be law-abiding do not need to be further motivated and punished. Those who should be excused are those who already have the appropriate motivation but who break the law *for other reasons* – because of a mistake, provocation, and so on. This means we should only punish those who have some character defect – a motivational state that inclines them to harm others without justification – that is, who have evil characters.

It might be argued that if there were not laws prohibiting us doing wrong, we would all break the law. If this is the case, then we would have to conclude that we all have motivational defects (in the sense I have outlined), and that punishment and the threat thereof is aimed at all of us. There is nothing inconsistent with this. If the only thing that is preventing us from killing our fellow man is the punishment that would follow, then I think it would be fair to say that we *were* all evil characters (having motivational defects).

Ralph has led an exemplary life. He is a caring man, regularly spending weekends offering his services as a physician free of charge to the poor. But he falls on hard times. He gets wrongfully sued, loses his reputation, and is unable to pay for his child's health problems. One day, feeling despondent, he takes some heroin from his hospital and sells it to pay for his child's operation. He deeply regrets what he has done, and thereafter works in a drug rehabilitation clinic free of charge to atone. His action is discovered and he is charged. Should he be punished? Utilitarianism suggests he should not. This is because he has a good character that needs no further deterrence or reform. CR also argues we should not punish him because he is not an evil character – he does not deserve to be punished for a minor lapse of his character in extreme strain. If Ralph continued to display this character flaw, becoming a hardened drug pusher, his act would not be momentary lapse of a good character but a reflection of an evil one. But as there is a lapse of normal good character under extraordinary circumstances, both CR and Utilitarianism justify excusing him.

It may be difficult to decide when someone's action represents a lapse of his normal character, or a true reflection of his basic character. A change in behaviour is not sufficient to represent a change in character. Thomas appears to be an altruist, constantly offering to help the most miserable. Actually, he really despises weakness and does not care for others. The problem is that he feels inferior, and being in a position of power over the weak helps to compensate. If he changes one day to overtly exploiting others, this seems to represent a change of character but actually does not. On the other hand, whatever we do is a function of who we are, so that even a lapse in normal character can be interpreted as consistent with the person's underlying character. If we steal heroin under pressure, this is a function not only of the pressure, but also of who we are and where we draw the line. This seems to imply that every lapse represents the person's underlying character. But we define a person's character by what emerges in a normal range of circumstances. When these become abnormal, we no longer conclude that the person's behaviour in these circumstances reflects his character. Under extreme deprivations, we would all behave badly, but it would be misleading to say that we are all 'evil' characters underneath. For this reason, when a person acts in abnormal circumstances in an uncharacteristic way, we should conclude this was a lapse in his normal character. In such circumstances, both Utilitarianism and CR recommend we excuse him.

Character Retributivism holds that a person only deserves punishment if he freely does wrong (unjustifiable harm) because of his evil character. This theory agrees with Utilitarianism that punishment and the threat thereof should be directed at evil characters (people with motivational defects). Retributivism justifies excuses because excuses show that the person was not an evil character, and only evil characters deserve punishment. Utilitarianism justifies excuses because accepting excuses is the best way to both preserve our liberty and prevent harm by reducing crime. On both accounts, excuses are exactly those psychological states that show that the harmful act was not committed by an evil character.

7

CAUSALITY AS AN EXCUSE

DOES CAUSALITY EXCUSE?

If our actions are determined by our characters, and we have no control over what characters we have, are we responsible for our actions? If our behaviour is governed by causal laws, are we responsible? Determinism is the thesis that every event is the consequence of universal laws acting on prior events, and if it is true, it seems to undermine responsibility (Honderich, 1993). If I am only responsible for those actions where I could have acted otherwise, how can I act otherwise if my actions are determined by antecedent conditions and causal laws? I can only act otherwise if I violate causal laws (which I cannot as they are universally true). The existence of the causal laws seems to rule out responsibility.

If determinism does not rule out responsibility, does being caused by a disease undermine responsibility? If our behaviour is under the causal control of our rational deliberations and choices, we seem responsible. But if our behaviour is the product of an illness instead, it seems reasonable to excuse us. Is this correct? Does this mean any mental abnormality (including an abnormal personality) causing our behaviour provides an excuse? Do only certain sorts of causal explanations provide excuses? And if so, how can we distinguish those that do from those that do not?

CRIME IS DESTINY

While some criminals offend only once, repeated offending is a feature of a small minority. Nevertheless, the vast majority of crimes are committed by such recidivists. Of men born in England in 1953: 31 per cent were found guilty of at least one offence by the age of 28, but 86 per cent were found guilty only once (Walker, 1987). Most significantly, 70 per cent of all offences were attributable to 6 per cent of its members with six or more offences to their credit. This pattern is not true of England alone. In the USA, most offences are committed by those who offend more than five times (Wolfgang *et al.*, 1972). These chronic offenders made up 6 per cent of males and committed 56 per cent of the offences. Why does this group of recidivists turn to crime?

Mednick and Finello (1983) argue that such individuals suffer from an inherited disorder of the autonomic nervous system making them bad at fear, and that this defect leads to poor avoidance learning and antisocial personality disorder (psychopathy). This theory does not purport to be a complete account of the aetiology of crime. It does not even take all the biological factors into account. Crime is also associated with head injuries, low IQ, low cortisol levels, high testosterone levels, poor parenting, low socio-economic status, frontal lobe dysfunction, physical unattractiveness, and so on (Raine, 1993). But while the theory might be simplistic, the moral dilemma raised by the existence of a biological explanation for crime remains the same.

It might be objected that criminality cannot be inherited because what counts as a crime is socially constructed. What is a crime in one society is not a crime in another, and hence it is unlikely that there is a single genetic factor accounting for disparate behaviours. In addition, it might be argued that while we can make it a crime to vote Tory, it is unlikely there is a gene for this behaviour. But these objections are weak. The fact that the content of crimes can vary does not mean there cannot be a single factor predisposing individuals to break the law (whatever it may be). I think there is a gene that predisposes individuals to cheat – that is, to break the rules whatever they are. Such a gene will play a role in crime – the breaking of social rules – whatever they are. If we did make voting Tory a crime, it would still be the case that one type of person would repeatedly break this law. The fact that crime is socially constructed does not mean there are not biological factors predisposing to it. I will now present some evidence for the genetic theory of criminality.

There is ample evidence that criminality is inherited. The first attempt to show this was a twin study published by Lange (1931) under the title *Crime as Destiny*. Identical twins share 100 per cent of their genes and non-identical twins only 50 per cent. If a trait is genetically determined, more identical twins will share it than non-identical twins, or, in technical jargon, the concordance for the trait will be higher among monozygotic twins. Lange found that the concordance for criminality among thirteen identical twins was 77 per cent versus only 12 per cent in seventeen non-identical twins. This result has been replicated many times, supporting the thesis that criminality is genetically determined. In a study of 3,586 Danish twins, Christiansen (1977) showed that concordance for criminality in identical twins was 35 per cent versus 12 per cent for non-identical twins. If all the twin pairs studied so far (numbering around 6,000) are pooled, the concordance for identical twins is 51 per cent compared to 20 per cent for non-identical twins (Raine, 1993).

Adoption studies support these conclusions. If the sons of criminal fathers are more likely to be criminals than the sons of non-criminal fathers even though both have been adopted, this is strong evidence for genetic determinism. Crowe (1975) found that 6 out of 46 adopted-away offspring of female offenders were convicted of crimes whereas none of a control group broke the law. Hutchings and Mednick (1977), using the Danish Adoption Register, found that where the biological father had a criminal record, the adopted-away son had a 21 per cent chance of breaking the law compared to an 11 per cent chance if the biological father was non-criminal.

Recidivists generally suffer from antisocial personality disorder (Hare *et al.*, 1988: 268): 'Psychopaths generally had significantly more convictions for assault, theft, robbery, fraud, possession of a weapon, and escaping custody than did non-psychopaths.' They engage in a wider range of offences, attract more convictions, and spend more time in prison than non-psychopaths (Hollin, 1992). This criminal type is heritable. Cadoret (1978) compared 190 adoptees from parents with persistent antisocial behaviour to a control group of adoptees whose biological parents were not antisocial. Twenty-two per cent of the adult descendents of antisocial parents had psychopathic personalities while none of the controls had.

Cleckley (1982) defined the psychopath by the following traits: He has superficial charm and such little anxiety that he is at ease in situations that would unsettle the average person. He has no sense of responsibility or shame, and a cavalier attitude towards telling the truth. He commits antisocial acts with no regret, and exercises poor judgement. He is incapable of love and attachment, and does not respond to kindness and makes no genuine suicide attempts. He has an unrestrained sex life. He fails to have any life plan and follows a persistent pattern of self-defeat. We can explain these features by supposing psychopaths are no good at fear (Gray, 1971). If the psychopath has such a low autonomic reactivity that he has little anxiety, he will have such confidence as to exude charm. He will not feel threatened by most situations, including the threat of punishment. He will develop little respect for the law or a moral conscience which arises from learning to fear punishment or disapproval. Eysenck (1977) argues that what we call 'conscience' is a set of conditioned emotional responses – the association of fear (from punishment) with the thought of doing wrong. Because a psychopath is deficient at this, he is not held back from crime. Without fears for the future, he is imprudent. Lacking any concern that he make the same mistake again, he will not learn from his mistakes and be condemned to repeat them. His poor judgement arises from not fearing certain consequences enough. He has few regrets because he worries little about missed opportunities. Without fear, he develops little concern for himself, and without this, he develops little concern for others.

Gray (1975, 1976, 1981) has subsequently postulated a Behavioural Inhibition System (BIS) with the function of inhibiting behaviour that has been punished. According to this up-dated theory, poor socialization occurs because of a reduced ability to learn to inhibit punished behaviour, and this is a result of an inability to be anxious (fearful). This in turn is a result of reduced brain levels of serotonin and norepinephrine. Cleckley was aware that psychopaths had little fear:

> Regularly we find extraordinary poise rather than jitteriness or worry, a smooth sense of physical well-being instead of uneasy preoccupations with bodily functions. Even under concrete circumstances that would for the ordinary person cause embarrassment, confusion, acute insecurity, or visible agitation, his relative serenity is likely to be noteworthy.
>
> (Cleckley, 1982: 267)

This is a perfect description of someone not good at fear. This explanation of psychopathy is plausible, but it assumes the only thing preventing people from exploiting others is fear, that by nature people are selfish and without sympathy for others. This is wrong (Wilson, 1993), and therefore this theory cannot be the whole story. Other defects of the psychopath, such as a defect in moral reasoning, a defect in feeling sympathy, and a defect in prudential reasoning, will be explored in Chapter 9. However, let us assume for the moment that the defect in fear provides a biological explanation for the psychopath's lack of sympathy.

There is evidence that psychopaths are bad at fear. Lykken (1957) compared psychopaths to normal subjects in an avoidance-learning task. Psychopaths made the most errors when learning a sequence of coloured lights, with wrong answers receiving a shock, providing some support for the hypothesis that psychopaths are less motivated to avoid aversive stimuli because they are less fearful. Schachter and Latane (1964) argued that if this was right, then increasing their anxiety should make them learn better. Using the same task, they studied the effects of the stimulant drug adrenalin on psychopaths. When the psychopaths were injected with adrenalin, they showed a great reduction in the number of shocked errors, but the non-psychopathic prisoners were adversely affected. These results support the hypothesis that psychopaths are not good at fear and therefore do poorly at learning to avoid aversive stimuli.

More evidence that psychopathy is due to low autonomic reactivity comes from Hare (1982) who presented prisoners with numbers (1 to 12), warning them they would be shocked at 8. He measured anticipatory fear by skin conductance – the more fear, the sweatier the palms and the lower the skin conductance. The psychopaths showed little anticipatory fear until just before the number 8, while the non-psychopaths showed a strong response early in the number sequence. 'Although these findings must be interpreted with caution, they are at least consistent with most clinical statements about the psychopath's general lack of anxiety, guilt, and emotional "tension" ' (Hare, 1970: 57). Lidberg *et al.* (1984) observed adrenalin blood levels just before men appeared in criminal court for trial. If subjects are anxious, adrenalin is secreted into the blood. He found psychopathic criminals had no elevation in adrenalin unlike non-psychopathic criminals. Lippert and Senter (1966) compared psychopathic delinquents to neurotic ones, telling them that they would experience a shock in 10 minutes. The neurotic subjects showed much anticipatory anxiety while the psychopaths showed none. This low autonomic reactivity predicts recidivism. The pulse rate increase (which occurs in fear) in anticipation to stress was studied in a group of 11-year-olds (Wadsworth, 1976). Those who later (at age 21) showed severe delinquency had a lower pulse rate response at age 11. This demonstrates that those who become recidivists (psychopaths) display a poor autonomic response to stress (making them bad at fear). This has been replicated by Raine *et al.* (1990) who studied the autonomic reactivity of 15-year-olds. They discovered that low arousal correctly predicts which subjects would be criminals at aged 24 with a 75 per cent accuracy!

In summary, there is evidence that most crimes are committed by a small group of recidivists, that they suffer from a personality disorder making them bad at fear and avoidance learning, and that this is due to inherited disorder of autonomic arousal. We are all motivated by egoistic desires which bring us into conflict with others. Society sets up moral and legal rules which serve to inhibit such impulses. Such inhibition is learned by punishment or the threat thereof only if the person has the capacity to experience fear. The fear associated with such impulses serves to inhibit them, and if psychopaths are not good at fear because of this autonomic disorder, they will be unable to inhibit their antisocial impulses. Should we then blame them for their crimes? Since their behaviour is determined by their character, should we not excuse them?

DOES CHARACTER EXCUSE?

Clarence Darrow persuaded many juries to find a defendant not guilty because he was not responsible for his character and therefore his actions. 'If any of you', Darrow would say, 'had been reared in an environment like that of the accused, or had to suffer from his defective heredity, *you* would now be standing in the dock.' Wrongdoers, he said, were disordered: 'I do not believe that people are in jail because they deserve to be. They cannot feel the moral shocks which safeguard others. Is [a man] to blame that his machine is imperfect?' But does the causal explanation of a man's actions by his character show he is not responsible for his actions? Nagel (1979: 27) argues that a person is not in control of character formation, and since his choices depend on his character, he is not responsible for them either: 'Everything seems to result from the combined influence of factors, antecedent and posterior to action, that are not within the agent's control. Since he cannot be responsible for them, he cannot be responsible for the results.' Is this correct?

This is too large a question to be dealt with adequately in one short chapter. But if we are to understand whether the Causal Defence provides an excuse, we need to sketch an answer. In what follows I will suggest that far from determinism undermining responsibility, it supports it. Character determinism seems essential for moral responsibility. Someone is worthy of praise or blame if the origin of his actions can be traced to his character. If a man steals because of greed, he is blameworthy, and if he is charitable because of generosity, he is praiseworthy. If his acts are only accidentally related to his character, he does not deserve praise or blame. If a person hurts someone else, and this was not caused in any way by a violent or indifferent character, he is not blameworthy. As Hume argues:

> Actions are by their very nature temporary and perishing; and where they proceed not from some cause in the characters and disposition of the person who perform'd them, they infix not themselves upon him, and can neither redound to his honour, if good, nor infamy, if evil. The action itself may be blameable; it may be contrary to all the rules of morality and religion: But the person is not responsible for it; and as it proceeded from nothing in him, that is durable or constant, and leaves nothing of that nature behind it, 'tis impossible he can upon its account, become the object of punishment or vengeance . . . 'Tis only upon the principles of necessity, that a person acquires merit or demerit from his actions, however the common opinion may incline to the contrary.
>
> (Hume, 1962: 459)

Only if the person's actions issue from his character is he responsible. Moreover, it is only reasonable to have an institution of punishment if the person's character is causally connected with his deeds. If Mother Theresa were an evil person, and only did good deeds by accident, would we praise her? Conversely, if Hitler was a good person, and only did evil in spite of himself, would we condemn him?

This is further illustrated by the fact that the paradigmatic act we should excuse is one that is 'out of character'. If Mother Theresa uncharacteristically does something bad, we are not inclined to punish her because she is a good character. She should not be blamed for behaviour only accidentally related to her character. Retributivism and Utilitarianism both advocate that we excuse someone when his evil actions are not the consequence of his (good) character. If someone does evil because he is ignorant or out of control, we do not punish him because his actions do not flow from an evil character. The institution of defences is based on the thesis that it is just to blame only those whose actions reflect their evil characters, and upon the fact that punishment is only effective when directed towards those with motivational defects – that is, those who are evil characters.

The idea that we should not punish a person for actions flowing from his character rests on a deep mistake. It supposes that the object of praise or blame is a *characterless person*. But in judging whether it is fair to punish someone for acting in character, we are not considering punishing some characterless person for behaviour he did because of some accidental possession of his character. It is not characterless persons but people with fleshed-out characters who deserve things. Characterless persons deserve nothing – only determinate characters do.

We are responsible, then, for those actions that are are caused by our characters. If actions do not issue from our characters – from our enduring desires, values and beliefs, they are not ours, and we cannot be praised or blamed for them. This means that our behaviour must be governed by causal law if we are to be responsible. If an agent's rational deliberations are not causally sufficient for his making a choice, then either it is a matter of chance that he makes his decision or some other cause outside himself is responsible for that decision. If it was a matter of chance that he made the decision, he is not responsible. If the additional cause came from outside himself, he is also not responsible. As Ayer (1954: 102) puts it:

> Either it is an accident that I choose to act as I do or it is not. If it is an accident, then it is merely a matter of chance that I did not choose otherwise; and if it is merely a matter of chance that I did not choose otherwise, it is surely irrational to hold me morally responsible for choosing as I did. But if

it is not an accident that I choose to do one thing rather than another, then presumably there is some causal explanation of my choice: and in that case we are led back to determinism.

My choices are either random or determined by my reasons, and it is only randomness that threatens responsibility. Causality, on the other hand, is required for responsibility.

BIOLOGY OF EVIL?

It might be argued that we are only responsible if we have the ability and opportunity to do otherwise, and that if determinism is true, none of us can do otherwise. As Kenny (1978: 31) asks:

> I do X freely only if I have the opportunity not to do X and the ability not to do X. Can this power ever be present if physiological determinism is true? Can I have the ability and opportunity not to do X if I am in a physiological state from which, in conjunction with physiological laws, it can be deduced that my body will move in such a way that I will do X?

We have seen that a psychopath's behaviour is determined by his low autonomic reactivity. This ensures he is not able to form a conscience. Does this mean that he is unable to stop himself breaking the law? Or is he simply disinclined to stop himself?

> There are those who doubt whether the scandalously antisocial condition of the psychopath is truly attributed to his incapacity, as opposed to his disinclination, to behave better. In order to establish, therefore, the desired conclusion by reference to some physiological condition or phenomenon, it is necessary to show, not only that that condition or phenomenon is suitably correlated with psychopathy, but also that it is relevantly disabling.
>
> (Flew, 1973: 77)

Flew argues, as we have, that a condition prevents a person from doing otherwise if he is provided the opportunity and incentive to do otherwise, wants overall to do otherwise, but fails. Establishing the existence of abilities or disabilities in this sense *presupposes* the behaviour is caused. To show that A can do otherwise, we must see whether different circumstances induce different behaviour. But this assumes determinism. Thus showing that some action has physiological causes does nothing to prove that the person could not have done otherwise. We have shown that the psychopath's lack of sympathy has a cause. Does this mean that he is unable to do other than harm people? Physiological factors cause the psychopath to be incapable of sympathy for others. But this only means that he is unable to feel or desire otherwise, just as Mother Theresa cannot be unsympathetic or desire to inflict suffering. It does not imply that he cannot do otherwise. The question of whether a person is able to *feel* or *desire* otherwise is different from whether he is able to *act* otherwise. If a psychopath is given some short-term incentive (like a policeman at his elbow) to do otherwise, he will act otherwise. Thus he is responsible for his actions in spite of the fact that he is not responsible for his character. He can do otherwise even though he cannot feel or want otherwise.

This means that attributing to someone the ability to do otherwise presupposes determinism, and is not undermined by it. It also means that there is a biology of evil. Those who repeatedly commit offences do so because of an inherited biology. This does not mean they are not evil, that they have a disorder which excuses them from their evil deeds. This would only be true if they could not do otherwise, which they can. All it means is what we should have known anyway – that any persistent pattern of behaviour, good or bad, will have a cause, most likely in the neurological basis underlying that person's character. Psychopaths cannot want otherwise, but they are still able to do otherwise. This means that they are responsible for their actions, and are evil even though their evil has a biological basis. Evil, or the indifference to the well-being of others, has (like everything else) a biological basis. We can and should undertake a scientific study into the nature of evil (Peck, 1983).

EXCUSED BY DISEASE

If behaviour were the random product of some stochastic (indeterministic) process making us choose this action one moment and a different action the next, we would not be responsible. It is only where actions are caused by our characters that we are responsible. Conversely, when a person is caused to behave in a different way, for example by an epileptic seizure, he is not responsible. This suggests that being responsible has something to do with having one's behaviour caused in one way rather than another. Even the idea that only rational agents are responsible implies that it is only when an agent's behaviour is caused (by his rational deliberations and choices) that he is responsible. It is this central idea that underlies the Durham defence: If the homicide was the offspring or product of mental disease in the defendant, he is not guilty by reason of insanity. This rule works best in automatism. Here the mental disease is causally sufficient for the resulting behaviour. There is no way here for the person's will or reasons to intervene. If the resulting behaviour has nothing to do with the agent's reasons, deliberations, and decisions, it seems wrong to hold him responsible for that action.

For behaviour to be excused on the basis of mental illness, it is necessary that it be *caused* by a mental illness. Spike has exhibitionism and likes to expose himself to school girls. He also thinks he is entitled to the easy life, and robs a bank. He is caught, and argues he should be excused because he is suffering from a mental illness (exhibitionism). We have no temptation to excuse him, and the reason is obvious: his mental illness has nothing whatsoever to do with his offence. Blake has a paranoid illness. He believes that the FBI are experimenting on his brain. He also works as a stock broker and does some insider trading. He is caught and pleads NGRI. There is no temptation to excuse him because his psychotic illness has nothing to do with his behaviour. As Kenny notes:

> Let us suppose that an academic suffers from paranoid delusions that his colleagues are constantly plagiarizing his work, and that they are denying him unjustly of the promotion that is due to his talents . . . Suppose that while subject to these delusions he makes careful and efficient plans for the secret poisoning of his mother-in-law so that he and his wife can enjoy the large fortune which they stand to inherit by her death. It does not seem at all obvious that his mental disorder should excuse him from criminal responsibility for a premeditated murder which has no connection with it.
>
> (Kenny, 1978: 83)

If mental illness is to excuse, it is necessary that it cause the behaviour.

Many insanity defences forget this. The Infanticide Act does not require the infanticide to be caused by the puerperal illness. Suppose Jane is psychotic in that she believes that her neighbour is persecuting her. She also wants to marry someone but has a newborn from another relationship that her new man does not like. Being the callous woman that she is, she kills her child. There is no temptation to excuse her because her psychosis had nothing to do with her crime. Similarly, the Butler Commission's proposal is flawed: 'We propose that the special [insanity] verdict should be returned if at the time of the act or omission charged the defendant was suffering from severe mental illness or severe subnormality' (Home Office, 1975: 227). There must be a causal connection before mental illness can excuse. Even the most severe psychotic illness may leave many areas of mental functioning intact, as we can see with Kenny's example, and will not provide all behaviour with an excuse.

We must differentiate mental illnesses that are sufficient for the resulting behaviour (such as epilepsy) and mental illnesses (such as sexual disorders and schizophrenia), that are only necessary. Epilepsy is sufficient to cause the behaviour because once the person has a seizure; no other causal factor is needed to explain it. Schizophrenia is not sufficient to cause behaviour because it only causes a delusional belief, which is not sufficient to explain the behaviour. Let us start with mental illnesses sufficient for behaviour. When mental illness is sufficient for behaviour independently of the agent's desires and beliefs, that behaviour is called an automatism. Automatisms provide an excuse providing the person has not deliberately induced it. Thus if a mental illness is causally sufficient for the behaviour, the person has an excuse. There is one caveat – if someone knows that he will be violent during an epileptic seizure, and wants to hurt his wife, he might stop his medication. Even though his epilepsy is sufficient to explain his violence, he is responsible (Fingarette and Hasse, 1979). Only if a person has no control over the occurrence of such disorders, does he have an excuse.

What of mental illnesses that are only necessary for the behaviour? They constitute the vast majority of cases. A mental illness may cause a delusional belief, but this is not sufficient for the behaviour based on it. M'Naghten's psychosis made him believe the Tories were persecuting him. This was not sufficient to causally explain his behaviour. The final action is a causal result of the delusional belief, other beliefs, his desires and values, and so on. For example, had he believed emigrating to Australia would have solved the problem, he would have behaved differently. This means that the disorder is only necessary for the behaviour. Similarly for mental illnesses that cause perverted desires, such as the desire to have sex with dead bodies. This does not itself cause the behaviour – desires do not spontaneously bring about actions without the agent having beliefs about the best way to satisfy the desire, and deliberating over the consequences of his action for his other desires. Such mental illnesses are only necessary for the behaviour. This means that being caused by such mental illnesses cannot excuse on its own. Jed has panic attacks and goes to a psychiatrist. Therapy is successful but expensive. Jed cannot afford it and decides to rob a bank. During the robbery, he shoots the teller. Is he responsible? He would not have shot the man had he not had the mental illness (without the latter, he would not have needed the psychiatrist, would not have run up a debt, and would not have needed to rob a bank). But no one thinks that Jed should be excused because his mental illness was causally necessary for his behaviour. Pete has a fetish for shoes and collects them. Bored with his present collection, he steals some. His sexual disorder plays a causal role in this theft – without the disorder, he would not have stolen the shoes. But Pete's disorder does not excuse.

The problem runs deeper. What prevents us introducing the Greed Defence? Or the Selfishness Defence? Scrooge embezzles his clients' money. When charged, he pleads that his behaviour was the 'product of greed' and that he should be excused. We might think that a person should be excused when a disease causes his behaviour because he cannot help being ill. But Scrooge cannot help being greedy also. All of us have no (little) control over our characters. Some men are attracted to women, some not. Some men are thrill seekers, others not. We have little control over this.

> My genetic inheritance and the circumstances of my upbringing may be factors over which I exert little control, but I exert no less control than anyone else. To show that a personality disorder should excuse a person from responsibility for his actions, it is not enough to show that he bears

no responsibility for his disordered personality; it would be necessary to show that he bears less responsibility for developing a disordered personality than the rest of us bear for developing the personalities that we have. But as long as we are all equally capable or incapable of influencing what sort of personalities we have, then there is no reason to excuse persons with personality disorders. They are no less responsible for their character, and their actions, than are the rest of us.

(Elliott, 1994: 99)

The central issue is whether we can control our actions, whatever the control we have over our personality. If we can, we are responsible; if we cannot, we are not. The fact that our behaviour is caused by features of our characters (like desires and values) over which we have no control does not rob us of our responsibility. So lacking control over factors that cause our behaviour cannot be the criterion that enables mental illness to excuse. We have no control over the fact that we have two arms, but these are factors causing what we do.

If, on the other hand, we explain why Pete has an excuse by arguing that he was overwhelmed by his fetish, and lost control of himself, we have produced a valid excuse, but we have thereby abandoned the Durham Rule. We are no longer saying he should be excused because a disease *caused* his behaviour, but because the disease made him *lose control*. Similarly, if a person argues that he was overwhelmed by his desire to have sex with dead bodies, and therefore was not responsible for killing, he has abandoned the Causal Defence. He is no longer arguing that he should be excused because he has a disorder (necrophilia) which gave him the sexual desire for dead bodies. He is saying that this desire was of a nature and degree that he was not able to control himself. This is to use another defence entirely.

The Greed and Selfishness Defences must fail because responsibility requires our behaviour to be caused by our desires, beliefs and deliberations. Where our behaviour is random and unconnected to our characters, we are not responsible. It is indeterminism not determinism that is the real threat to responsibility. But if having one's behaviour caused (by one's deliberations and reasons) is necessary for responsibility, then it cannot undermine responsibility. All a person would have to do

148

to undermine responsibility would be to show that he acted because of reasons. If I stole money because I wanted to be rich, my desires (and values and beliefs) are causes of my behaviour, but they are hardly excuses!

We can justify the view that being caused by a disease should not excuse on both Utilitarian and Retributive grounds. On Utilitarian grounds, even if Jane received treatment for her post-partum psychosis, she would remain an evil character. She does not care enough about the lives of others and is prepared to kill in order to get what she wants. Such a person needs reform and the rest of us need protection from her. In addition, a message has to be delivered to all those who are tempted to do what they like just because they happen to be mentally ill. On Retributive grounds, even though Jane is ill, she is also evil, and she committed the offence because she was evil (and not because she was ill). Justice requires that she be punished. Similarly, Jed and Pete do what they do because of their characters, and therefore deserve punishment. If they were good characters, their having an illness would not constitute a reason to harm others. As they need deterrence and reform (independently of treatment), they should be punished.

To see this more clearly, consider this example. Nick is a good man, but a mental illness gives him the desire to kill other people. Since he is a good person, he finds himself experiencing an alien desire to do something he judges morally unacceptable. He tries to do something about it, going for psychiatric help and warning the police. If he did not, this would show that he was overwhelmed by the desire or that he is not the good person we supposed. If he is overwhelmed by the desire, he would have an excuse – not on the basis that the desire was caused by the disorder, but on the basis that he lost control. The fact that the desire is caused by a disease on its own does nothing to excuse. On the other hand, if Nick is unwilling to act on the desire, he would stop himself from acting on it and get help. If he is happy to act on the desire, he shows himself to be an evil character and deserves punishment. Either way, the fact that a desire is caused in an abnormal way (by a disease) does not excuse him. Only if the disease causes the subversion of his whole character would he have an excuse. In particular, if it changes his moral beliefs, we might excuse him on the basis of a change in character. But this is also to abandon the Durham

Rule and use a different excuse. On its own, being caused by a disease does not excuse him.

But there is a kernel of truth in the Durham Defence. This is the idea that if behaviour is caused in one sort of way, the person is responsible, and if it is caused in another, he is not. When someone 'could have done otherwise', his behaviour is caused by his enduring desires (from his character) and his rational deliberations. If it were not, other incentives would not influence his behaviour and he would be unable to do otherwise. If his behaviour is caused by such factors, he is responsible. On the other hand, if it is caused by other sorts of causes, like epileptic seizures, overwhelming desires, and so on, he is not. But the problem with the Durham Defence is how to choose the causal chains that permit us to judge that the agent is responsible for the behaviour so-caused. Why should we choose behaviour that is caused by rational deliberation? The answer is difficult to find unless we say that such behaviour is not performed under ignorance and compulsion. But if we argue thus, we are no longer claiming that it is the type of cause that determines who is responsible, but the absence of exculpating ignorance and compulsion. We are forced to abandon the Durham Defence in favour of other insanity definitions.

There is another flaw in the Durham Defence. It places the legal decision of guilt or innocence outside the hands of the jury and into the hands of a specialist psychiatrist. As Reid (1960: 119) says:

> Durham is a medical test. The jury must accept the expert testimony of the alienists, and if psychiatric opinion changes overnight, a person convicted as a result of the obsolete opinion may be entitled to another jury trial at which the jury cannot 'arbitrarily reject' the new opinion. Shifts in medical theory and even in medical nomenclature may determine the conduct of trials and the fate of defendants.

But the decision about guilt or innocence is a legal decision, not a medical one. Guilt, innocence, and responsibility are not diagnostic categories appearing in psychiatric nosologies. They are moral concepts implying that a person ought or ought not to be punished. But by defining NGRI in terms of causation by a mental illness, the psychiatrist is given the job of deciding guilt or innocence. But he has no authority to make such moral or legal pronouncements. He can diagnose the presence of mental disorder, but that is all. While he may be trained to judge 'He is a bad case of Schizophrenia', he is not trained to judge 'This is a terminal case of Impaired Responsibility' or 'This person has a disorder of his faculty of Responsibility'! Deciding whether someone is NGRI is to make a moral judgement – it is to say that he does not deserve punishment and should be excused, which is distinct from making a medical diagnosis. The decision about responsibility is a moral and legal one, and one a psychiatrist has no expertise to make. Such matters must be left for the jury. Therefore, insanity should not be defined by the Durham Rule.

Determinism does not undermine responsibility. In fact, the causation of our behaviour by our characters, rational deliberations and choices is necessary for responsibility. Furthermore, causation by a disease does not undermine responsibility unless the disease is sufficient for the behaviour (and the person is not responsible for the disease). Where it is necessary, we need the traditional criteria for responsibility to decide whether a person is responsible. Being caused by a disease is not an excuse *per se*. This means that a person can be inclined to be indifferent to others as a result of a biological disorder, but still be responsible because he can do otherwise even though he cannot want or feel otherwise.

8

THE REDUCTIONIST THEORY

WHAT'S SPECIAL ABOUT MENTAL ILLNESS?

Causation by a mental illness is not sufficient to count as an excuse. Is there anything about a mental illness that makes it sufficient to excuse? Reductionism is the thesis that there is not, and that mental illness only excuses via ignorance and compulsion.

> Mental illness should not itself be an independent ground
> of exculpation, but only a sign that one of the traditional
> standard grounds – compulsion, ignorance of fact, or
> excusable ignorance of law – may apply . . . [T]here is
> nothing very special about mental disease as such. We
> hardly need the separate insanity defence at all if we accept
> the propositions that mentally ill people may be subject to
> internal compulsions, that mental illness can cause inno-
> cent ignorance, and that both compulsion and innocent
> ignorance are themselves excuses.
>
> (Feinberg, 1970: 274–7)

Morris (1982: 11) is another reductionist, arguing 'there is no need for the M'Naghten or Durham Rules, because [cases of insanity] clearly fall within general criminal law exculpatory rules. The actor simply lacks the *mens rea* of the crime.' Reductionism is plausible, but is it correct? I will argue that it provides sufficient conditions for an excuse, but that it is not a complete account of why mental illness excuses.

152

THE M'NAGHTEN RULES

The M'Naghten Rules constitute the most influential definition of insanity, being used in England, New Zealand, India, Pakistan, Australia and many states of America. They form part of the ALI test of insanity, and a broad interpretation of them is used in Canada. The test is cognitive, excusing the mentally ill offender on the basis of ignorance: A person is NGRI if he is suffering from a disease of the mind producing a defect of reason such that he does not know what he is doing or that it is wrong.

Like the excuse of ignorance, the M'Naghten Rules embody the As-if Rule. In formulating the Rules, Judge Tindal said that the deluded offender 'must be considered in the same situation as to responsibility as if the facts with respect to which the delusion exists were real.' The As-if Rule explains why we feel differently about the following two cases: Adam comes to believe his neighbour is an alien from another planet intent on killing him. Seeing no alternative, he kills him in self-defence. Adolf is a Neo-Nazi who wants to kill Jews. He comes to believe his neighbour is a Jew because he wears a hat, and kills him. Both murders occur as a result of a delusion, and neither would have occurred had the person not been suffering from a mental illness causing this delusion. However, only Adam has an excuse because had his belief been true, his action would not have been wrong. If the neighbour had indeed been an alien intent on killing him, self-defence would have been justified. Conversely, Adolf has no excuse because had his belief been true, he would not have been justified in killing the Jew. It is because he is an evil man that he lacks an excuse.

What decides whether a person is responsible is our *explanation* of his action. We explain Adam's behaviour on the basis of his good character and his delusion. No reference is needed to an evil character, and therefore we excuse him. On the other hand, a reference to Adolf's evil character is essential to explain his evil deed. Therefore, he is responsible and deserves punishment. Both Retributivism and Utilitarianism agree that it is when a person is not evil that he has an excuse. According to Retributivism, if the person is evil, he deserves punishment even though also mentally ill, and Utilitarianism tells us that if he is evil, then even after we treat his mental illness, he is still a danger to society (because of his evil character). Even if we

153

treated Adolf's mental illness, he would still deserve punish-ment because of his evil character, and would still constitute a danger to society.

What about the following difficult case: Fritz is also a Neo-Nazi who wants to kill Jews. His neighbour is in fact a Jew, but Fritz comes to believe that he is part of an international conspiracy to establish the reign of Satan on the earth. In order to save the world, Fritz kills his neighbour. Does he have an excuse? He has an evil character, because he does not think certain races deserve to live. However, in explaining why he killed his neighbour, we need no reference to his evil character. On the contrary, we need a reference to a good impulse – his desire to save the world. Therefore, he has an excuse and we are not inclined to punish him. It is only where a reference to the offender's evil character is *essential* in explaining why he did the harmful deed, that he does not have an excuse. If he is only acci-dentally evil, we should not punish him.

Exculpatory ignorance must also satisfy the Responsibility Rule. Sam suffers from paranoia. When he stops his medication, he believes others are against him and retaliates. He wants his rival out of the way and so stops his medication, hoping to 'beat the rap' with an insanity plea. He has no excuse because he is responsible for his ignorance. Ignorance must also satisfy the Disability Rule to excuse. This automatically obtains if someone is deluded. A delusion is a conviction a person is unable to correct because of his irrationality. This is why the Rules refer to a defect in reason. If the person is able to reverse his ignorance, he is responsible. Gary suffers from Narcissistic Personality Disorder. He has a grandiose belief that obedience of the law is for losers. He thinks special people like him are above the law. He is not deluded. He knows he is quite ordinary – in fact, it is because he feels inferior that he inflates his own importance. He *chooses* not to correct his false belief because he likes feeling special. When he breaks the law, he does not have an excuse because he is quite able to correct his false belief. Only if he is unable to correct his ignorance does he have an excuse.

Of course, someone might suffer from narcissism to a degree that he is overwhelmed by his desire to feel important, and is unable to correct his false belief. But once this happens, he will be suffering from a delusional disorder that makes his ignorance exculpatory. Between the extremes of someone with a mild degree of narcissism who can easily correct his false beliefs, and the person with the severe narcissism leading to a delusional disorder, there is every shade of grey. There is every reason to think that nature does not come in black and white, and that many will have varying degrees of difficulty becoming aware that their grandiose beliefs are false. So too with every other disorder leading to ignorance. While only those who are unable to correct their false beliefs have a (complete) excuse, it is reasonable to argue that those with less severe disorders nevertheless have a partial (moral) excuse. They are not as blameworthy as those who freely choose to remain ignorant. But whether the law should move towards this graded concept of guilt we will leave to the Conclusion to discuss.

The M'Naghten Rules define a person as NGRI if he 'does not know what he is doing is wrong'. This could mean: (1) he mistakenly thinks it is against the law, (2) he mistakenly thinks it is contrary to socially accepted morality, (3) he mistakenly thinks it is morally right, and (4) he fails to appreciate that it is contrary to the law or socially accepted morality. The first interpretation does not provide an excuse. Boris becomes psychotic in the Middle East and believes it is legal there for a husband to do whatever he wants to his wife. When she burns his supper, he kills her knowing it is morally wrong but assuming it is not illegal. He does not have a (moral) excuse. Even if it was not against the law, he still commits an evil deed. Ignorance of the law, at least for such offences, is no excuse if the person knows it is morally wrong. If a Neo-Nazi becomes deluded that killing Jews is now legal, and sets about this task with relish, he should still be punished. Moreover, as the Butler Commision (Home Office, 1975: 218) note: 'Knowledge of the law is hardly an appropriate test on which to base ascription of responsibility to the mentally disordered. It is a very narrow ground of exemption since even persons who are grossly disturbed generally know that murder and arson are crimes.'

The second interpretation seems valid, and different from the first, as Stephen (1883, 149) illustrates:

> A kills B, knowing that he is killing B, and knowing that it is illegal to kill B, but under an insane delusion that the salvation of the human race will be obtained by his execution for the murder of B, and that God has commanded him

(A) to produce that result by these means. A's act is a crime if the word 'wrong' means illegal. It is not a crime if the word 'wrong' means morally wrong.

Angus, a psychotic patient I cared for in Scotland, killed his father believing him to be the Devil. Straightaway he phoned the police to tell them to prepare a ticker-tape parade, so convinced was he that he had done something socially acceptable. Angus has an excuse – if his father was the Devil, he would not have acted contrary to socially accepted morality. As Gordon (1978: 353) writes: 'If A kills a man in the belief that he is killing the devil he is entitled to be acquitted since it is, presumably, no crime to kill the devil.'

In a contrasting case, Peter Sutcliffe, the Yorkshire Ripper, killed thirteen women from 1975 to 1981. In his trial, four psychiatrists (for the defence and prosecution) agreed that he had paranoid schizophrenia. He had acted on hallucinatory instructions from God and believed he had a divine mission to kill prostitutes (Prins, 1986). The court decided he was responsible for his actions and found him guilty of murder. He did not have an excuse – even if God had instructed him to kill prostitutes, it would have been a violation of common morality to have acted on such instructions (without good reason). This is different from the man Stephen described as having to kill in order to save the world. If we had to kill an innocent person to save the world, our common morality suggests we should. If an innocent person was unknowingly carrying a mutant virus that would wipe out the human race, and the only way to stop him infecting others was to kill him, common morality would suggest that killing him would not be wrong. Hence, if a psychotic person kills another person while deluded that this is necessary to save the world, we do not judge him to be evil, and would excuse him. But killing others only because God has told us to do so would not be judged as acceptable by our common morality. Hence such deluded persons do not have excuses.

The third interpretation is incorrect. If a sane person does something morally acceptable to him knowing it is socially unacceptable, he lacks an excuse. Similarly for deluded offenders. Chaulk and Morrissette were two youths who robbed and killed an elderly man in Winnipeg. They believed they had the power to rule the world and that ordinary law and morality did not apply to them. According to their subjective morality, killing the old man was acceptable, but they knew society would not approve. The judge ruled that 'moral wrong is not to be judged by the personal standards of the offender but by his awareness that society regards the act as wrong,' and they were found guilty (Rogers and Mitchell, 1991: 124). Even if something is subjectively acceptable, we are not entitled to do it if we know it offends against socially accepted morality. If someone has an excuse whenever he believes that what he was doing is subjectively acceptable, everyone would have an excuse. Fingarette (1972: 154) agrees:

> If the word 'wrong' means something like 'judged to be morally wrong by the person's own conscience,' we then have an interpretation that is surely in itself an unacceptable legal test for the absence of *mens rea*. It would undermine the foundations of the criminal law to allow that a person who violated the law should be excused from criminal responsibility because, in his own conscience, his act was not morally wrong.

Someone has an excuse if his mental state shows he is not an evil character. Angus is not an evil character because killing the Devil is not wrong. Chaulk and Morrissette are evil because killing an elderly man is an evil thing to do. After Angus has been treated, he does not have an evil character that makes him a danger to others. But Chaulk and Morrissette constitute a danger even after treatment because they lack concern for others. This explains why we feel uncomfortable excusing the Yorkshire Ripper who acts on instructions from God to do something he knows is socially unacceptable. Similarly, Adolf is not entitled to kill Jews even if his conscience tells him it will make the world a better place. Our legal codes are there to protect us against such fanaticism, not to sanction it.

On the fourth interpretation, a person appreciates what he is doing is wrong not only if he has a cognitive awareness that the act is wrong, but also if he experiences the usual moral sentiments associated with that act. This is the law in Canada: 'Emotional, as well as intellectual, awareness of the significance of the conduct is in issue' (Milliken, 1985: 327). But this is not the sort of move we want to make – it implies we cannot convict the psychopath or the cold-hearted offender. As Schopp (1991: 33) notes:

This requirement, however, would seem to exculpate the cold or vicious criminal who victimizes innocent people without experiencing sympathy or remorse. Yet, the insanity defence certainly is not intended to exculpate such criminals. Rather, these are just the people that the criminal law – and the prison system – are designed to deter.

In fact, the Canadian formulation quickly led to trouble. Kjeldsen, a sadistic psychopath with a long history of sexual attacks, committed a carefully planned murder, and then argued that he was a psychopath, and that his lack of emotional empathy prevented him from appreciating the nature and quality of his act. The Supreme Court of Canada was forced to narrow their definition of 'appreciate' in order to uphold the conviction. So this interpretation is wrong. If appreciating the consequences of one's actions implies that one has sufficient empathy for others (implying that one is motivated not to harm them), every criminal would be M'Naghten insane and have an excuse! Not only would this interpretation excuse the hard-hearted criminal, but it would also excuse soft-hearted criminals who are only able to commit offences because they 'hide' the vivid details of what they are doing from their awareness. Sly is only able to commit pension fraud because he avoids imagining the hardships he will cause his victims. He does not 'appreciate' what he is doing because he does not experience the usual emotional reaction to such behaviour, but he is not M'Naghten insane! Many crimes may only be psychologically possible because the criminal deliberately avoids awareness of the victim's suffering, but the perpetrators do not have an excuse.

The M'Naghten Rules also define a person as NGRI if he 'did not know what he was doing'. This can mean either (1) he did not know *exactly* what he was doing, or (2) he did not know some *morally significant* feature of what he was doing. The first interpretation cannot be right. Anyone with a delusion does not know some aspect of what he is doing. Adolf did not know he was killing a Gentile when he killed his neighbour. But this does not excuse him. On the other hand, Angus did not know some morally relevant feature of what he was doing. He did not know he was not killing the Devil. Because the second formulation is a rewording of the As-if Rule, it is correct. Someone is M'Naghten insane and has an excuse only if he did not know some morally significant feature of what he was doing, and did not know that what he was doing was contrary to socially accepted morality.

While the M'Naghten Rules excuse some deserving cases, they do not excuse all cases with cognitive impairments; that is, reductionism is incomplete. There are some cases where the delusion does not satisfy the As-if Rule but where we still consider that the defendant should be excused on cognitive grounds. M'Naghten, himself, knew what he was doing (in the morally significant sense) in that he knew he was killing a man and that it was against the law and social morality. He believed he was being persecuted by the Tory party, and had turned to his father, the Sheriff-Substitute, and the Lord Provost for help, but had received none. Believing he could not elude the Tories, and believing they planned to murder him, he killed what he thought was the PM. Even if he was being persecuted, killing the PM in self-defence is not justified. We only allow pre-emptive strikes in self-defence when the attack is immanent and there is no alternative, which was not the case here. The As-if Rule tells us we should not excuse him.

But we are still inclined to think that M'Naghten deserves to be excused. Why? Perhaps he has an excuse not captured by the traditional excuses. A madman is not a sane man with false beliefs – he lacks the rationality to reflect dispassionately on his beliefs and reason clearly about the courses of action that are open to him. Because his ability to reason is more generally affected, he is unable to see clearly the options that are open to him, and this may provide him with a unique excuse. If M'Naghten was unable to see that he had an alternative, he would have an excuse.

> An ordinary offender might be expected to distinguish between a situation in which there is an immediate threat to his life, and one in which there is a plot to kill him at some stage. But there is no reason to believe that M'Naghten had the capacity to distinguish between those situations in which there was no alternative but to kill in self-defence, and other situations in which various evasive actions to save one's life might be taken.
>
> (Ten, 1987: 124)

If this failure excuses, Reductionism can explain this by showing that this reduces to further ignorance. M'Naghten's defective reasoning – his inability to see other options – can be seen as a further delusional belief that he had no option. If we then apply the As-if Rule to both his delusion that his life was in danger *and* the delusion that he had no alternative, it turns out that he does have an excuse. If the Tories were really planning to kill him, and the only way of avoiding this was to shoot the PM, this would be justified. The excuse falls under the category of ignorance, and we need no further explanation.

While the excuse of ignorance explains why such cases are excused, it does not explain why all deserving cases of cognitive failure should be excused. Arnold shot Lord Onslow because he believed Onslow had sent imps and devils to disturb his sleep. Arnold knew what he was doing and that it was against the law and social morality. His ignorance does not satisfy the As-if Rule: If Onslow had been disturbing his sleep, this would not justify his death. Yet do we really think Arnold should not be excused? As Lord Onslow himself felt, it was inhumane to punish him. We have two options here: we can argue that we should not excuse Arnold and therefore we have no exception to the M'Naghten Rules, or we can argue that we should excuse him, and that the M'Naghten Rules are incomplete. Moral intuitions are unreliable here because they differ. But suppose that prior to becoming ill, Arnold had been a gentle and caring man, always thinking of others. Then he had become ill, acquiring the persecutory delusion and a selfishness making him care only about his own peace of mind. Here our intuitions suggest quite strongly that we should excuse Arnold – he is a good person underneath. Suppose, instead, that prior to becoming ill he had been an uncaring and self-centred person, with prior convictions for assaulting those who got in his way. Then he had become psychotic, and discovering that Onslow was interfering with his sleep, he had concluded that this justified Onslow's death. Here we have little inclination to excuse Arnold because he is an evil character. But if we excuse Arnold in the first variation, this means that the M'Naghten Rules are incomplete.

There are non-cognitive reasons why we might want to excuse a mentally ill offender. If we had reason to believe that M'Naghten or any other mentally ill offender was in the grip of such a powerful emotion or delusion that he was unable to prevent himself acting on it, we would excuse him not on the basis of ignorance, but because he had lost control over his behaviour. This is not captured by the M'Naghten Rules which hold that

> a person whose insanity consists merely in delusions is still capable of choosing to act in conformity with the law governing the situation as he perceives it ... According to the better medical knowledge available now, however, the fact of the matter is that such persons in the grip of their delusions are normally so severely incapacitated that they cannot even choose to act otherwise.
>
> (Gross, 1979: 127)

Whether medical knowledge shows this or not, reductionism is not thereby undermined. If we excuse someone because they were unable to do otherwise, we rely on the traditional excuse of compulsion.

THE IRRESISTIBLE IMPULSE TEST

Many insanity defences have a volitional prong, excusing on the basis of compulsion. Irresistible impulses were accepted as excuses in English law with the Homicide Act, and the ALI standard contains a volitional prong. But most courts have been reluctant to accept such a test because of the empirical difficulty of distinguishing between irresistible and unresisted impulses. Of course, talk of irresistible impulses is misleading. It is not so much that an impulse is so powerful that it cannot be resisted – it is that the person's control is so weak that he cannot resist acting on the impulse. But however we formulate it, there is still the problem of deciding when a person is unable to resist the impulse and when he chooses not to do so.

When Byrne strangled a young woman in a YMCA hostel, his defence argued that he suffered from sadistic sexual impulses he could not control. He was convicted, but at Appeal it was ruled that the inability to exercise sufficient self-control is a defence (when due to an abnormality of mind). At the Appeal, the Lord Chief Justice observed:

> In a case where abnormality of mind is one which affects the accused's self-control, the step between 'he did not resist his impulse' and 'he could not resist his impulse' is, as the evidence in this case shows, one which is incapable

161

of scientific proof. A fortiori, there is no scientific measurement of the degree of difficulty which an abnormal person finds in controlling his impulses. These problems, which in the present state of medical knowledge are scientifically insoluble, the jury can only approach in a broad, common-sense way.

(Kenny, 1978: 41)

How do we tell the difference between an impulse which is irresistible and one which is not resisted? Wootton (1981) argues we cannot because 'it is not possible to get inside another man's skin'. Kenny goes further:

If someone succumbs to the temptation of committing a criminal act there is no way even in principle of deciding whether he is a man of normal strength of will who is giving way to impulses which are stronger than normal, or is a man of unusual weakness of will giving way to normal impulses. If evidence is given to show that on many occasions he has indulged in criminal behaviour, this may be taken with equal justice as evidence of chronically imperious impulses, or of chronic unwillingness to exercise self-control. If, on the other hand, evidence is given to show that this is a wholly uncharacteristic lapse in a life of otherwise unblemished rectitude, this in its turn may be taken with equal justice as evidence of impulses no stronger than normal, or of a degree of self-control well beyond *l'homme moyen sensuel*. Where the same behavioural evidence can be taken with equal justice as evidence for contrary mental phenomena, it is clear that the alleged mental phenomena are metaphysical fictions.

(Kenny, 1978: 42)

Is this argument correct?

There is some reason to think so. We know that there is something different in the brains of those who act on aggressive impulses – they are low on the neurotransmitter serotonin (Virkkunen, 1992; van Praag, 1991). But does this mean that a low serotonin is the physical basis for choosing not to resist aggressive impulses, or the basis for the inability to resist those impulses? This discovery cannot help us decide whether the person is unwilling or unable to resist. Nevertheless, Kenny's argument is not conclusive. First, the fact that we cannot decide which of the two options is correct is no surprise. Scientists always have the option of saving a theory in the face of conflicting data (Quine, 1960, 1969). If we see someone acting self-destructively, do we argue that he wants (consciously or otherwise) to kill himself and is adopting appropriate means to this end, or do we argue that he does not want to kill himself but is mistaken about what he is doing? How could we decide? We could give him a gun – if he kills himself, we might conclude the first theory was right. But again, we can still stick to the second theory and argue that he thought the gun was unloaded. And so on. Take this example from the history of science (Shapere, 1974). Aristotle held that a force was required to keep an object moving. This implied that when a projectile is released, it should drop to the ground (because the force acting on it has stopped). But when it did not drop, Aristotelians did not reject their theory. They simply argued that there was a force still acting on it – air was displaced from the front of the projectile and rushed in to push the projectile from behind! The fact that we have difficulty deciding between two options does not make irresistible impulses metaphysical fictions. If it does, then all our scientific concepts are metaphysical fictions.

Second, although any theory can always be 'saved', we can still have grounds for adopting one theory over another. In the first example discussed above, we could ask the man what he wants to do, and in the second example, we could tie a streamer to the projectile and see whether it is pushed forward by the 'wind'. These answers are not conclusive either, but they do provide evidence supporting one theory over the other – to sustain the alternative becomes too implausible. We have defined the capacity to do otherwise so that it can be settled in an empirical way. To decide whether an impulse is irresistible, we provide a person with the opportunity and incentive to do otherwise. We can also observe whether he tries to resist the impulse, and whether he is remorseful and disappointed in himself afterwards. If this happens, it becomes more and more implausible to argue that he chose not to resist the impulse. Ten writes:

Consider now the case of an offender who kills . . . [W]e see him disturbed before the killing, confessing to having homicidal desires which he does not understand or identify with, and seeking help. When he kills, there is no motive, no interest of his which is served by the killing, and there is only remorse and total confusion that he should have committed such an act. It is as if the impulse to kill is like an alien force with a life of its own while he is merely a helpless spectator having no control over it. Under these circumstances we can indeed say that he had an 'irresistible impulse' to kill.

(Ten, 1987: 132)

Contrary to Kenny, we *can* have evidence for one view over another.

Nevertheless, the law is reluctant to allow an insanity defence based on such a notion. The American Bar Association (ABA) and the American Psychiatric Association (APA) have both supported insanity defences that focus on the defendant's capacity to appreciate the wrongfulness of his conduct and do not include volitional tests (Schopp, 1991). The ABA recommended that the defendant be exculpated only when 'as a result of mental disease or defect, that person was unable to appreciate the wrongfulness of such conduct'. The APA also advocated adherence to a standard declaring someone NGRI when 'as a result of mental disease or mental retardation he was unable to appreciate the wrongfulness of his conduct at the time of the offence'. Both have opted for cognitive tests primarily because they think that experts lack the capacity to distinguish irresistible from merely unresisted impulses. We will see in Chapter 13 that we have reason to doubt this conclusion.

We have defined an irresistible impulse as one that the person fails to resist even when provided with sufficient incentive. Considered absolutely, there are no irresistible impulses. People losing control under provocation can always be provided with an incentive (like a policeman at his elbow) sufficient to inhibit their impulse.

Strictly speaking, no impulse is 'irresistible'. For every case of giving in to a desire, it will be true that, if the person had tried harder, he would have resisted it successfully. The psychological situation is never – or hardly ever – like that of the man who dives from a sinking ship in the middle of the ocean and swims until he is exhausted and then drowns. Human endurance puts a severe limit on how long one can stay afloat in an ocean; but there is no comparable limit to our ability to resist temptation.

(Feinberg, 1970: 283)

To avoid concluding that there are no irresistible impulses, we relativized the notion of ability to standard circumstances. I do not have the ability to run 100 metres in under 10 seconds if I achieve this feat with drugs, the fear of God, and a gale-force wind! Similarly for the ability to restrain one's impulses. Marks (1969: 141) argues:

> A patient cannot be expected to muster her energies so that she treats every minor shopping expedition as she would a fire in the house. Not only agoraphobics but everybody can perform unexpected feats in an acute crisis; it would be unrealistic to demand such feats constantly of everybody as a matter of routine, and in an agoraphobic who has much anxiety any minor sally outside the house requires great effort, trivial though it would be for a normal person.

Only if we refer to standard circumstances can we say that the agoraphobic is unable to leave the house. If we allow a fire in the house to count as a standard circumstance, we have to conclude she is able to leave the house, which prevents us making a useful distinction between an agoraphobic and a normal person. Similarly for the ability to restrain oneself. While there may be no absolutely irresistible impulses, once we relativize the notion to standard circumstances, there are such impulses. Note that we are not committing ourselves to the unjust 'objective standard' here. We are not saying that someone has an excuse only if the reasonable man would have been overwhelmed too. If the person is given an incentive (one that would produce in him sufficient motivation to resist), but is unable to do so (even if a reasonable person could), he will lack the ability to control his impulses, and will have an excuse.

In Dahmer's trial, his psychiatrists argued that he was over-whelmed by his necrophilic desires. However, when it was shown that he was able to stop himself acting on his necrophilic impulses to conceal his actions from the police, and his family, and to allow himself to get maximum pleasure (he committed the crimes on the weekends giving him two full days to enjoy the bodies), it was evident that these impulses were far from irresistible. The inhibition of the impulses by such situations shows that he was not overwhelmed. Nilsen was charged with the murder of eleven men. Like Dahmer, he kept the bodies for days afterwards, having sex with them. He too was able to interrupt his murders when a policeman arrived on the scene, when it was not convenient for him, and when he wanted to let his victims live, and this shows us that he was not out of control (Masters, 1985). This illustrates that we construe the threat of punishment as a standard circumstance. If a person would have modified his behaviour with the threat of punishment, we conclude he was able to do otherwise and does not have an excuse. As a Canadian judge explained in 1908:

> The law says to men who say they are afflicted with irresistible impulses: 'If you cannot resist an impulse in any other way, we will hang a rope in front of your eyes, and perhaps that will help.' No man has a right under our law to come before a jury and say to them, 'I did commit that act, but I did it under an uncontrollable impulse,' leave it at that and then say, 'now acquit me'.
>
> (Low *et al.*, 1986: 15)

If hanging a rope in front of him inhibits the impulse, then the person is responsible. But if someone has 'lost control', and acts in spite of the policeman or noose being there, this shows that he is unable to do otherwise and we should excuse him.

Some may think that necrophilic desires are intrinsically irresistible. This is false. Someone can have necrophilia in that he is aroused by the idea of sex with dead bodies, but may lack the nerve to act on such desires. There is nothing about a sexual impulse that makes it irresistible. If this were so, every sexual offender would have an excuse. As Feinberg (1970: 282) argues:

> There is no *a priori* reason why the desires, impulses, and motives that lead a person to do bizarre things need necessarily be more powerful or compulsive than the desires that lead normal men to do perfectly ordinary things. It is by no means self-evident, for example, that the sex drives of a paedophiliac, an exhibitionist, or a homosexual must always be stronger than the sexual desires normal men and women may feel for one another.

In addition, if a person recognizes that he is having trouble controlling whatever sexual impulses he has, he should go for help. If he does not, he has chosen his own satisfaction over the well-being of others. In which case, he is an evil person deserving of punishment.

However, just as we have argued that there are degrees of ability to correct false beliefs, providing partial excuses, so we might argue that there are degrees of being in control of one's impulses. In between the extremes of being able to do otherwise in any circumstances and being unable to do otherwise even if extraordinary incentives are provided, there are many shades of grey. While the person who cannot resist in standard circumstances has a (complete) excuse, those who are able to resist but who still have some difficulty have a partial excuse. They are not as blameworthy as the person who commits the offence in total control of his impulses. While we might accept they have a partial (moral) excuse, whether the law should accept degrees of guilt is another matter which we will discuss in the Conclusion.

There are some cases where a volitional test may provide a valid excuse. Premenstrual Syndrome (PMS) can dramatically reduce a woman's capacity to control her impulses. English killed her lover while suffering from severe PMS, and was found not guilty of murder on the grounds of diminished responsibility (Whitlock, 1990). However, anyone knowing that she experiences difficulties controlling her impulses during the premenstrual period should take precautions against herself becoming violent then. Being violent during PMS is much like taking alcohol when you know this makes you dangerous. Whenever a person suffers from a condition making her predictably violent, she assumes responsibility because she knows what will happen. Nevertheless, there are many other cases where we judge that the person was not in control, and should be excused for that reason. For example, many psychotic patients harm themselves (and sometimes others) because they are terrified of being tortured to death by some conspiracy. From their description of the events, there is every reason to believe that the fear was overwhelming, and while they knew what they were doing was wrong, they could not stop themselves. One of my patients in Canada was so terrified that he would be tortured to death that he became panic-stricken and frantically tried to kill himself with whatever means was available. His delusions were so overwhelming that he lost control over his behaviour. Though he committed no offence, he was not responsible for his behaviour because his impulses were irresistible.

The excuse of compulsion explains why such patients have excuses. But it does not explain why all deserving cases of volitional failure should be excused. When McCullough, a high school student with kleptomania, was apprehended for stealing, the following stolen objects were found in his possession: silverine watches, old brass watches, old clocks, razors, cuff links, watch chains, pistols, combs, jack knives, pocket mirrors, bicycle wrenches, padlocks, clippers, bicycle saddles, keys, scissors, mouth organs, rulers bolts, washers, calipers, violin strings, penholders, spoons, pulleys, and more (Fingarette and Hasse, 1979). He had no interest in owning these objects, yet he risked things that he did have an interest in (like his freedom) by stealing them. There was no evidence that this senseless desire was overwhelming. Yet he hardly seems to be the sort of person we regard as responsible for his actions.

We can strengthen this case if we expand the story. Suppose that prior to suffering from kleptomania, McCullough was a law-abiding and caring person. However, following the loss of his parents, he had developed the incomprehensible desire to steal things, even completely useless things. He knew it was wrong and knew he could resist such impulses, but felt so miserable that he no longer cared. Before the loss, he would have worried about the harm a theft would do to others. Now nothing mattered. McCullough is a fundamentally good character, and we feel he should be excused. However, it is not the case that he was suffering from irresistible impulses; rather it is because he underwent a temporary change in character that he has an excuse. But this means that not all cases of volitional insanity can be captured by the traditional excuse of compulsion.

MENTAL ILLNESS AS DURESS

There are two formulations of the 'incapacity to conform one's conduct to the law' (Schopp, 1991). In the first, we imply that a person would not have done otherwise had the circumstances differed in standard ways sufficient to make him want to do otherwise – he suffers from 'irresistible impulses'. In the second, we mean not that he could not have done otherwise, but that he could not have been expected to do otherwise. On this reading, the volitional test really becomes the defence of duress. We have seen that when a person is faced with awful options – such as helping terrorists versus allowing them to kill his family (duress), and facing death from starvation versus killing another person to stay alive (necessity) – while he might not have a complete justification for doing the wrong thing, it would be inhumane to punish him. This is because we cannot expect such people to be super-human. When conforming to the law requires someone to be a hero or a saint, we should not punish those who do the wrong thing. We partially excuse them and exempt them from the harsh punishment deserved by those who freely break the law.

Perhaps a mental illness is an excuse on this basis? Note that the acceptance of this defence does not undermine reductionism. Reductionism is the thesis that we do not need a separate insanity defence, and that the reasons why mental illness can excuse are derived from already existing defences in the law. Robert, who becomes deluded that he is being persecuted by a gang of thugs, believes that if he does not do something evil, like stab an innocent person, they will torture him to death. He also believes that there is no way out of this dilemma, and that even if he went to the police for protection, the gang would still ensure that he met a sticky end. He succumbs to the dilemma and stabs a girl. Does he have an excuse? He was not in the grip of an irresistible impulse in that he would have conformed his conduct to the law had a policeman appeared. His ignorance does not satisfy the As-if Rule – even if his beliefs were true, his act was wrong. But if we judge that only a hero would have resisted such a threat (had it been true), then it seems unreasonable to punish him. Where it is extremely difficult to resist doing the wrong thing, we judge that the person is less blameworthy, and has a partial excuse. Given that we partially excuse such people (even from murder) when they are really in such a dilemma, we should also partially excuse Robert who is deluded that he is in such a dilemma.

This argument shows that a person's delusions can place him in exactly the same situation as someone operating under duress or necessity. And if the latter exempt a person from punishment, then so should the former. However, Elliott (1991) argues that this explains why we should excuse those suffering from 'volitional disorders' such as kleptomania, pyromania, or pathological gambling. He argues that duress consists in being faced with equally aversive alternatives (such as choosing between harming someone else and being harmed oneself), and that such patients also face such choices (between satisfying a morally abhorrent desire and experiencing the discomfort of leaving that desire unsatisfied). If they act on the desire, they experience guilt and shame, but if they resist, they experience extreme discomfort. But the trouble with this model is that there are many situations where a normal person faces aversive alternatives but where he does not have an excuse. Much ordinary criminal behaviour is like this. A person with a weak moral character faces the option of breaking the law (and doing something he knows is wrong), or facing extreme hardship (by doing without the profit his criminal activity will bring). Someone may face a life of poverty if he does not sell drugs, or face ruining his political career if he does not blackmail a former lover. But because it is reasonable to expect everyone to resist these temptations, (or perhaps because having such temptations reflect an underlying evil character), their predicament does not excuse. So why should the predicament of those with volitional disorders excuse? Many alternatives are as aversive to the sane person as the alternatives facing the volitionally disordered patient, and if the former do not have an excuse, then neither do the latter.

Elliott argues that there is a difference between the cases where the criminal succumbs to temptation and where the volitionally disordered patient succumbs to his impulse. The criminal wants to have his desire (for wealth or sex with children), whereas the patient does not want to have the desire (to steal, or gamble). But this may not be true. The paedophiliac may on occasion regret that he does not have normal heterosexual desires, but he is still responsible. Conversely, the kleptomaniac may want to satisfy the urge to steal (when he has it). So this distinction will not stick. Elliott also argues the volitionally disordered patient could claim that he has some (though not complete) justification for doing what he did. He might concede he did a bad thing, but argue that he should not be punished as severely because he did it to avoid the suffering caused by not satisfying the desire. But once he does this, one can see immediately how weak the defence becomes. Imagine the hardened criminal arguing to the judge: 'I suffer so much when I don't have violent sex, my Lord, that this partly justifies the suffering I give others!' Of course this is nonsense.

For the defence of duress to work in mental illness, the person must be deluded and not just suffer from a 'volitional disorder'. Schopp agrees, and concludes that affective states like depression are not of themselves sufficiently aversive to constitute an aversive state no reasonable person could resist avoiding:

> When one examines carefully the types of cases in which it seems natural to conclude that the actor could not have done otherwise due to depression, the depressive disorder usually includes cognitive dysfunction that renders it unreasonable to expect the actor to do otherwise in the light of his distorted understanding or reasoning.
>
> (Schopp, 1989: 87)

But even if we accept that duress can count as a defence in mental illness, there will still be cases where a person will have no excuse of ignorance or compulsion, or the defence of duress, but still have an excuse. Alex gets depressed. When the time comes to fill in his tax form, he cannot be bothered. He knows it is against the law not to complete it, and is not immobilized by the depression. He simply no longer cares what happens to him. His depression does not distort his cognitions, or give him any impulse he cannot resist, or place him in a situation analogous to duress. Yet we are not inclined to punish him because his depression has induced a change in character – he is not his usual self and would not have done this were it not for the change induced by the depression. This means that traditional excuses cannot account for all cases where mental illness excuses.

Reductionism is the thesis that insanity excuses in virtue of the traditional excuses of ignorance and compulsion (and the traditional defences). There are nevertheless some cases of insanity where we regard the person as having an excuse, but where the person's actions do not satisfy either the M'Naghten Rules, the Irresistible Impulse Test, or the defences of Duress and Necessity. They have an excuse, but do not suffer from exculpatory ignorance or compulsion. Some delusions do not satisfy the As-if

Rule, and some impulses are not irresistible, but they still have exculpatory power. This is because some people should be excused because they acted out of character. Thus Reductionism does not provide both necessary and sufficient conditions for excuses. It is incomplete.

9

IRRATIONALITY AS AN EXCUSE

RATIONALITY AND RESPONSIBILITY

According to what I call Rationalism – the theory that irrationality excuses – there is a deep connection between irrationality and excuses. We regard someone as responsible only if he has a fair opportunity to avoid punishment. As Radden (1985: 54) puts it, those who are rational 'have the ability to avoid errors of judgment and action: the power to engage in the kind of scrutiny, reflection, and checking which would allow them to do so . . . In contrast, the exculpating unreason exhibited by the insane results from an inability to avoid such errors.' If a person is irrational, he is unable to calculate the consequences of what he is doing, and cannot infer that he faces punishment if he breaks the law. In addition, if a person's behaviour is not under the control of his rational deliberations, he does not have a fair opportunity to avoid punishment because he is unable to control himself. Therefore, if someone is irrational, he is not responsible.

Retributivism holds that it is only just to punish someone if he could have done otherwise. A person can only do otherwise if he is able to take into account the consequences of his actions and able to control them. Therefore someone must be capable of rationality if we are to justly punish him. Utilitarianism supports this conclusion. It holds that there is only a point to punishing those who are rational. It is only worth deterring someone who is able to be influenced by that deterrence – that is, if he is able to take account of the consequences of his actions. This means that he must be rational. Duff (1990: 102) puts it this way:

> In holding someone responsible for his actions, we suppose
> that he is in some relevant sense a 'free' agent; that he has,

in the traditional terminology, 'free will'. Now the meaning of 'free will', as a precondition of responsibility, is a matter of long controversy. I think it can best be explained, however, in terms of the concept of rational agency: an agent is 'free' in so far as his actions are guided by his understanding of good reasons for action.

Someone is responsible if he can do otherwise, which implies that he is rational. This Rationalism is plausible, but is it correct? We will see.

SUBSTANTIVE IRRATIONALITY

Rationalists argue that ignorance and compulsion alone do not explain why it is just to excuse the mentally ill. In M'Naghten's case:

> He made no mistakes about what he was doing – he knew he was shooting, and he knew that he was killing – nor was he ignorant of the legal and moral prohibitions against killing. Finally, there is no very persuasive case for saying that M'Naghten was compelled to do what he did. True, under the facts as he believed them to be, he had a hard choice to make. He believed that he was being persecuted by Peel and others and that if he did not strike first, he himself would be hurt or worse. Yet for a sane person such beliefs, even if true, would not give rise to any valid duress defence (there being no threats of immediate harm), nor can such preemptive strikes be justified as self-defence. The short of it is that M'Naghten should flunk not only the test that bears his name, but all the standard insanity tests with the exception of Durham. Yet I think our intuition is that someone like M'Naghten, who was very crazy, should not be responsible.
>
> (Moore, 1984: 223)

Fingarette argues that mentally ill offenders are irrational and therefore should be excused:

> An insane person has 'lost his reason'. Hadfield was a man who wished to be put to death in order to play his God-ordained role as the new Christ. He was an irrational man. His attempt to assassinate the king was well thought out,

but it was an irrational act. The psychotic mother, agonizingly depressed, feeling that the world was filled with suffering and sin, tortured by the conviction that her child faced a life of nothing but suffering and sin, skillfully arranged matters so that she could undisturbedly put her infant to a relatively quick and painless death. She was irrational. Her mood and attitude were irrational. Her act was irrational. She had indeed lost her reason. Her conduct, however, was self-initiated, voluntary, skillfully carried out toward the clearly conceived end she had in mind.

(Fingarette, 1972: 176–7)

If M'Naghten, Hadfield, and the psychotic mother have excuses, then we must reject Reductionism. The question we now face is whether their irrationality explains why they have an excuse.

We will first examine the idea that mental illness causes substantive irrationality, and this is why it excuses. Fingarette believes that emotions and desires can be irrational (and provide excuses):

Conduct is insane, crazy, mad, irrational when it is not shaped in the light of certain norms. These norms are not only norms of correct inference or valid argument; they are norms regarding what emotions, or moods, or attitudes, or desires are in some sense suitable or proper with respect to certain other aspects of one's situation . . . [I]t is irrational in the sense that concerns us, to giggle or chuckle pleasedly at the sight of a mangled body, to feel pleasure at the death of a loved one, to feel gloomy upon succeeding in an important venture, to step nonchalantly and knowingly in front of a racing train, to desire to maim oneself.

(Fingarette, 1972: 183–4)

According to Fingarette, someone is insane if he is irrational, and he is irrational not only if he is unable to arrive at rational beliefs and subject his behaviour to rational control, but also if he is motivated by irrational emotions and desires.

Can emotions be irrational? We might argue that an emotion is irrational if the belief on which it should be based is either absent or irrational (Foot, 1978). When I am frightened by a spider, my emotion is based on the belief that I am in danger. The emotion is rational if the spider is a black widow (making

175

the belief rational), but irrational if the spider is a harmless house spider (making the belief irrational). If I am terrified of the house spider while not believing I am in danger, my emotion is also irrational. On this basis, we can argue that emotions can be irrational. But does this mean that a person fearful of house spiders is insane? What if Gertrude attacks a person showing her such a spider? Is she NGRI? If Gertrude believes her life is endangered, she has an excuse, but not because her fear is irrational, but because her ignorance satisfies the As-if Rule – she would be justified in defending herself if her life were threatened. Contrast her with Bob who also has an irrational fear of spiders, and attacks the spiders in his house with cyanide fumes, knowing full well the risk to others. Someone is killed. Bob does not have an excuse because he does not suffer from exculpatory ignorance – he knew of the risks to others. Irrational emotions *per se* do not excuse.

Fingarette argues that the psychopath is irrational because he fails to be sympathetic to others.

> Individuals with psychopathic personalities may manifest a bizarre insensitivity or a purposefully cultivated but now deep-rooted callousness that enables them to commit crimes of peculiarly inhuman or cruel kinds. Could it be said, then, that on the whole each 'lacks capacity for rational conduct in regard to the criminal significance of the act' because of a gross incapacity for emotional responsiveness? . . . If the facts do show chronic generalized failure to develop human relationships – i.e., a generalized incapacity to respond with feeling to the sufferings, agonies or death of human beings – then we do indeed have grounds to view the individual as criminally irrational.
>
> (Fingarettte and Hasse, 1979: 237)

But is it irrational not to care about others? Moreover, does this excuse? Suppose in 2010, someone expresses sympathy towards his damaged robotic house-cleaner. Is this feeling rational? We might say that the emotion is irrational because the belief on which it is based – that robots have feelings – is irrational. But what of the psychopath who does not care about others so that, when they are in pain, this does not matter to him? What is the source of irrationality here? It is not that he believes others do not experience pain. He knows they do, but does not care. He is like the man not fearful of the black widow spider because he has nerves of steel. There is nothing irrational about the psychopath lacking sympathy and, therefore, in Fingarette's own terms he is not insane. But even if we judged that he is irrational, if he kills another person because he lacks sympathy, but knows what he is doing and is in control of his action, why would we want to excuse him? Retributivism argues that we should punish a person if he freely commits an offence because of his evil character, and not caring about others is what we *mean* by evil character. Hence it is appropriate to punish him. Utilitarianism too argues that the psychopath is paradigmatically the sort of case that needs deterrence, reform and incapacitation. Both theories support our not excusing him.

What about the irrationality of desires? If desires can be rational, we will have two sorts of rational action. An action is formally rational if it is what the agent believes to be the best means to his ends. On this concept of rationality, it is not rational or irrational to choose one end rather than another. As Hume remarks in his famous passage:

> 'Tis not contrary to reason to prefer the destruction of the whole world to the scratching of my finger. 'Tis not contrary to reason for me to choose my total ruin, to prevent the least uneasiness of an *Indian* or person wholly unknown to me. 'Tis as little contrary to reason to prefer even my own acknowledg'd lesser good to my greater, and have a more ardent affection for the former than the latter ... In short, a passion must by accompany'd with some false judgment, in order to its being unreasonable; and even then 'tis not the passion, properly speaking, which is unreasonable, but the judgment.
>
> (Hume, 1962: 416)

Fingarette defines insanity in terms of substantive rationality. Someone is substantively rational if he not only chooses the best means to his ends, but also if his ends or desires themselves are rational.

But when is a desire irrational? There are a number of theories. According to the *Objective Good Theory*, an end is irrational if it is not worth desiring. Culver and Gert (1982: 35) argue that 'an irrational desire involves both wanting to suffer some evil and *not* having an adequate reason for doing so'. But what is an 'adequate reason'?

> It is a reason that is adequate to make some particular self-harming action rational . . . If I cause my leg to be amputated in order to get rid of an annoying Plantar's wart, that would count as a very irrational action because I am inflicting on myself several very great evils: pain, permanent disability, and increased risk of death (through a wound infection) for an inadequate reason. However, if I allow my leg to be amputated because I have a malignant osteosarcoma in the femur and amputation may prevent metastatic spread, then I have an adequate reason for acting, because the pain, disability, and probable death associated with metastatic bone cancer are at least as significant as the evils associated with the amputation.
>
> (Culver and Gert, 1982: 30)

An irrational desire is wanting to suffer an evil without avoiding a greater evil or gaining a greater good.

This implies that we can objectively rank evils such as death and goods such as pleasure into a hierarchy independent of subjective preferences. Only with such an objective hierarchy can we get the notion of substantive irrationality off the ground. If someone has a different hierarchy and does what is (formally) rational in his own lights, he is substantively irrational if he does not avoid the greater evil as determined by the objective hierarchy. Some patients have such a hatred of invasive procedures, like giving samples of blood, that they would rather risk death (from undetected disease) than subject themselves to such procedures. Such individuals are substantively irrational on this view because their desire hierarchies are irrational. If death is a greater evil than 5 minutes of pain according to the objective hierarchy, it will be substantively irrational to prefer death to avoid that pain. Even if someone hates pain so much that he would rather be dead than experience it, so that avoiding pain is (formally) rational, he is substantively irrational. His hierarchy of preferences is, by definition, irrational.

This theory has problems. Any ranking of goods and evils is based on a system of values not necessarily shared by all agents. If I train heavily, experiencing pain and lost opportunities in order to achieve my dream of winning an Olympic medal, it is because I judge this good to be worth more than the evils I suffer. But will the objective hierarchy agree? What will the objective ranking say of the man who risks death by attempting to climb K2 solo without oxygen, or who risks death by spending the longest time living up a pole so that he can get into *The Guinness Book of Records*? Any decision here depends on our values, and what justification do Culver and Gert have for saying that an agent is irrational simply because he does not have the same value hierarchy that they have? This concept of substantive rationality implies that anyone with different values is irrational!

Once we recognize that the 'objective' ranking of goods and evils is based on one set of values, there will be a number of different hierarchies reflecting different value systems. If substantive rationality is to be a form of *rationality* and not another way of talking about values, we need to know why it is rational for someone with one set of values to make choices governed by another. It will not help to argue that rationality requires the adoption of one hierarchy because it is only in this hierarchy that one good or evil is 'really' of more benefit or harm than another. Even if we could show this, it is, as Sartre remarked: 'Even if God existed, it would not matter.' Even if there were values that corresponded to some 'reality', why should this matter to someone who values different things? Values are necessarily relational – values cannot exist independently of some being for whom they are important. But if we cannot have absolute values (independent of any beings), why is it rational to pursue someone else's values rather than one's own?

Fingarette's notion of insanity depends on this flawed notion of substantive rationality. He illustrates his argument with one case:

> Fish, the complacently habitual child killer and child eater, was found sane under a traditional insanity test, but he was in fact a very paradigm of insanity. His emotional reactions and desires were in some respects so distorted that he had not the capacity to act rationally insofar as these came into play. However, his intellectual and perceptual capacities were not ever substantially impaired, nor was he, apparently, dominated by depressed or manic moods. When he ate children or stuck sharp objects into his body, he knew

179

what he was doing, and he knew that what he was doing was contrary to law and public morality. He acted voluntarily ... Yet we do not strain language at all ... to say that his conduct was grossly irrational. And it is this notion that is the ground of our intuitive but very clear perception that he is insane.

(Fingarette, 1972: 177)

Fish's values are so seriously flawed that Fingarette concludes he is irrational and insane. He similarly concludes that psychopaths are insane. Bavidge (1989) concludes that the psychopath is not responsible for his actions because he fails to live in a 'worthwhile world', and Fingarette and Hasse (1979) argue that psychopaths are 'not rational in regard to law' because they do not value human life.

If someone can be excused on the basis that he holds different values, every criminal has an excuse! When a person breaks the law or a moral rule, it is because he has different values. When a person steals, or murders, it is because he does not care sufficiently about the suffering he causes. But this does not mean that all criminals should be excused. This would make the category of the criminal or evil person disappear. A psychopath might justify his conception of cruelty in terms of survival of the fittest. Why should we think he is not responsible simply because he holds different values? If only extremely deviant values imply a loss of responsibility, this argument precludes extreme evil (Wootton's paradox). But extreme evil *is* possible. Why should someone who does not care very much about others (because he runs them over in his car by accident, but cannot be bothered to stop) be evil, someone who cares even less (because he decides to kill his wife so that he can be free to keep the house and marry his mistress) be more evil, but someone who cares nothing at all about others (because he is willing to rape and kill numerous women) not be evil at all? Since being evil consists in not caring sufficiently about others, it is hard to understand why someone who does not care at all about others should inexplicably cease to be evil. But if extreme evil is possible, this account of responsibility must be wrong.

According to the *Informed Desire Theory*, a desire is rational if one would want it if one knew all the facts. Rawls (1971: 416) argues: 'A person's future good on the whole is what he would now desire and seek if the consequences of all the various courses of conduct open to him were, at the present point of time, accurately foreseen by him and adequately realized in imagination.' But Fish's desire to torture and eat children may not be based on any mistaken beliefs. Moreover, even if it were irrational, he is still responsible. If I think that money will bring me happiness, but am mistaken about this, and rob a bank, killing the teller in the process, why should I have an excuse? I knew I was breaking the law and was in control of my conduct, so why should my making a mistake about what I 'really wanted' provide me with an excuse?

Brandt (1992: 46) argues for a variant of this theory according to which a desire is rational if it survives cognitive psychotherapy:

> I mean by saying that a certain desire is irrational for a given person, that the person would not continue to have the desire if he got before his mind vividly, with firm belief, not necessarily just once but on a number of occasions, all the relevant propositions the truth of which can be known to him, at the very same time at which he was reflecting on the object in a desiring way.

If a desire survives repeated exposure to the facts accessible to a person, it is rational. If Jane wants to go back to her boyfriend, her desire is irrational if it would fade with repeated recall of how abusive he is. But many desires Fingarette considers irrational may be unaffected by cognitive psychotherapy. Fish's desire to inflict pain on others may remain undiminished by his awareness that it arose because he was abused as a child. Conversely, most of our desires might turn out to be irrational on this account. If we knew the origins of our desires, they might not persist. Moreover, even if irrational desires are ones not surviving cognitive psychotherapy, if Pollard robs banks (when this desire would not survive the realization he is doing it to be punished), if he knows he is breaking the law and is in control of his actions, he is still responsible.

According to the *Intelligibility Theory*, a desire is only rational if it is intelligible. Moore (1984: 19) argues that 'if the desire is so bizarre as to be unintelligible to us – say, a desire to keep one's elbow in mud all afternoon for no further reason – we cannot understand the action as that of a fully rational agent'. What makes a desire unintelligible? 'We judge a desire to be unintelligible when we reach the limits of our empathic understanding, that is, where we cannot understand how any *person* could want what he claims he wants.' We are able to empathize with someone's desires when we recognize that we have the same actual or potential desires. But how do we decide when a desire (actual or potential) is shared? We might not share the necrophiliac's desire for sex with corpses, but we do share the desire for sex with whatever makes him sexually aroused. If we make his desire abstract, we share the same desires and can empathize with him. Or we might understand his desire to have sex with a corpse as a desire to have control over his sexual object, and we might recognize in ourselves such a desire. But if we allow ourselves to identify with some abstract feature of the desire, we can empathize with anybody. The same problem arises for potential desires. We have the same potential desire as someone if we would acquire that desire if we had his experience. If we are trying to identify with a sadist, and imagine ourselves being brought up by an abusive mother as he was, we can see ourselves coming to hate women and wanting to hurt them, and can empathize with the sadist. But then almost any desire, no matter how bizarre, will become intelligible.

But even if this criterion were useful, why should someone with an unintelligible desire have an excuse? If Dahmer's desire to eat his victims so that they can live on in him is unintelligible, why should this count as an excuse? After all, an unintelligible desire is simply one which we do not or would not share. Why should being different be an excuse? Moreover, it is impossible to see how someone who commits a serious offence will *not* be different. How could someone who deliberately kills another person in cold blood for personal gain not be different? Such a person lacks the normal desire to avoid harming others. But his different desires do not excuse. If they do, we will obliterate the distinction between the mad and the bad. As Moore (1984: 207) puts it: 'There is such a thing as evil in the world. Believing this, it becomes important not to confuse unintelligibility (madness) with incorrectness (badness) in the major premises of the practical reasoning of human beings.' But an evil person is someone who by definition has desires that are different from ours. If having different desires is grounds for an excuse, the distinction collapses.

Feinberg (1970) is conscious of the pitfalls of defining intelligibility in terms of our 'imaginative capacities'. He opts for a definition in terms of the pursuit of ends that do not serve the good of the agent.

> McCullough's sick desires were not for his own good, material or otherwise. He stole objects that could do him no good at all and assumed irrational risks in the process. The desire to steal and hoard these useless trinkets was a genuine enough desire, and it was his desire, but it does not follow that it was a desire to promote his own good.
>
> (Feinberg, 1970: 287)

But can we be sure we suffer from no imaginative failure? We may have difficulty understanding why someone wants to punish himself, but if we see he is trying to assuage his feelings of guilt, we see what interest of his is being served. Perhaps McCullough pursued some end we have not understood. Perhaps he pursued a relief from tension. Before we can conclude that the desire does not serve any of his interests, we must first understand it, and if Feinberg has given us reason to doubt our ability in this arena, we have reason to suspect we may be unable to decide whether a desire is not intelligible.

According to the *Alien Desire Theory*, a desire is irrational if it is alien. Bavidge (1989: 74) argues that the psychopath is not responsible because he 'relates to his own personality in a way which is different from normal, and which prevents him endorsing his own actions ... The whole import of his is contained in one remark of Dennis Nilsen: "I cannot judge or see myself in any of it".' There seem to be two ideas here: A desire is alien if (1) a person does not identify with it, or (2) he does not endorse it. What does it mean to identify with one's desire? It means seeing it as part of oneself rather than some alien part of one's character. What do we mean when we judge that it belongs to some alien part of one's character? It means not approving of it; and this is what not endorsing it means. But this cannot be the basis for an excuse. This implies many criminals have an excuse because they know that what they are doing is wrong. Even if Nilsen did not endorse his desires, he lacks an excuse.

Feinberg (1970: 289) regards the hallmark of an alien desire as the 'actor's lack of insight into his own motives ... [H]e may think that "exposure for exposure's sake" is what appeals to him in the idea of public undress, whereas really what appeals to him is the public "affirmation of masculinity".' This cannot be right. First, many of our normal desires are as obscure to us as abnormal ones are to criminals. Do I really understand why a woman's shape arouses me any more than a sadist understands why inflicting pain arouses him? But even if I do not understand my desires, I am still responsible when I act on them. If Tim thinks he wants to get rich quickly by committing fraud, but really wants to embarrass his father, he is still responsible because he knows what he is doing and is in control of his actions. Furthermore, should it turn out that all our theories of human motivation are wrong (which is likely given the fate of all theories), this does not prove that we were never responsible! Suppose sociobiology is correct – all our desires and behaviour are directed towards maximizing our biological fitness. We find beautiful women beautiful because our genes know that their best chance of getting into succeeding generations is to tag along with such women's genes – our children will be attractive like her and likely to be married and have children. But this does not mean that those unaware of such motivations are not responsible.

The attempt to show that an offender is not responsible because of substantive irrationality fails not only because this notion of rationality is suspect, but because substantive irrationality, even if it exists, is not sufficient for exculpation.

FORMAL IRRATIONALITY

Radden (1985) argues that mental illness excuses because it leads to irrationality. Like Fingarette, she holds that exculpatory ignorance and compulsion are not enough to explain why mentally ill offenders deserve excusing. She argues that non-psychotic depression and paranoia excuse without exculpating ignorance or compulsion. Therefore,

a test for criminal insanity will be proposed which by passes reference to the traditional notions of knowledge and control in favour of the broader notion of unreason . . . Persons charged with a criminal offence should be found not guilty by reason of insanity if it is shown that their act resulted either from a pervasive defect of mind manifested in their not holding and acting upon

184

sufficient reasons or not holding consistent beliefs and desires, or an inability to control their actions.

(Radden, 1985: 135–61)

Radden correctly points out that the paranoid patient irrationally ignores conflicting evidence when arriving at his paranoid beliefs. She concludes that because of this irrationality, he has an excuse.

Some argue that psychotic patients are no more irrational than normal people, and therefore that their irrationality cannot excuse (unless it excuses us all). Healy (1990) argues that it is the psychotic's abnormal experience (auditory hallucinations and passivity experiences) and not his irrationality that explains his abnormal beliefs. When the psychotic explains his auditory hallucinations providing a running commentary by saying he is being spied upon, he is being no more irrational than the rest of us. But if the schizophrenic is no more irrational than most, we cannot excuse him on the grounds of irrationality, and the Rationalists are in trouble. But psychotic patients *are* more irrational. Chapman and Chapman (1988: 176) note:

> The reasonableness of a belief should be judged in part by the range of evidence considered . . . The non delusional person takes the usual step of considering more information about the world than the anomalous experience itself, while the delusional person responds to the experience as if it were the only datum available.

Because of this, it is theoretically possible for irrationality to count as an independent excuse for the mentally ill. But before we examine these arguments, we must distinguish different kinds of rationality. First, there is inductive rationality, or reasoning from evidence to a hypothesis going beyond that evidence, and, second, there is deductive rationality, or reasoning from premises to a conclusion contained in those premises. There is a third kind which I call practical rationality. Someone has this sort of rationality if he possesses both inductive and deductive rationality, holds consistent beliefs, possesses consistent and transitive desires, is able to think of the options facing him, and uses a rational principle to select the best course of action. Does a failure of any of these sorts of rationality excuse?

Let us start with inductive irrationality. Rick is paranoid. He sees a friend purchasing a gun and remembers an argument with him the day before. He infers that the man is against him and ignores evidence to the contrary. When he next sees his friend, he considers his life to be in danger and kills the friend in self-defence. Does he have an excuse? It seems that he does, but this is because he is suffering from exculpatory ignorance. His ignorance satisfies the As-if Rule. This is not a case where irrationality excuses independently of the M'Naghten Rules. What about cases where paranoia does not satisfy the M'Naghten Rules? Suppose Ethan uses the coffee machine at work, and it malfunctions, spilling coffee all over him and making his work mates laugh. He infers that they are deliberately humiliating him and decides to take revenge by killing them. He lacks an excuse – if this is the sort of thing he thinks is an appropriate response to humiliation, he is an evil man deserving punishment. His irrationality does not excuse because his ignorance does not satisfy the As-if Rule.

Radden's argument with non-psychotic depression is similar. Jenny is depressed and sees the world in negative terms, irrationally ignoring the positive things. Her mother is suffering badly from terminal cancer, and when she finds a pamphlet from EXIT – the organization assisting suicide – she concludes that she wants to die. Believing that her mother needs her help, she kills her. Jenny is irrational and has a (partial) excuse, but her irrationality does not excuse independently of the M'Naghten Rules. If her mother had really been suffering interminably and wanted to die, her act of assisted suicide would not have been evil. If affective disorder does excuse because of the irrationality it causes, it does not do so independently of the M'Naghten Rules. To see this, we need only take a case of depression not satisfying the M'Naghten Rules. Suppose Deidre is depressed. When the casting director does not stop the auditions after her screen test, she infers the worst. She decides to make the director pay, tampering with his car and causing an accident. Does her irrationality provide her with an excuse? No. Even though Deidre is irrational, she shows a callous disregard for life and deserves punishment. Radden fails to produce an example of mental illness where irrationality excuses independently of the M'Naghten Rules.

These examples suggest that irrationality is like ignorance – not any irrationality counts as an excuse. Irrationality must satisfy an equivalent of the As-if Rule – it excuses only in those cases where, had the reasoning been correct in arriving at that conclusion, the person would not have done wrong. If Rick was correct to reason that his friend was about to kill him, he would not have done wrong by killing in self-defence. We excuse Jenny because, if her reasoning were correct, her act would have been justified; but this is not true of Deidre or Ethan. The irrationality of Jenny and Rick shows them to be good characters, unlike Deidre and Ethan, and thus they have an excuse. Irrationality must satisfy the As-if Rule to excuse. Consider these cases: Tony wants to kill his uncle. He sees a person take a pill and die. He commits the inductive fallacy of *post hoc, propter hoc* and infers that the tablet is poisonous. Actually, the man dies coincidentally of a heart attack. He gives the tablet to his uncle, who chokes on it and dies. Even though he is (inductively) irrational, he lacks an excuse. In contrast, Frank thinks that sweating helps cure disease. He observes patients sweating from fevers and then recovering, and overgeneralizes. He puts his sick child in a sauna to help her diabetes and she dies of dehydration. Frank is also (inductively) irrational but this time he has an excuse. Irrationality only excuses if the act was justified had the reasoning been correct.

Irrationality must also satisfy the other rules required of exculpatory ignorance. Only those irrationalities that we cannot help will excuse. Radden is aware of everyday irrationalities: 'Our inductive or evidential reasoning is subject to error in countless ways: we jump to conclusions, we overgeneralize in ways which are unwarranted, we fail to connect and draw conclusions which are indicated, and we persist in holding beliefs without sufficient evidence' (1985: 73). Does this sort of irrationality excuse? Suppose Mark believes he is entitled to the profits of his company. He has made some good deals, but he ignores the fact that others have too. He deceives himself that it would not be theft to steal. Does he have an excuse because he ignored evidence that theft was not justified? What of Sally who chooses to ignore the evidence that her son is a murderer, and helps him escape the police? In cases of everyday irrationality such as self-deception, we take the person to be responsible for his irrationality because it does not satisfy the Disability Rule. Mark and Sally are responsible because they are able to reverse such illogicalities – their reason is not paralysed. Radden accepts this, saying of the irrationality of the insane: 'Because it is so pervasive, their unreason is unavoidable – and, as such, exculpating.' If irrationality does not satisfy the Responsibility Rule, it will also fail to exculpate. If a paranoid patient deliberately stops his medication, allowing himself to become irrationally paranoid and violent, he does not have an excuse. This is because his irrationality does not satisfy the Responsibility Rule.

Why must irrationality satisfy exactly the same rules as ignorance before it excuses? Is this a massive coincidence, or is there some other explanation? The answer is that whenever irrationality excuses, it excuses *because* it produces exculpatory ignorance. This explains why the same rules apply to exculpatory irrationality as exculpatory ignorance. The most reasonable conclusion to draw is that irrationality is not an independent excuse – it only excuses via ignorance. Both ignorance and irrationality ultimately excuse by showing that the person has a good character, and it is this that explains why the same rules apply to both. For example, the As-if Rule is valid for both ignorance and irrationality because only those with that sort of ignorance are good characters. Radden has failed to produce an example where someone should be excused on the basis of irrationality but who also fails to satisfy the M'Naghten Rules.

Thus inductive irrationality *per se* does not provide an excuse. What of deductive irrationality? Dudley reasons thus: 'If my mother is healthy, her skin will be shiny. If I paint her skin, it will be shiny. Therefore, if I paint her skin, she will be healthy.' He paints her skin and she dies of hyperthermia. He is irrational because he commits the fallacy of affirming the consequent. We are inclined to excuse him, but only because his irrationality satisfies the As-if Rule – if painting did make his mother healthy, he would not have done anything wrong. In contrast, Paul reasons thus: 'This man has a long nose. All Jews have long noses. Therefore this man is a Jew.' As a result, Paul (who is anti-Semitic) kills him. His (deductive) irrationality does not excuse because it fails to satisfy the As-if Rule – even if his reasoning were correct, killing a Jew is evil. Hence we may conclude that Formal Irrationality is not an independent excuse.

PRACTICAL IRRATIONALITY

Moore defines mental illness in terms of irrationality. He also accepts that only rational agents are responsible, and therefore concludes that the mentally ill are not responsible:

> To be mentally ill is to be very seriously irrational . . . Yet why does severely diminished rationality preclude responsibility? It is because our notions of who is eligible to be held morally responsible depend on our ability to make out rather regularly syllogisms for actions. Only if we can see another being as one who acts to achieve some rational end in light of some rational beliefs will we understand him in the same fundamental way that we understand ourselves and our fellow persons in everyday life. We regard as moral agents only those beings we can understand in this way.
>
> (Moore, 1984: 44)

Only agents with (minimal) practical rationality are responsible. We might define minimal practical rationality by following this rule: If I desire G and believe B is the best means to achieve G, I ought to do B.

To illustrate why this is wrong, let us look at the maximizing rule of rationality. Someone is maximizing if he maximizes the satisfaction of his most important present and future desires. Suppose someone chooses not to follow this principle. The father about to risk almost certain death in a rescue attempt to save his daughter may know he is being irrational in this sense. He knows he and his daughter will probably die. He also knows he is emotionally resilient, and that after a year he will recover from her death, move on, have another daughter, and be happy. In spite of this, he chooses to make the rescue attempt. He is being irrational (in this sense), but he is still responsible because he *chooses* to be irrational. It might be countered that he still has the *capacity* for rationality, and that if he lacked this, he would lack responsibility. But being incapable of practical rationality does not imply a lack of responsibility. When an evil person is irrational in planning a murder, he is still responsible. Alistair wants to kill his parents to inherit. He knows the best way to do this is to engineer a car accident. He cannot be bothered to set this up, and strangles them instead. He lacks the capacity for practical rationality, but does not have an excuse.

Minimal practical irrationality only excuses the most disturbed offenders. A person has to be extremely ill before minimal practical rationality is impaired. M'Naghten, Hadfield, and Hinckley all had practical rationality. Given M'Naghten's irrational belief that the Tories were after him, he followed the minimal practical rule of inference and did what he saw as the best means to his goal of ending the persecution. If minimal practical irrationality is an excuse, it will not apply to such individuals. But is it an independent excuse? Erving has severe schizophrenia which muddles his thinking. He wants to rescue his drowning neighbour and believes the best means to this end is to throw him the life line. But he follows this principle: If you desire G, and B is the best means to achieve G, then you ought to do non-B. He fails to throw the rope to his neighbour and he drowns. Does Erving have an excuse, and is the excuse independent of the excuses of ignorance and compulsion? His irrationality satisfies the As-if Rule, demonstrating that he is not an evil man deserving punishment. But is his practical irrationality an independent excuse?

Rationalists hold that this failure of rationality is not equivalent to ignorance. Lewis Carroll (1972) argues that we have to make a distinction between beliefs and rules of inference. If we are trying to infer 'B' from 'A' and 'If A then B', we need the *rule*: 'If "A" and "If A then B", infer "B".' If a rule were equivalent to a belief, we could simply add this proposition to the two premises: 'If "A" and "If A then B", then "B".' However, adding another proposition to the premises will not allow us to infer 'B' (so Carroll argues), unless we add this rule: 'If "A" and "If A then B" and "If 'A' and 'If A then B' ", then "B", infer "B".' Therefore, rationality is not equivalent to knowledge. But this argument is flawed. We do not understand the proposition 'If A then B' unless we realize we can infer 'B' from the truth of 'A'. Understanding the belief is one and the same as accepting the rule. If this is right, then being irrational is reducible to holding an irrational belief, and hence irrationality is not a separate excuse from ignorance. If, from his desire for G and his belief that B is the best means to G, the agent fails to reason that he should do B, this is the same as possessing the mistaken belief that if he desires G, and if B is the best means to obtaining G, then he has a reason to do not-B. It is part of the meaning of 'best means' that if B is the best means to G, and an agent desires G, then he should do B. Irrationality reduces to ignorance.

So far we have looked at minimal practical rationality. Moore posits other requirements for a fully rational agent: he not only selects the best means to his ends, but also reasons according to the correct inductive and deductive rules of inference (that is, is formally rational), acts only on rational desires (that is, is substantively rational), has no inconsistent and intransitive desires, and no inconsistent beliefs. Radden also argues that a person will not have full practical rationality if he has inconsistent desires and beliefs. I would add that if an agent is not able to perceive the most obvious courses of action open to him, he lacks full practical rationality. We will now see whether the lack of these other elements provides an excuse.

Let us start with inconsistent beliefs. Karen believes that arsenic will kill her mother. She also believes that it will only paralyse her. She wants her mother dead and so gives it to her anyway. Her mother dies. The fact that Karen had inconsistent beliefs in no way excuses her. And the reason is obvious. We do not excuse people whose evil characters have led them to freely commit unjustifiable harm. Karen is such a person and deserves punishment. She is also in need of deterrence and reform. What of cases where the person is good and intends to do something beneficial, but fails to do so because of inconsistent beliefs? Neil wants to rescue a stranger who has slipped into the river. He believes that throwing a rope will save the man, but also believes that the rope will weigh him down. From any two inconsistent beliefs, Neil realizes we can infer any proposition. He infers the belief that throwing him a rock will save him. He does so and the stranger drowns. Neil has an excuse but not because he has inconsistent beliefs. He believes the rock will save the stranger, and because this ignorance satisfies the As-if Rule, it excuses.

The case for inconsistent desires excusing is even harder to see. Most of us are ambivalent – when we desire something, it is not wholeheartedly as there are aspects of the desired object we do not like. This is so common as to be normal. There is hardly any action not done under some degree of ambivalence. Kane wants to murder his mother-in-law to inherit her money, but also feels some sympathy for her. We want to go to University, but do not want six years of hard study. We are all divided selves. This means that when we desire to do something, we also desire not to do it. Ultimately, we do something because we consider the desire to do it more important. But the fact that there is some degree of ambivalence in all our actions does not show that we are not responsible for what we do. If it did, we would all cease to be responsible.

Moore also requires that desires be transitive for a person to be rational. But desires are rarely transitive. I may prefer ice-cream to mint chocolate, mint chocolate to coca-cola, but coca-cola to ice-cream. But this does not mean I am not responsible for choosing coca-cola over ice-cream! A criminal may prefer committing fraud to robbery, robbery to blackmail, but blackmail to fraud. If faced with a choice between fraud and blackmail, and he chooses blackmail, what reason could there be for not holding him responsible? It is certainly rational to organize desires in a hierarchy because this makes complex decision making easier. But this is different from the intransitivity of desires providing an excuse.

The last element of full practical rationality is the ability to perceive the available courses of action. If a person is unable to figure out what options are open to him, and chooses his course of action from a very limited and incomplete set, he will fail to be fully rational. Will he also have an excuse? M'Naghten believed that the Tories were planning to murder him. If he had full practical rationality, he would have realized that a host of options faced him – getting help from the police, going to Australia, and so on. It appears, however, that he did not consider all the options available to him. In Anglo-American law, self-defence is justified if there is no alternative. If M'Naghten had no alternative, killing to save his life would have been justified. The As-if Rule tells us that his inability to arrive at alternatives is an excuse – he is not evil if he kills because he believes he has no choice. But this failure does not constitute an independent excuse. The belief that he had no alternative can excuse because of ignorance. Compare these cases: Jack is reasoning how he might get his rival in love out of the way. He can only see one option – murder. Is this inability to conjure up other options a form of irrationality that excuses? No. He is an evil character deserving of punishment. Conversely, Jill believes that her family is going to be tortured slowly to death. She is only able to see one option – to kill them humanely herself. Here her inability to think of options excuses – if she knew there were options, she would not have an excuse. The ignorance of options excuses her (unlike Jack) because it shows that she is not an evil person. But once again irrationality does not excuse independently of ignorance. Hence Practical Irrationality is not an independent excuse.

MORAL INSANITY

Pritchard (1835) first used the term 'moral insanity' to describe 'a perversion of the natural feeling, affections, inclinations, temper, habits, moral dispositions and natural impulses, without any remarkable disorder or defect of the intellect and reasoning faculties and particularly without any insane illusion or hallucination'. The psychopath, so described, creates a difficulty for our traditional set of excuses because he knows that what he is doing is wrong and can control himself. Yet many (Pritchard, 1974; Duff, 1977; Elliott, 1992) argue that he should be excused. There are three arguments: first, that he suffers from moral ignorance; second, that he is incapable of moral reasoning; and, third, that he is unable to calculate the consequences of his actions.

The traditional argument against using moral ignorance as an excuse for psychopaths is that they know their actions are contrary to socially accepted morality. But these authors argue that the psychopath is unable to sympathize with others, and therefore cannot *really* understand that his actions are wrong. Ryle (1967: 75) says 'there seems to be an incongruity in the idea of a person's knowing that something wrong had been done, but still not disapproving of it or being ashamed of it'. Elliott and Gillett (1992: 57) argue: 'Morality involves more than simply knowing what society's moral norms and values are. It also involves endorsing and internalizing them.' Pritchard (1974: 640) argues: 'It cannot be denied that psychopaths have some kind of understanding of moral concepts. However, since they are devoid of moral sentiments, they can at best be said to have an "intellectual" understanding.' In the sense of understanding required, 'understanding *is* a kind of caring'. Duff (1977: 194) writes: 'An understanding of moral concepts and values requires not just an intellectual recognition of the criteria by which others make moral judgments, but a *concern* for such values.'

This is a dangerous argument. It implies that if a person does not have the same moral sentiments as us, he cannot really understand that what he is doing is wrong, and therefore has an excuse. If 'real' moral understanding requires the actual concern for the values in question, then holding different values implies a

193

lack of moral understanding and an excuse. On this view, endorsing alternative values is necessarily to suffer from moral ignorance and to have an excuse. No one can be evil: every person knowingly doing evil has a different set of values. But if this means that he has an excuse, he cannot be evil, and the distinction between good and evil disappears. But we know there are evil men. Those who do not see the importance of Jewish lives, or unborn lives, do not disagree with us because they are ignorant. There are no facts about which they are mistaken. They disagree because they hold different values.

Duff (1977) argues that the psychopath cannot have an understanding of what he is doing to others because he lacks any values himself: 'A psychopath, who shares in no values himself, is incapable of such understanding.' But this is too hasty. The psychopath *does* operate with a system of values – he takes his own present needs to be more important than anything else. If having a set of values is necessary for understanding wrongdoing, then the psychopath is not disqualified. Duff argues further that because the psychopath does not understand the meaning of love and friendship, he cannot understand what it is to ruin a love or friendship, and therefore we cannot blame him if he does. This is like arguing that if a mentally retarded person does not know what life is, he should not be blamed for ending it. But this argument is weak. A psychopath might not understand what love and friendship are, but he does understand that these are desired objects and sources of pleasure for others. He knows what it is to desire things and derive pleasure from things, and this is all the understanding he needs to make him responsible. Duff argues the psychopath cannot understand what it is to harm another's interests because he 'exhibits no conception of interests of his own which reach beyond his present moment'. But the fact that he has this basic interest allows us to say that he has some conception of what it is to violate the interests of others.

One might be tempted to push the analogy with the mentally retarded person. If the psychopath lacks feelings for others, is this not similar to his not perceiving others as people? But if the mentally retarded person does not understand that others are people with feelings, goals, interests and desires, he will have an excuse if he harms them. If he does not understand they are sentient creatures, but thinks they are just like machines, his ignorance excuses because it satisfies the As-if Rule. But the psychopath clearly does not think of people in this way. His plans clearly take into account the reactions of others, and this presupposes that he sees them as people. The psychopathic sadist knows what his victims will hate because he can put himself in their position. He has the cognitive ability to understand they are persons. The problem is that he does not care about them, but lacking sympathy for others is not sufficient to excuse.

We might argue that moral understanding requires grasping the Golden Rule of 'Do unto others as you would have them do unto you', and that the psychopath fails to grasp this rule. But what of those accepting Hillel's Rule: Do not do unto others as you would have them not do unto you? Or those acknowledging that one man's meat is another man's poison and adopting the Rainbow Rule: Do unto others as they would have you do unto them? Do they fail to possess moral understanding? While all these rules share some principle of reciprocity, they are different, and it is a mistake to argue that moral understanding is only to be had if one particular rule is accepted. Hare (1963) argues that the hallmark of moral beliefs is that the person be willing to universalize them. The distinction between a mere preference and a moral point of view is that the person is willing to approve that everyone act in that way. But our psychopath might accept that someone else has the right to treat him as an object if they so choose, and that it is up to everyone to look out for themselves. We cannot deny the psychopath is defective here in such a way that he has an excuse.

The second argument assumes that the psychopath has a defect in his moral reasoning. As Duff (1977: 195) puts it, 'we cannot hold him answerable for his actions, any more than we can a young child.' This argument is based on the theories of Piaget (1948) and Kohlberg (1976) who argue that moral development is achieved by progressing through a series of cognitive stages. Psychopaths supposedly have an arrested moral development, leaving them with defective 'moral reasoning' that prevents them from being able to tell right from wrong. This theory has been tested by presenting hypothetical moral dilemmas (such as the dilemma of a husband having the choice of stealing a drug to save his dying wife) to delinquent and control groups, and the results do show that delinquents operate at a lower level of moral development than controls (Thornton, 1988; Henggeler, 1989). But the interpretation that such differences are due to defects in moral reasoning is circular: delinquents are not particularly moral individuals, and so it is hardly surprising that they exhibit 'lower' levels of moral reasoning. If being egocentric implies having a lower level of moral development, then it follows by definition that someone who does not care about others will have a lower level of cognitive development. But this does not imply that he is egocentric *because* he has some cognitive defect. The egoist might argue with equal plausibility that pursuing one's own interests is right, and that those who think otherwise have failed to arrive at the appropriate moral stage and therefore have defective moral reasoning. We cannot regard the failure to arrive at some preferred moral position as implying a defect in moral reasoning without begging the question.

This does not mean that it is impossible to show that egoism is not the result of a defect in reasoning. However, in order to do this, the defective moral reasoning would have to be part of a moral general cognitive failure. If a person does not take other people's feelings into account, and this because he does not in general take *any* consequences of his actions into account, we can make a case for saying that egoism is the result of a *defect* in reasoning. And this brings us to the third argument. The psychopath seems to be peculiarly indifferent to his own future (Cleckley, 1982). Elliott and Gillett (1992) note that the psychopath is 'characteristically imprudent'. Can we argue that this is due to a defect in reasoning rather than a difference in values? Some might argue that it is necessarily irrational not to care about one's future. But suppose I know I will be brainwashed into becoming a Nazi and set about killing Jews. Should I take steps now to ensure that this future interest is satisfied? No. But why not? Because I do not care for such a future self. Only if I care for my future self or identify with his values, is it irrational to ignore my future interests. If the psychopath does not identify with his future self – he only cares about his present self – we cannot conclude that he is being irrational.

In any event, there is little evidence that psychopaths have no awareness of the consequences of their actions for their own interests. They commit their crimes in private and take steps to avoid detection, showing they have an interest in their futures.

Moreover, imprudence can hardly count as an excuse. If Daly imprudently steals from his rich (but terminally ill) uncle without waiting to inherit legally, he is responsible for what he does and should be punished even if he is incapable of being prudent. If Winston kills someone for sexual pleasure, but imprudently fails to eliminate the evidence, he is still responsible. This failure of far-sightedness or practical rationality does not excuse these men – they are evil and deserve punishment.

The conclusion that the psychopath does not deserve to be excused receives support from Retributivism and Utilitarianism. Retributivism argues that we should punish him because he is the paradigmatically evil person who freely does wrong. He knows that what he is doing is wrong, and is able to do otherwise (if it suits him). He should therefore be punished. Duff thinks Utilitarianism justifies not seeing psychopaths as responsible. He believes that it is not possible for the psychopath to see his own values as wrong because he is not open to rational persuasion, and this is required for responsibility. But there are many good people who are not open to rational persuasion to change their values either. We could not get Mother Theresa to accept that being cruel to people is good for them, but this does not mean she is not responsible. The Utilitarian argument should not be based on the idea that people can be 'converted', but on the idea that they can be deterred. Utilitarianism concedes that the psychopath is not capable of reform in the same way that saints are not capable of corruption. However, the psychopath is able to be deterred, and will stop what he is doing when he faces imprisonment. He is exactly the sort of person from whom we need protection. Therefore, he must not be excused.

STATUS EXCUSES

Moore argues that madness is a status excuse:

> Each of these three tests [M'Naghten Rules, the Irresistible Impulse Test, and the ALI test] shares a common and fundamental defect: They assume that legal insanity is an *excuse* for the particular acts done, not a general *status* attached to a class of human beings who are not accountable agents. Worse, they assume that insanity is not even a special excuse but is collapsible into the traditional excuses

of ignorance or compulsion. There is, in such a view, nothing special about being crazy; one's responsibility is affected only if one can avail oneself of one of the two traditional excuses . . . The problem with each of these views is that they fail to capture our moral intuitions about what it is about crazy people that precludes responsibility.

(Moore, 1984: 222)

What is a status excuse?

Someone has a status excuse if he falls into a certain category of person. Childhood is a status excuse. If a person is a child, then he has an excuse irrespective of his mental state and capacities at the time of the offence. But the problem with status excuses is that we require an explanation why a particular category has this status. In the case of children, we have an easy explanation. We do not hold children responsible for their actions because they do not fully understand the consequences of what they do. Clark and Marshall (1952: 123) state: 'A child is not criminally responsible for his acts or omissions if he is of such tender years as to be incapable of distinguishing between right and wrong, and of understanding the nature of the particular act.' We grant a status to a particular category of person if the traditional excuses (of ignorance or compulsion) apply to that category. On the other hand, when a child *does* know what he was doing (and is in control of his actions), we are inclined to ascribe responsibility. Status excuses are not a new category, but depend for their justification on the traditional excuses already articulated.

We can see this more clearly if we examine a chauvinist proposal to introduce masculinity as a status excuse. Someone might argue that testosterone deprives a person of control over his aggressive impulses. In America, 87.5 per cent of violent crime is committed by men, and those committing violent crimes have the highest blood testosterone levels (Gibbs, 1995). Olweus studied 58 healthy 15- to 17-year-olds, measuring their testosterone levels and assessing their aggressiveness by both objective and subjective ratings, and concluded that 'dimensions reflecting intensity and/or frequency of aggressive responses to provocation and threat were most clearly and directly related to testosterone' (Olweus, 1987: 280). But the argument to make masculinity into a status excuse is only faintly plausible because it appeals to the traditional excuse of compulsion – if being a male did mean lacking control, being a male would be an excuse.

Status excuses depend on specific excuses. If Moore objects that specific excuses also require justification, we can easily provide one. According to Retributivism, a person deserves punishment if he freely does wrong because of his evil character. Being evil consists in not caring sufficiently about others. If a good person does something harmful because of ignorance or compulsion, he does not do it because he is evil, and therefore has an excuse. According to Utilitarianism, someone who does wrong only because he is ignorant or compelled does not need any deterrence, reform, or incapacitation. He is already well motivated to avoid doing evil. For these reasons, ignorance and compulsion are excuses. On the other hand, someone who commits an evil act because he is male still has an evil character deserving punishment and requiring reform, deterrence and incapacitation.   \

It is difficult to defend the notion of Substantive Rationality, and any account of responsibility based on it is suspect. A person does not lack responsibility simply in virtue of his having an 'irrational' desire. Formal irrationality only excuses if it conforms to the As-if, Disability, and Responsibility Rules. The best explanation why it must satisfy the same rules as exculpatory ignorance is that irrationality only excuses *because* it produces exculpatory ignorance. Irrationality is therefore not an independent excuse. Lacking minimal practical rationality counts as an excuse, but not independently of exculpatory ignorance. Lacking the ability to discern the options available also excuses, but again this excuse reduces to having exculpatory ignorance. When inconsistent beliefs excuse, they only do so via exculpatory ignorance. For all the Rationalist's efforts, practical irrationality does not excuse independently of the traditional excuses. Irrationality does not constitute an independent excuse.

10

THE CONCEPT OF DISEASE

INSANITY WITHOUT ILLNESS

It is paradoxical to claim that a mental illness is not required for someone to be excused on the basis of insanity. Successful insanity defences require the offender be mentally ill, so how can mental illness not be essential? Let me explain. Someone with kleptomania has an excuse because he is unable to control his conduct, but someone who finds his wife in bed with his best friend, and is so overwhelmed by emotion that he is unable to control his impulses, is in the same position as the kleptomaniac. Both are overwhelmed by impulses. It would be absurd to argue that the person committing the crime of passion acquires a mental illness lasting a few minutes, but it would not be absurd to say that he was temporarily insane. Similarly, a person with a mental illness that so clouds his reason that he shoots a person, mistaking him for a pumpkin, has an excuse. Someone terrorized by Halloween pranksters might be so terrified that he thinks his life is in danger and if he fights back, he also has an excuse on the basis of ignorance. Extreme terror is not a disease, but it would not be absurd to say he was temporarily insane. If this is right, a person can be excused on the basis of (temporary) insanity without suffering from a mental illness.

In order to support this, we need to define a mental illness or a disease. First, a disease is a process rather than a static defect (Reznek, 1987). Someone suffering from Down's syndrome is not able to reason clearly, and may not understand what he is doing. If he commits a crime in this state, he will have an excuse. One such mentally retarded offender I encountered in Scotland threw a baby into a toilet without realizing that the child would drown.

He was not suffering from a mental illness, but was suffering from a static handicap or disability. Something is a disease only if it progresses – if it has an onset, a course, and an outcome. It is something that evolves and changes over time. Fixed disabilities like Down's syndrome do not qualify as diseases.

Second, a disease does harm (Reznek, 1987). There are various categories of harm – pain (or other unpleasant mental states like nausea or depression), disability, disfigurement, and death (Culver and Gert, 1982). These are harms because they all make the person worse off. This element makes the concept of disease irreducibly value-laden – diseases are those conditions we are better off without. Let me explain. Some patients suffering from hypomania are filled with such a sense of well-being that they do not see their condition as an illness. Because they value being high and energetic, even at the cost of increased impulsivity and risk-taking, they do not classify the condition as a disease. Other patients with epilepsy have their 'pleasure centre' stimulated by their epileptic focus, and have resisted treatment because they value the pleasure derived! If we had these conditions, perhaps we would not view them as diseases. Whether we do or not depends on whether we see ourselves as worse off with these conditions, and this depends on our values.

Throughout history, strange conditions have been viewed as diseases because of the values of the classifiers. Benjamin Rush, father of American psychiatry, saw runaway slaves as suffering from the disease drapetomania, and slaves who destroyed their master's property out of frustration as suffering from dysaesthesia aethiopsis (Engelhardt, 1974)! On the other hand, because we regard such behaviour as a normal reaction to an abnormal institution, we regard such behaviour as healthy. Masturbation was at one time considered to be due to the disease Spermatorrhoea, and was subjected to such treatments as bromide and amputation (Curling, 1856). Political dissidents in Russia were seen as suffering from a unique mental illness – sluggish schizophrenia – and treated involuntarily with neuroleptic drugs in asylums (Bloch and Reddaway, 1977). It is not hard to see the influence of value judgements on what counts as normal behaviour.

What counts as a disability depends on our values. Some of the things we are unable to do are not disabilities because we do not value doing them. Someone not able to furrow his tongue is not disabled because we do not think this is a valuable talent. But someone unable to walk has a disability because we value being able to walk. Thus a stroke causing paralysis is a disease, but a condition preventing us furrowing our tongue is not. Of course, if furrowing our tongue did have a central role in our lives – if it was the only way we could operate a blow-pipe to kill prey and stay alive – then lacking this power *would* be a disability. What counts as a disfiguration depends on our values too. Dubos (1965) describes a South American tribe, most of whom suffer from dyschromic spirochaetosis. Because they like the rose-coloured spots it causes, they do not regard it as a disease. In fact, so fond are they of the spots that they exclude anyone lacking them from marriage. Many African tribes deliberately inflict pathological scar tissue or keloids on their bodies because they like the result. To us, such changes are disfigurations, and we therefore classify the conditions causing them as diseases. We also value avoiding conditions that cut our lives short prematurely, and therefore classify such conditions as diseases. This is because we value longevity. Whether a process is a disease depends on whether we are worse off with it.

Third, a disease is an abnormal process (Reznek, 1987). There are many conditions that we are better off without but which are not diseases because they are normal. For example, pregnancy is a disabling condition but not a disease because it is normal. Labour is a painful condition but not a disease because it is normal. Ageing is a process that disables and kills, but because it is normal we do not regard it as a disease. Only if the process causing the harm is abnormal is it a disease.

Fourth, a disease is a condition that does not have an obvious external cause (Reznek, 1987). If I am freezing cold, I am relatively disabled, but this is not a disease. If I am tied up in chains, I may be completely disabled, but I am not diseased. The causes of these disabilities are obvious external factors and not internal states. For this reason, the disturbances caused by emotions such as terror and jealousy do not qualify as diseases. They have obvious external causes such as the discovery of one's spouse in bed with one's best friend. Similarly, hypnosis can be disabling in the sense that the hypnotized subject may be unable to perceive reality accurately or control his behaviour. But because it has an obvious external cause, it is not a disease.

Fifth, a disease is an involuntary process or process over

which we have no control (Parsons, 1951). Suppose we came across an unusual tribe called the Somnoleths. We notice that when they become upset, they slip into an unrousable but temporary state called a Comaspell. We assume that Somnoleths suffer from a strange disease. However, after we get to know them better, they let us into their secret. They can choose to go in and out of this state whenever they want. They remain aware of what is going on but become totally detached, and can choose to wake up when they want. They prove this to us by inducing and reversing Comaspells at will. A Comaspell is not something that happens to them, not something over which they lack control – it is something they *do*. Once we discover it is a form of action rather than an affliction, it becomes incoherent to say it is a disease. To be a disease, it must be a condition we cannot reverse or initiate at will.

The fact that our notion of disease has this conceptual dimension can been inferred from the fact that many people have difficulty accepting the disease status of mental disorders. This is because they are seen as conditions that sufferers can reverse by an act of will. Depressed people are told to 'pull themselves together' or 'snap out of it' as if it is possible for them to reverse their condition by an act of will. On the other hand, if depression were seen as involuntary, it would be accorded disease status. Whenever we see a condition as something that can be reversed by an act of will, it ceases to be a candidate for a disease. As Parsons (1951) put it, a sick person 'cannot legitimately be expected to get well simply by deciding to be well, or by "pulling himself together".'

A disease, then, is an abnormal involuntary process without an obvious external cause that does harm. What can we say of conditions like a jealous rage or extreme terror? They are processes that the person cannot reverse by an act of will. They harm in that they impair judgement and control. They are sufficiently uncommon to be abnormal. They are also not static states; they evolve. But they have obvious external causes, and therefore are not diseases. This means that a person can suffer from temporary insanity without suffering from a mental illness. We will be inclined to excuse him on the same basis that we are inclined to excuse those who are insane but they will not be mentally ill. In fact, in many jurisdictions, these sorts of mental states are treated as cases of insanity. As Gunn (1991: 20) puts it:

'It is theoretically possible for a jury to decide that someone is insane even though the doctors would not call him or her mentally disordered, although this is unlikely.'

IS CRIME A DISEASE?

There is a concern that once a disease is defined in value-laden terms, anything can legitimately be labelled a disease and the way is open to such abuse as the persecution of political dissidents. If some process is a disease simply because it has undesirable consequences, what is to stop society labelling any minority group as ill because they are deemed undesirable? Kendell (1976: 508) notes:

> To accept . . . that the attribution of disease, mental or physical, is fundamentally a social value judgement would mean that we could never criticize Russian psychiatrists for incarcerating sane political dissidents in their beastly asylums: they would be perfectly entitled to regard political dissent as a mental illness.

It would be more attractive to define disease in terms of something objectively discoverable, like a biological malfunction (Boorse, 1976). It is a factual matter whether a biological malfunction causes political dissidence and we could settle such disputes unequivocally. But it is a mistake to understand disease in terms of a biological malfunction (Reznek, 1987). Without rehearsing all the arguments here, it is possible for natural selection to endow any species with a self-destruct system that functions to perpetuate the species (Goosens, 1980). Stress-induced arrhythmias might have the function of killing individuals and preventing the population exhausting the food supply, but they are still diseases. Deciding whether something is a disease depends on whether *we* are better off without it, not on whether our *genes* are better off without it. The same applies to psychiatric conditions.

Is crime a disease? Or rather, is a condition predisposing to crime a disease? Low autonomic reactivity causes harm (to others if not to the person himself), it is abnormal, it is an involuntary process (it cannot be reversed at will), and it does not have an obvious external cause. Hence it is a disease. Raine (1993: 5) says that 'serious, recidivistic criminal behaviour is a disorder in much the same way as depression, anxiety and schizotypal personality are currently conceptualized as disorders'. He shows that criminal behaviour is a valid construct correlated with many biological and social variables – genetic factors, low serotonin and norepinephrine levels, left-handedness and reduced lateralization, defects in the frontal lobes, lower resting heart rates and electrodermal responses, head injury, ugliness, low cortisol levels, raised testosterone levels, poor avoidance learning, low IQ, child abuse, inconsistent parenting, large families, bad schools, and so on. He concludes:

> Based on these findings, it is argued that there are good reasons to believe that a variety of social and biological factors exist that predispose the individual toward criminal behaviour. In combination with the fact that criminal behaviour also meets a number of the definitions of disorder, it is concluded that there is reasonable evidence to directly support the view that crime is a disorder.
>
> (Raine, 1993: 292)

Does this mean we should excuse all criminals? Raine (1993: 312) thinks so:

> If we accept that crime is a disorder, acknowledge that there are clear predispositions that form the basis for recidivistic crime, and acknowledge that in most cases these predispositions are beyond the individual's control, then the implication is that criminal offenders should not be punished.

Is this right?

No. While the process predisposing to the criminal act is involuntary, it does not follow that the criminal act itself is involuntary, and it is only this that allows the disease of crime to excuse. If the disease of crime consists in a low serotonin level which loosens a person's social restraints, it does not follow that when he is in any situation contemplating breaking the law that he cannot inhibit his impulses should there be an advantage to do so. Only if he is 'unable to do otherwise' should we conclude that he has an excuse. Just as we might argue that necrophilia is a disease, but hold a person responsible for harming others in the pursuit of satisfying these sexual needs, so we might argue that being a criminal is a disease, but hold a criminal responsible for his law breaking. The disease of crime *predisposes* a person to recidivism, but he is responsible for any single crime because, if the circumstances were different in standard ways providing him with the motivation to do otherwise, he would. This means that for any single crime, he can do otherwise and is therefore responsible.

SAVING DURHAM

Having a cause for one's behaviour does not excuse, otherwise acting because of reasons would excuse. But perhaps being caused by a disease excuses. If so, we need to ask what it is about a disease that enables it to excuse. Diseases are processes we cannot reverse at will. If our behaviour is caused by factors we cannot reverse at will, do we cease to be responsible? No. All of us have little control over our characters. Some are attracted to members of the opposite sex, some not. Some enjoy danger, some not. We have little control over this. But the issue is not whether we have any control over our desires but whether we can control our actions. If we can, we are responsible, and if we cannot, we are not. The fact that our behaviour is caused by remote factors which form our characters and over which we have no control does not rob us of responsibility. Lacking control over the remote factors that cause our behaviour cannot be what it is that enables mental illness to excuse.

Perhaps being caused by a biological process is what enables a disease to excuse. However, this cannot be right. The desire for sex is clearly a biological process, but we are responsible for how we satisfy this desire. Hence, mental illnesses cannot excuse because they are biological processes. Perhaps being caused by an abnormal process is what enables a disease to excuse. But what would tempt us to say this? Should Einstein not be praised for his discoveries because they were caused by his abnormally high intelligence? If someone is abnormally strong, this does not provide him with an excuse for killing people. More relevantly, if someone has an abnormal desire to have sex with dead bodies, there is no reason to excuse him. If I have an abnormal desire to collect hubcaps, this does not excuse my stealing them. Being caused by a harmful process cannot explain why disease excuses either. My signing up for a suicidal mission is a harmful process but I am still responsible for my decision. Knowing what a disease is does not show that being caused by it excuses.

RELATIVITY OF THE INSANITY DEFENCE

Does our disease classification determine what are excuses? With the exception of 'temporary insanity', in order to be NGRI someone must be mentally ill. This suggests that how we classify conditions is critical in determining whether someone can be excused on the basis of insanity. Let me illustrate. Someone is prejudiced if he believes without justification that a group of people are inferior. If someone believes blacks have lower IQs than whites as a result of unbiased research, he is not prejudiced. On the other hand, someone is prejudiced if his emotional need to see others as inferior leads to his distorting the evidence. Suppose Jock knows that his daughter needs a heart to save her life. He thinks that blacks are no more developed than apes. He kills a black girl to take her heart for his daughter. Does prejudice provide an excuse? His ignorance satisfies the As-if Rule – we are justified in sacrificing an ape to save the life of a human (with apologies to animal liberationists). Thus if blacks were no more developed than apes, we would be entitled to sacrifice a black to save a white. But Jock's ignorance does not provide an excuse because it does not satisfy the Disability Rule. Jock has the ability to discover that blacks are as developed as any other human. Therefore, he does not have an excuse.

Suppose psychiatrists drafting DSM V argue that prejudice should be classified as a disease called Prejudice Disorder (PD). They argue that a prejudiced person is the victim of a deep-seated sense of inferiority such that his ego is unable to tolerate the idea that others are his equal. He has to ensure that they are inferior. This need and fear, supposedly, are severe enough to paralyse his reason so that he is unable to correct his view of the minority group against whom he is prejudiced. If Jock suffers from PD, his ignorance will satisfy the rules for exculpatory ignorance (the As-if, Disability, and Responsibility Rules). But does he have an excuse?

There is a fact of the matter whether a person is unable to reverse his ignorance. If there was a fact of the matter whether Somnoleths could reverse their Comaspells by acts of will, there is a fact of the matter whether someone is unable to remove his prejudice. Before we can classify prejudice as a disorder, we must first discover whether it can be reversed by an effort of will – and if it can, it cannot be a disease. This means we cannot give a condition any excusing power by *deciding* to classify it as a disease. It will only have excusing power if we *discover* it to be involuntary. How do we discover this? We decide that Somnoleths are not the victims of Comaspells because they go into Comaspells if we provide them with an incentive to do so. Similarly, to discover whether prejudice is within a person's control, we see whether he reverses it when we give him an incentive. Suppose Jock falls in love with a black woman. He now has an incentive to remove his ignorance. We then present him with sufficient information to undermine his prejudice, and see whether he overcomes it. If he does, then a prejudiced person is able to remove his ignorance, and it cannot qualify either as a disorder or as an excuse. Whether something excuses does not depend on its disease status – its disease status depends on whether it can excuse – that is, on whether it is involuntary.

To illustrate further that the disease status of a condition does not determine its excusing power, let us take the phenomenon of shared delusions. Psychiatry accepts that when a person (or family) share the delusion of a sick partner, they suffer from the disorder called *folie à deux*. However, if a whole community share the delusion of their crazed leader, they are precluded from suffering from any illness. This is because a delusion is defined in terms of an irrational conviction *not shared by that person's subculture* (Gelder *et al.*, 1989). Leaving aside the reasonableness of this definition, it follows that when a whole community, like the followers of Jim Jones or David Koresh, share the delusions of their leader, they cannot be described as deluded. I believe such followers are suffering from a disorder I call *folie à cult*. Does the disease status of their beliefs affect their responsibility? Suppose a follower of David Koresh is convinced the FBI are followers of the Devil, and kills an FBI agent. Whether he has an excuse does not depend on whether we classify his belief as delusional, or on whether we classify him as suffering from *folie à cult*. It depends on whether his ignorance satisfies the rules for exculpatory ignorance. While it satisfies the As-if Rule, the real question is: 'Does it satisfy the Disability Rule?' If he can correct his erroneous belief, he has no excuse. Whether he has an excuse depends on this and not the disease status of *folie à cult*.

We must look at a recent debate over the disease status of alcoholism to see how this works in practice. This debate turns on whether addictive behaviour is involuntary – i.e. whether the alcoholic is unable to stop himself drinking. Jellinek argues in his *The Disease Concept of Alcoholism* that 'loss of control' is the essence of alcoholism: 'The disease conception of alcohol addiction does not apply to excessive drinking, but solely to the loss of control which occurs in only one group of alcoholics and then only after many years of excessive drinking' (Jellinek, 1960: 674). But subsequent researchers have challenged the idea that alcoholics have no control over their behaviour, thereby challenging the disease concept. This does not challenge the idea that alcoholics have an addiction or a bad habit. But it does challenge the idea that the behaviour is involuntary and thereby a disease. In one classic experiment, subjects (who were addicted to alcohol and accustomed to drinking a quart of whisky a day) were allowed to perform a boring task that would earn them measured amounts of alcohol. They could earn an ounce of bourbon in anywhere from 5 to 15 minutes. Although they could have earned enough to become totally intoxicated, they did not. Heather and Robertson (1981:·84) conclude: 'All these observations are inconsistent with the concept of loss of control in the sense of an inability to stop once drinking has commenced, and with the related concept of craving in the sense of an uncontrollable urge to consume more and more alcohol during a drinking session.' The amount of alcohol consumed was a function of how 'costly' the subject perceived the procurement of alcohol to be. Far from there being an impulse that 'overwhelmed' the subjects, they adjusted their behaviour according to their other needs.

In another experiment, alcoholics were given the choice of access to alcohol versus removal from a pleasant social environment – most subjects limited themselves to moderate drinking in order to remain in the pleasant environment (Cohen *et al.*, 1971). These studies show that the drinking of alcoholics is no different from other behaviour in that it is subject to influence by incentives (like privileges, sociability, boredom, and so on).

> On any particular occasion the heavy drinker may drink heavily, or moderately, or may not drink at all, or may start drinking and then voluntarily stop. The choice depends on situational factors (such as the drinker's mood and feelings of frustration, satisfaction, threat) and the social setting. The choice also depends on the rewards or deprivations the drinker believes will ensue, on his or her beliefs about the

effects the alcohol will produce, on the cost or inconvenience of obtaining a drink, and so on – all the reasons and motives that affect anyone's decisions about personal conduct.

(Fingarette, 1988: 45)

Fingarette concludes that alcoholism is not a disease but a way of life: 'Instead of viewing heavy drinkers as the helpless victims of a disease, we come to see their drinking as a meaningful, however destructive, part of their struggle to live their lives' (Fingarette, 1988: 66). The issue over the disease status of alcoholism turns on whether the person is in control of his behaviour or not.

This is the nub. Whether someone can reverse a condition by an act of will is an ability. Someone has an ability to do X if he does X when we provide him with the incentive and opportunity to X by changing the circumstances in standard ways. Addictive behaviour is not involuntary because standard incentives such as the desire to remain in a pleasant environment are sufficient to get him to inhibit his impulse to take another drink. But what are standard incentives? If I lift a car when my daughter's life depends on it, we cannot conclude I am able to lift such a weight. But if I lift up a car when I am offered £50, then I do have this ability. If an alcoholic is dissuaded from drinking when his life is threatened, we cannot conclude that he has the ability to stop. But if he is dissuaded by ordinary incentives like the avoidance of boredom, he does have the ability to stop. As experimental studies have demonstrated, it is a *fact* that an alcoholic has control over his drinking. What of prejudice? We know that prejudice can be extremely difficult to reverse. We have all had the experience of trying to enlighten a prejudiced person. But if it turns out that ordinary incentives can reverse it, then we cannot view it as a disorder (or an excuse). It is not our classificatory practice that determines whether prejudice is an excuse – it is its reversibility. There is a fact of the matter whether we can overcome prejudice, a fact that depends on whether standard incentives plus the relevant information achieve enlightenment. Whether a person has an excuse depends on this, not the disease status of a condition.

This means that a person who suffers from alcoholism cannot claim that he could not help getting drunk. He cannot argue that his intoxication is involuntary. And therefore he cannot argue that if he commits an offence while he is intoxicated – perhaps because he does not know what he is doing or because he has lost control of himself – he should be excused on the grounds of involuntary intoxication. His getting drunk is something that is within his control, and therefore he should be punished for any offence he commits during this state. Of course, we might concede that his staying sober is less within his control than someone who is not addicted to alcohol, and that for this reason his intoxication is less voluntary and therefore that he has some excuse – he is not as blameworthy as someone not addicted to alcohol, or someone committing the same offence while sober. While this is correct, and we might concede that the person has a partial excuse because of it, whether we should allow this to count as a legal excuse is another matter which we will discuss in the Conclusion.

If some condition is a disease, not every consequence is involuntary. For example, a phobia is a disease because the irrational fear cannot be reversed by an act of will. If the phobia is mild, the phobic has a choice whether to avoid certain situations. His avoidance of these situations, while a consequence of the disease, is not involuntary. Similarly for crime. Raine (1993) and Diamond (1962) assume that disorder implies an excuse. Even Wootton (1978) assumes this when she generates her paradox: she argues that extreme evil implies a disorder which implies a lack of responsibility. While a disorder is something over which we have no control, this does not mean that all behaviour arising from it is outside the agent's control (and for which he deserves an excuse). I have no control over the fact I find women sexually attractive, but I am still responsible for how I satisfy my sexual appetite. This is important, especially when we consider whether personality disorders excuse. A personality disorder is a disturbance in the way the person thinks, feels, and behaves. For example, a psychopath does not care about others. Although his behaviour is a consequence of this indifference, it does not follow that his behaviour is involuntary. He can stop his behaviour at any moment he chooses. If we give him an incentive to stop harming others and he stops, it follows that he is in control of his behaviour. Psychopathy is a disorder because he cannot reverse his uncaring attitudes at will. He does not choose to be indifferent, just as we do not choose to care. But he does choose to act on these emotions. Not all actions that are a consequence of mental disorder are involuntary.

Labelling the process leading to indifference as a disorder amounts to not valuing it, and this does not give the process any power to excuse. We classify the psychopath's inability to feel sympathy as a disability because we think this ability is worth having. On the other hand, the psychopath might argue that having the power to feel sympathy makes one weak. It prevents one from being single-minded in the pursuit of one's own desires and makes one vulnerable to distraction by the needs of others. Being able to form a conscience prevents us from doing what we want. This relativity of values does not make excuses relative. Whether psychopathy excuses does not depend on whether we judge we are worse off with the condition, that is, on whether we consider it to be a disability. It depends on whether the condition, disease or not, causes exculpatory ignorance or compulsion. If someone is unable to develop human feelings for another person, or to put it another way, if he is able to remain uninfluenced by the needs of others, this says nothing about his ability to control his actions. Someone with psychopathy might be incapable of sympathy, but as long as he is capable of acting otherwise, he is responsible.

If the disease status of a condition makes the difference between being responsible and not, we are faced with a paradox. A sinner and a saint are similar in many respects. Both have biological processes that explain their characters. The psychopath has a defective autonomic nervous system, and the saint an overdeveloped autonomic nervous system. Since both characters are rare, the causes will also be rare, so that both characters are due to abnormal biological processes. The causes of their characters are not obvious either. The only crucial difference is that the one process is labelled a disease and the other is not. We admire the saint and not the psychopath, and so only classify the latter as diseased, but the psychopath admires the sinner and classifies things differently. It is implausible to argue that this labelling decides the issue of responsibility.

Imagine a monastic tribe who classify sexual desires as pathological. These values determine what counts as human good and well-being, what counts as harmful, and hence what counts as pathological. This difference in values and classification has no implications for responsibility because we are not overwhelmed by normal sexual impulses. Whether we act on them is influenced by standard incentives, and for this reason they are within our control. Classifying them as pathological does not imply that we are not responsible for our sexual behaviour. It may lead to us to view sexual desires as alien, and we may decide not to act on them. But this change in identification does not mean we are not responsible. What is important is not whether a person identifies with the desire, but whether he is able to control it. Our disease classification does not determine what counts as an excuse. Whether an impulse is an excuse does not depend on whether we classify it as pathological, but on whether standard incentives get the person to behave otherwise.

SEXUAL SADISM

According to current legal wisdom, serial killers are sane. Generally they are not found NGRI, but they number among the most seriously disturbed people. Henry Lee Lucas, convicted of eleven murders, wrote:

> I hated all of my life. I hated everybody. When I first grew up and can remember, I was dressed as a girl by mother. And I stayed that way for two or three years. And after that I was treated like what I call the dog of the family. I was beaten; I was made to do things that no human being would want to do. I've had to steal, make bootleg liquor; I've had to eat out of a garbage can. I grew up and watched prostitution like that with my mother till I was fourteen years old.
>
> (Norris, 1988: 152)

He was the son of Anderson, an alcoholic who lost his legs when he fell under the wheels of a freight train in a drunken stupor, and Viola, the daughter of a Chippewa Indian. Their marriage was dreadful, and Viola, a sometime prostitute, forced Anderson to watch her having sex with many customers. One night in 1950, unable to take any more, Anderson crawled into the snow and died a few days later of pneumonia, leaving his son, Henry, to face his mother's brutality. Viola beat him mercilessly with broom handles, pieces of timber, and any weapon she could find, telling him that it was for his own good, and preventing him crying. She forced him to watch her having sex with countless men, and on one occasion, shot a customer in the leg with a shotgun after having sex with him, splattering the blood all over Henry. She also fitted Henry in girl's clothing and forced him to go to school in them, where he was teased by his peers. The brutalization continued throughout his life, sometimes leaving him semiconscious for days. The torture occurred on an emotional level too, with Viola destroying everything to which he was attached. He was very fond of a pet mule as a child, and on hearing of his fondness, she promptly got out her shotgun and killed the animal!

This disturbed upbringing soon produced disturbed behaviour. Henry began to cut animals' throats and perform bestial acts on the carcasses. He caught small animals and skinned them alive for pleasure. At 15 years old he claims to have committed his first murder, killing a 17-year-old girl when she resisted being raped. He began his career as a convict soon afterwards following his apprehension for breaking and entering. Soon after discharge, he killed his mother, and was sentenced to 40 years for second degree murder. He was recommended for parole in 1970 even though he warned the prison officials and the staff psychologist that he would kill again. The State of Michigan, facing prison overcrowding, went ahead, claiming he was rehabilitated. A few miles away from the prison he found his first victim and killed her. Thus began a killing spree that took him across much of the Southwest and into Florida, abducting children, raping young girls, and killing whoever was convenient. He gained sexual potency only after he had bludgeoned and strangled his victim into a coma or death, enabling him to have intercourse with the victim's body.

Charles Manson was the son of Kathy Maddox and one of her lovers. From the outset, Manson received no parenting from his mother. He was handed from pillar to post while she worked on the streets. When she was convicted of armed robbery and sent to prison, he went to live with relatives. An uncle rebuked him for missing his mother, and sent him to school dressed as a girl, where he was teased mercilessly. When his mother was released, she made Manson live with her. He slept with her in the same bed, and was forced to witness her having sex with men and women. Finally unable to raise him, she placed him with the Catholic Gibault Home for Boys. Any infraction of the rules met with severe beatings, and Manson was consistently whipped for repeated attempts to be with his mother. At the age of 12, he ran away, and lived by stealing and eating out of garbage cans. By the age of 14, he was sent to a state institution, the Indiana School for Boys at Plainfield. Here Manson was brutalized by a guard who repeatedly had other boys torture and beat him while the guard masturbated. Manson was also repeatedly gang-raped by other inmates at the guard's instigation.

After escaping he was re-arrested for stealing cars. Over the next 15 years he was in and out of prison for a variety of crimes from fraud to pimping. Finally, he made it to San Francisco in 1967 when thousands of young people flocked there to take drugs and make love. Manson attracted drop-outs and drifters who were hopelessly confused about their lives and looked to Manson as a mentor and saviour. A year later, the killing began, the Manson gang taking orders from their leader and steadily gaining confidence. In the month between 27 July and 26 August 1969, Manson's tribe slaughtered at least nine people in southern California. This tally included Polanski's wife Sharon Tate and four guests. The following night, Manson's gang killed and mutilated another couple in their LA home.

Lunde and Sigal (1990) collected twenty such serial killers from 1970 to 1985. All had a background with aberrant childhood experiences linking sex and aggression. The mothers, like Lucas's, were punitive towards their sons, administering severe beatings for minor offences. Some engaged in sex with a variety of men in their son's presence, while others found excuses to play with their son's genitals. Most could recall an inseparable mixture of sexual and aggressive feelings. As 5-year-olds, these men found themselves becoming aroused by violence on television. This progressed to having violent fantasies while masturbating.

> The behaviour reported was so flagrantly bizarre as to support the notion of some type of pathology. These subjects not only kidnapped, tortured, raped and strangled young men and women, they also committed acts of necrophilia, cannibalism, and mutilation. Some also took sexual organs or other parts of the bodies home and preserved them by freezing or pickling. The combination of the aberrant childhood histories and the incredibly bizarre adult behaviour leads us to conclude that we are dealing

with some as yet unnamed disorder or syndrome. It has occasionally been referred to as *'sexual sadism'*.

(Lunde and Sigal, 1990: 629)

To paraphrase Shakespeare, there are more disorders in the world than we ever dreamed of in our nosologies.

There is nothing unusual in describing new disorders. Medical knowledge progresses through well-defined stages (King, 1982). First, abnormalities called signs and symptoms are identified. These were first seen as discrete diseases. For example, the collection of fluid in the body (oedema) was called the disease of 'Dropsy.' Second, clusters of signs and symptoms called syndromes are identified. Oedema may be part of the syndrome of heart failure, or part of the syndrome of renal failure. Third, an underlying explanation for such syndromes is identified. For example, thiamine deficiency or beri-beri is identified as one of the causes of heart failure. Psychiatry follows the same pattern. At first, it identifies signs of mental disorder such as memory loss. Later, it recognizes well-defined syndromes such as general paresis of the insane (GPI). Finally, it identifies a pathological process causing the syndrome, as in the discovery that the spirochaete infection causes GPI. Current psychiatry is mostly stuck at the level of identifying syndromes, and only in a small minority of cases have we been able to identify the nature of the underlying disease process.

When we identify the cluster of signs and symptoms of sexual sadism, it is reasonable to argue that some underlying process exists to explain that clustering. If there was not, it would be a massive coincidence why certain properties are found together with a frequency much greater than chance. This pathological basis has something to do with the link between violence and sex in their upbringing, making violence sexually arousing. This violence isolates them and forces them into a rich fantasy life which reinforces the association. The humiliation from their mothers leads to a hatred of women and the satisfaction of this hatred in sadistic sexual fantasies. It also makes them feel inadequate, and so are unlikely to have any normal sexual experiences to undermine the connection between sex and violence. Instead, they can only achieve sexual gratification after killing. In such a cauldron the mind of the serial killer is born.

Some may see this as proving that serial killers are not evil but ill. There is the worry that psychiatry will find a syndrome everywhere and the category of evil will disappear. The elimination of whole categories with the advance of knowledge is not unusual. For example, nowadays we argue that there are no such things as witches and bewitching, only mentally ill women and epidemic hysteria. Perhaps psychiatry shows that our category of evil is obsolete and, like that of witches, should be jettisoned. But psychiatry does nothing of the sort. If sexual sadism is a disorder, all that follows is that people with the disorder have no control over finding violence sexually arousing. This does not mean that they cannot stop themselves acting on this sexual impulse. Only if this is true will the disorder constitute an excuse. Normal heterosexual men have no control over the fact that they find women sexually arousing, but this does not mean they cannot control their sexual behaviour. Many sadists satisfy their desires only in fantasy, or with women who play-act for them. So while we can argue that sexual sadists are sick or disordered, this does not excuse them.

Of course, just as reality does not come in black and white, so there may be different degrees of sexual sadism. It is possible for someone with sadistic impulses to find it extremely difficult to resist them. He might not have a complete (moral) excuse, but if he succumbs, he will not be as blameworthy as a person freely indulging his tastes. But if this is the case, we need evidence. We need to see the person wrestling with his desire, expending some effort to avoid giving in, and experiencing remorse when he fails to resist his sadistic desires. When it is unreasonable to expect someone to resist doing the wrong thing, he will have a partial excuse.

It follows from this that someone can be evil *and* mentally ill. Sexual sadists get sexual pleasure from the suffering of others and this inclines them to harm others. However, it does not follow from the fact that these inclinations are pathological that sadists are not responsible. If they can do otherwise – if standard incentives dissuade them from breaking the law – then even if they have a disorder that inclines them to sadism, they are responsible. They are evil *because* they have an illness making them want to harm others *and* because they choose to act on these desires. Illness does not imply the absence of evil.

THE CHARGE OF TAUTOLOGY

Wootton (1959: 233) argues that psychiatric explanations that exculpate are tautological: 'In the case of an anti-social act that is said to be due to mental illness, the existence of the illness cannot, without circular argument, be inferred solely from the fact that the act was committed.' Wootton argues that the explanation of antisocial behaviour by reference to an antisocial personality disorder – psychopathy – is tautological because it amounts to the explanation that antisocial personalities commit antisocial acts because they commit antisocial acts. If citing the underlying disorder is sufficient to excuse, then we could excuse anyone on this logic by simply defining the behaviour as a disease. But we cannot excuse someone so easily, and Wootton is wrong to think that the psychiatric disorders are defined in terms of the behaviour they explain.

If 'psychopath' meant 'person committing antisocial acts', then the explanation *would* be tautological. This assumes that our scientific terms have a descriptive meaning, but this is false (Reznek, 1987). Instead, they have a reference (Kripke, 1980; Putnam, 1975). 'Psychopathic personality disorder' does not have a meaning captured by a description but refers to whatever abnormality such people have that explains their behaviour. Terms like 'gold' refer not to the surface properties of gold but to the underlying structure that explains such properties. In this way, we can say that something is 'fool's gold' even though it has the same surface properties as gold. It is not gold because it has a different underlying structure – it is iron pyrite. Similarly, for 'psychopath'.

Before the underlying nature of an entity is discovered, any explanation referring to that nature is more of a promissory note than a fully realized explanation. Before we know what underlies psychopathic behaviour, our explanation of it by reference to a psychopathic personality disorder does not amount to much. In this sense, Wootton is right. But she is wrong to think that there is not something underlying psychopathic behaviour that explains it. Whenever we find a cluster of properties coinciding in an object with a greater frequency than expected by chance, it is reasonable to assume there is a common underlying cause. If someone has no sympathy, we are also likely to find an indifference to his own fate, an inability to reason in a far-sighted fashion, the absence of a conscience, and the inability to form intimate stable relationships. This cluster strongly suggests that there is a discoverable underlying abnormality (to which our term 'psychopathic personality disorder' refers). This abnormality may consist in a disturbance in the autonomic nervous system. And the fact that the explanation is incomplete does not mean that the condition cannot excuse. We do not know what schizophrenia is, but it is able to excuse because it causes exculpatory ignorance. We do not have to know the nature of schizophrenia to have evidence that the schizophrenic is unable to correct his delusions. Similarly, a personality disorder can in principle excuse even if our understanding of it is incomplete. If we had evidence that psychopaths were unable to control their impulses, we would have evidence that psychopathy provides an excuse even though we do not fully understand it.

This means that there is in principle nothing to prevent psychiatric categories from providing genuine empirical explanations of behaviour. And if they can do this, then they can explain why someone does something wrong. And if they can do this, then they can provide genuine excuses.

A MORAL OR SCIENTIFIC VERDICT?

Insanity is equivalent to the notion of a mental illness that excuses. As Moore (1984: 220) puts it: 'To be legally insane is to be excused from criminal responsibility. Each of these definitions of legal insanity thus is a test determining when an accused is or is not responsible in the criminal law. Each of the tests has a mental illness or some related concept as one of its elements.' Insanity is not equivalent to mental illness (except in the Durham Rule), but goes beyond it to imply that we ought not to punish the person. We commit the Naturalistic Fallacy – the fallacy of inferring a moral conclusion from factual premises – if we infer insanity from mental illness (Moore, 1903). Insanity is a moral notion, and thus not something that a psychiatrist is specially qualified to assess. Gunn (1991: 26) writes:

> The legal concept of insanity is determined not by doctors but by judges and juries. Insanity is what the layman says it is. Psychiatrists did not invent insanity, and they are not allowed to define it. Most importantly, but hardest of all for

psychiatrists to swallow, neither schizophrenia nor any other mental illness equals insanity. Schizophrenia is a medical concept, insanity is a legal one, they overlap, interact, but that is all.

A psychiatrist might be best placed to decide who is mentally ill, but he is not better able to judge whether someone deserves to be excused. As Morse (1979: 282) puts it: 'Questions of responsibility are moral issues; empirical evidence may indicate how hard certain choices are, but deciding which choices are too hard to impose responsibility is a social, moral and legal question.'

If disease is an evaluative matter, and a psychiatrist is best qualified to make such judgements, then why can he not be called upon to make another value judgement (that someone is insane)? But when he diagnoses the presence of a disease, he is not making a value judgement. Society expresses its communal values by accepting a particular nosology. Once this has been accepted, the individual physician has only to rely on the *facts* to decide whether any one condition falls into some already accepted category of disease. He is not being asked: 'Do you personally judge that this condition should be classified as a disease? Do you personally feel we are better off without such a condition?' Such questions are requests for value judgements. He is being asked: 'Given our current nosology, is this classified as a mental illness? Given our current social values, does this condition qualify as a disease?' This is a request for a factual judgement. So when the psychiatrist testifies in court that the defendant is mentally ill, he is not making a value judgement.

On the other hand, 'ultimate issue' testimony is different. The question here is not: 'Given our current moral values, does this condition meet the standard set for excusing the mentally ill?' Rather, the question is: 'Ought we to excuse this person on the basis of his mental illness?' A person is being asked to *express* his values, not to describe whether his judgement conforms to the prevailing moral view. There is a difference between describing something as an expression of prevailing values, and expressing or endorsing those values. When I judge that some person is good, I am not describing him as having those value-free properties the prevailing morality judges as worthwhile. I am approving of him. This is the difference between the role of the psychiatrist (who helps clarify matters of fact) and the jury (who decide moral matters). The Insanity Defence Work Group (IDWG) puts it thus:

> When, however, 'ultimate issue' questions are formulated by the law and put to the expert witness who must then say 'yea' or 'nay', then the expert witness is required to make a leap in logic [Naturalistic Fallacy]. He no longer addresses himself to medical concepts but instead must infer or intuit what is in fact unspeakable, namely, the *probable relationship* between medical concepts and legal or moral constructs such as free will. These impermissible leaps in logic made by expert witnesses confuse the jury. Juries thus find themselves listening to conclusory and seemingly contradictory psychiatric testimony ... These psychiatric disagreements about technical, legal, and/or moral matters cause less than fully understanding juries or the public to conclude that psychiatrists cannot agree. In fact, in many criminal insanity trials both prosecution and defence psychiatrists do agree about the nature and even the extent of medical disorder exhibited by the defendant at the time of the act ... Determining whether a criminal defendant was legally insane is a matter for legal fact-finders, not for experts.
>
> (IDWG, 1983: 14)

The gap between mental illness and insanity is the gap between fact and value, and there is no deduction we can make from the one to the other. To think otherwise is to commit the Naturalistic Fallacy.

Furthermore, the psychiatrist might be the expert on explaining behaviour by theories involving technical ideas like neurotransmitter deficiencies, repressed Oedipal desires, and frontal lobe damage, but this is not the sort of theory needed to decide whether someone has an excuse. Someone has an excuse only if he is ignorant, or overwhelmed, or acts unconsciously or out of character, and we do not need to know anything about serotonin levels or repressed Oedipal desires to judge this. We need only explain the person's behaviour in terms of his desires, his beliefs, his deliberations and his choices. The critical questions for responsibility are: Did he know what he was doing? Was he in control? Was he acting out of character? To answer these questions we only require Folk Psychology and not complex psychiatric theory. Our concepts of responsibility, desert, excuse, good, and evil, all depend on explanations within Folk Psychology. Since laymen are just as expert at employing this theory, they are just as qualified as the psychiatrist to decide insanity verdicts.

The attempt to make the notion of insanity technical and decidable by psychiatrists alone is misguided. The Durham Rule was not an adequate account of insanity for two reasons: having a cause is not an excuse (because rational actions are caused by reasons); nor is being caused by a mental illness an excuse (because sick desires do not excuse). If paedophilia gives someone a controllable desire to molest children, he might act because of his mental illness, but he is nevertheless just as responsible as the rapist who acts because of his sexual desires. Determinism does not undermine responsibility – it is a precondition for it. While someone has an excuse because his behaviour is caused in one sort of way (and is responsible if his behaviour is caused in another sort of way), this is not a helpful analysis because we decide what counts as the right sort of way by using concepts such as ignorance, compulsion, automatism, and change in character. These ideas have logical priority – it is they that are needed to select the right sort of causal origin, and so we cannot define excuses in terms of causes independently of such notions.

Diseases are not discovered, they are invented. Nevertheless, something is not a disease if it can be reversed at will. This is a factual matter, and therefore not any condition can be a disease. The disease status of a condition does not determine whether it excuses – this is determined by whether it causes exculpatory ignorance or compulsion. For this reason, changes in our disease classification will not influence what we regard as excuses. The fact that deviant behaviour is caused by a disease in no way undermines the fact that such individuals are evil. A person can be both evil and ill, and moreover, can be evil in part because he is ill.

11

CHARACTER CHANGE AS AN EXCUSE

DR JEKYLL AND MR HYDE

In Robert Louis Stevenson's story, Dr Jekyll recognizes that he has both a good and an evil side. He believes that if he can free his good character from the burden of restraining his evil impulses, his humanitarian work will be unhindered. He creates a potion so that his evil side can emerge unfettered in the evenings, leaving his good side to be productive during the day. We all know the rest. The potion frees his evil side in the form of Hyde who commits a series of offences. It is not that Hyde is clinically deranged – he knows what he is doing and is in control of his impulses. He simply takes delight in doing others harm. Hyde is the same person as Jekyll but they are not the same character. They share the same body and memory, thereby satisfying both physical and psychological criteria for personal identity (Williams, 1973). But they are different characters in that they do not share the same values, emotions, and attitudes.

A person's character consists in the set of dispositions that explain enduring patterns of thinking, feeling, and behaving. Someone is selfish, for example, if he is disposed to think only of himself, to feel little for others, and to pursue only his own interests. Someone is obsessional if he feels threatened by chaos, and takes active steps to impose excessive order on his world. A person's moral character consists in the set of dispositions that explain his ethical beliefs, his moral sentiments, and ethical conduct. Obsessionality is not part of a person's moral character, whereas selfishness is. This is because the disposition to be obsessional does not impact on others, whereas selfishness does.

223

I will argue that it is a change in moral character rather than character in general that excuses.

Is Jekyll responsible for Hyde's evil deeds? According to what I will call the Principle of Personal Liability (PPL), if A is the same person as B but a different moral character, A is responsible for offences committed by B and conversely. This principle dictates that Jekyll is responsible for what Hyde does because he is the same person. According to what I will call the Principle of Character Liability (PCL), if A is the same person as B but a different moral character, A is not responsible for the offences committed by B. This dictates that Jekyll is not responsible for what Hyde does because he is a different moral character. Let us see which principle is correct.

Jekyll knew what he was doing when he took the potion. He knew he would be releasing his evil side free from inhibitions. He knew Hyde would break the law, but was happy to go ahead. Jekyll does not have an excuse for what Hyde does because he knows what Hyde will do and is prepared to allow it. He is like the violent drunk who takes a drink. Even though he lacks control or knowledge during the offence, because he has prior *mens rea*, he is responsible. Similarly, Jekyll has control over becoming a different character and is responsible for what that character does. This conclusion suggests that PPL is correct. Because Jekyll is the same person as Hyde, he should be punished for what Hyde does. If we thought that a person with a specific character was the bearer of responsibility, then Jekyll would not be responsible for what he did as Hyde. Does this imply that PCL is false? No. It is precisely because we do *not* think that Jekyll is a different moral character from Hyde that we feel Jekyll should be punished. PCL requires that we should not punish Jekyll for what he does as Hyde *only if* they are distinct moral characters. If Jekyll chooses to release Hyde, knowing Hyde does not care about others, this can only be because Jekyll himself does not care. And this means, *contra hypothesi*, that Jekyll is not a different moral character from Hyde – they both care very little about others. Justice requires that we punish Jekyll for what he did as Hyde.

Let us examine some variations of the story. In the first, Jekyll is working on a cure for cancer. He takes a dose to test its safety and accidentally turns into Hyde. Hyde goes out and kills a stranger. Hyde knows what he is doing and is able to control his impulses. The next day he turns back into Jekyll and, appalled by what he has done, goes to the police. Should we punish Jekyll? Jekyll is a good character – he would not hurt anyone in pursuing his own goals. If justice requires we only punish evil characters, then Jekyll deserves to be excused. PCL seems correct.

But if Jekyll is the same person as Hyde, and Hyde knew what he was doing when he killed, and was in control of his impulses, then Jekyll also knew what he was doing and was in control. If a person knowingly and freely commits an offence, he is responsible. Therefore, Jekyll is responsible for what he did as Hyde. QED. But this objection begs the question. By assuming he was responsible for what Hyde did because he is the same person as Hyde, we assume PPL is correct. But this is precisely the issue at stake. We cannot discover which principle is correct by assuming that one of them is! When Jekyll commits the offence as Hyde, he is a different moral character – he has a different set of moral beliefs or values. As Hyde, he is aware of what he is doing and is in control. But his values are now radically different – so different that we describe him as a different character. Jekyll *can* control his behaviour and stop himself doing evil as Hyde, but as Hyde he no longer cares about others. His behaviour is no longer under the control of his (original) values. It is at least plausible to argue that we should not blame Jekyll for what he does as Hyde.

If this reasoning is correct, we will be accepting a new category of excuse. If a person undergoes a temporary change in moral character from a good person into an evil one, and commits some offence, then we should excuse him when restored to his normal self. If he is normally of good character, he does not deserve punishment. It was not as his good character that he committed the offence, and therefore he should be excused. This is true even if as the evil character he knows what he is doing and is in control of his actions. If PCL is right, a temporary change in moral character constitutes a new category of excuse.

The second variation is like the first except this time the change is irreversible. Hyde kills his uncle and is apprehended by the police. Should we punish or excuse him? According to both PPL and PCL – Hyde is the same person and character who committed the crime, and so should be punished. But it might be argued that we should excuse a person who commits an offence after undergoing a character change. According to this principle, if a person undergoes an irreversible change from a good character A into an evil character B, and the evil character B commits an offence, then the person should be excused. (This is different from PCL which only allows us to excuse the restored original character A if he commits an offence as character B. This implies that we can *restore* the original character.) We might justify this latter principle by arguing that a great misfortune has befallen the person when he changes from a good to an evil character, and we should not punish him for this misfortune.

Hyde introduces this as a defence in his trial. He argues we should not punish a person who could not help a character change that led to his committing a crime. We sympathize – he did not knowingly transform himself into Hyde, and he would not have committed the offence had he remained the character he was. But we should not accept the principle that a person should be excused because he had no control over developing X, and would not have committed the offence had he not developed X. Take the person developing a taste of violent sex as a result of witnessing a sexual assault. As a result of this new taste, he rapes. The fact that he has developed a taste for sadism, that he would not have raped had he not developed such a taste, and that he had no control over developing this taste, does nothing to excuse him. If he knew he was raping and was in control, he is responsible. Thus we cannot use this principle to excuse Hyde here. Moreover, the motivation for excusing a person undergoing a personality change is that he is a good character. But in this variation of the story, Jekyll's good character has gone forever. Instead, we are left with the evil character of Hyde relishing the prospect of eluding the law, and we have no inclination to excuse *him*. He cynically exploits our sympathy for Jekyll, hoping we will fall for his new defence. This character knew what he was doing and could control himself. We should not excuse him.

The third variation is exactly like the second, only we discover an antidote to the character transformation. Should we give it to him? Yes. A misfortune has happened to the person (when he was transformed into an evil person), and we have a duty to him to reverse that change. If he changes back into Jekyll, do we continue with the punishment? This would be singularly unjust – the character of Jekyll did not commit the offence, and as a good character, he does not deserve punishment.

226

These stories provide overall support for PCL. People with specific characters are the bearers of responsibility and not characterless people. When Jekyll is transformed involuntarily into Hyde who then commits an offence, we should not hold Jekyll responsible. This means that a reversible change in moral character is an excuse. If a person changes from a good character to an evil one, commits an offence, and then changes back, the good character has an excuse. Since it is unjust to punish a good character who committed no offence, we should excuse him. Where we cannot restore the original character, there is no good character to whom we are being unjust. Therefore we should punish him. If this is right, only a temporary change in moral character excuses.

JUSTIFYING THE NEW EXCUSE

Retributivism argues that we should punish only those who freely do wrong because of their evil characters. This means that it is unjust to punish a good person who has, for various reasons, done something bad. If he is a good person who only does harm because he is ignorant, or loses control, we should excuse him. We can also understand why we should excuse good characters operating under duress – while they are not ignorant or out of control, they are in situations where it is not reasonable to expect them to do otherwise. Similarly, if a good person changes temporarily into a bad person and commits an offence, the good character is not responsible for the evil deed, and it would be unjust to punish *him* when he recovers. Justice requires that we only punish evil characters, and thus we should excuse the good person who acted out of character. Retributivism justifies the excuse of a temporary change in moral character.

Utilitarianism also justifies it. The point of punishment is to affect those not sufficiently motivated to avoid harming others – that is, evil characters. This is why we do not punish a person who harms others by accident – if he is a good character who harmed only by accident, he is already motivated to avoid harming others (because of his good character). If he is a good person who harmed because of ignorance, we do not punish him because he too needs no further encouragement to avoid harming others. Punishment is aimed at those with motivational defects. If a good person does evil when temporarily not himself,

227

and is restored to his good self again, there is no need to deter *this* character from further wrongdoing since he is already so motivated. Neither is there any need to reform or isolate him. There is no point in punishing him. Thus Utilitarianism justifies the excuse of a temporary change in moral character.

For similar reasons, both theories do not justify the excuse of an irreversible change in moral character. Retributivism argues we should punish a person if he freely did wrong because of his evil character. Hyde freely did unjustifiable harm because of his evil character. For this reason, we should punish him. Of course, if we could restore Jekyll, then it would no longer be true that *he* did the harm because of *his* evil character, and therefore we ought to excuse him. But this does not apply when the change in character is irreversible. Utilitarianism also takes the pragmatic line – if Hyde is here to stay, then because he has an evil character he is in need of deterrence, reform, and incapacitation. If we excuse and release him, he will re-offend. Therefore, we have very good reasons to punish Hyde. Let us now see how these arguments apply to the world of non-fiction.

PROVOCATION REVISITED

Traditionally, provocation excuses because the person is unable to resist his impulses. We relativize the notion of ability to standard circumstances – if standard changes in circumstances induce him to resist, then he has the ability to resist. If only extraordinary changes do this, then he lacks the ability. If only a person's most important desires get him to do otherwise, he is unable to do otherwise because only extraordinary changes induce him to do so. But should we conclude such people are not responsible for their actions? There are two possible solutions. First, we can define ability in the absolute sense, allowing extraordinary changes to show that a person can do otherwise. This implies that the person acting on his most important desire can do otherwise, but also that those provoked can do otherwise too, and therefore lack an excuse. Second, we could argue that the person acting on his most important desire has the higher-order desire to act on this desire, or has the evaluation that this is his most important desire, while the provoked person does not, and that this explains why only the latter has an excuse. But this gets the phenomenology of provocation all wrong. When someone is so aroused by emotion that he retaliates, he may at that moment have the desire to act on his desire, or may be so upset that his values have changed, making retaliation the most important thing to him. He may not be the divided self that the traditional theory of excuses would have us believe. Does this mean we have to say that those who are provoked do not have an excuse?

The usual picture of a man provoked is of someone who acts against his better judgement, who wants to resist the impulse to retaliate but fails. But he may be so angry that he *changes* his priorities in the heat of the moment. If we examine the phenomenology of provocation, the provoked person acts with a united self – he is not torn and conflicted. He may say afterwards: 'I know that the most important thing was to walk away. But at the time the only thing important to me was to hit back, I was so mad!' Far from the old character losing control, what happens is that a new character emerges to take control. Extreme emotions change a person's desires, values and beliefs – that is, his character. Instead of arguing that the provoked person was not in control, we can say that he was 'not himself'. But if this is the correct way to describe provocation, we now have a new way to explain why such people deserve to be excused. We excuse those who are provoked because they are pushed to the point that they are no longer themselves. When they commit the offence, they are different characters. Their usual values, attitudes, and moral beliefs have been transformed by the extreme emotion of the moment. In that state, they do not have their usual concerns – all they care about is retaliating. They might be law abiding, caring people when not subjected to such pressures. But when provoked, they cease to care, becoming different moral characters. When the original character is restored – when the person has calmed down and cares once more about others – we have no inclination to punish *him* as he is a different character from the one who acted. The provoked person has the excuse of a temporary change in moral character.

What of those who are easily provoked? The law does not excuse them. As Lord Diplock clarified in Camplin's Appeal, the 'disposition to . . . lose one's temper readily will not suffice' to excuse. But why not excuse the irascible man when he becomes angry and changes into a different character? The reason is that when someone changes character at the slightest provocation, we regard the alternation between these two selves as *part* of his character. A person's character is defined by how he reacts in a *normal range* of circumstances. Only when a person changes character under extreme pressures can we justly claim that this reaction is not part of his normal character. When a person can swing immediately from one character to another, we regard it as part of his normal character to do this. Therefore he does not have an excuse.

Provocation may excuse, then, because it induces a temporary change in moral character. Because we are inclined only to excuse good characters, we should also excuse a good character who only turned bad under extreme provocation. Retributivism tells us we should only punish him if he did wrong because of his evil character. But because his character is good, we should excuse him. Utilitarianism argues that there is nothing to be gained by punishing him. As a good person who only does wrong under extreme provocation, he needs no further motivation to avoid harming others. Punishment is not needed to deter, reform or incapacitate.

AUTOMATISM REVISITED

Traditionally, automatism excuses because the person is unaware of what he is doing or is not in control. But many cases lack these excuses. Someone who has dissociated may act purposively, and while his actions are not under his conscious control, a sophisticated level of consciousness must be present to manage such complex tasks as driving a car or shooting a gun. We might argue that the behaviour is not under the control of *all* his beliefs and desires, and therefore, when he deliberates, he can only take part of his desires into account. If a wife dissociates and kills her abusive husband, she only acts on her desire to escape the abuse, and is unable to take other factors like her desire to avoid prison into account. It is this that robs her of responsibility – had her behaviour been under the control of all her desires, she would have inhibited it. But it is sometimes normal to act on a subset of our desires. A woman fleeing from a sex attack is in an emotional state that enables her to ignore her usual concern for her clothing, for pain, and so on. In such states, we have the same narrow vision of someone in a dissociative state. Should we say that we are not responsible for such actions?

To avoid all these problems but still explain why a person in a dissociative state should be excused, we can invoke the excuse of a temporary change in moral character. We are inclined to excuse the abused wife who harms her husband in a dissociative state because she has acted out of character. She was 'not herself' when she acted. The new character is only concerned about satisfying a single desire, and has lost her usual concerns for others and her own future well-being. She has a narrow set of values, making her a different moral character from her normal self. If this is the best way to describe the transformation, she has an excuse on the basis of a reversible change in moral character.

Similarly, while some cases of hypnosis are excused because of ignorance and compulsion, in some the person is aware of his surroundings but still has an excuse. Suppose a hypnotist discovers that a woman desires to kill her abusive husband. She also has other desires, like the desire to be good, which inhibits this desire. The hypnotist induces her not to care about others, thereby removing any inhibition to kill her husband, and she kills him. She has an excuse because she has been transformed into a different moral character. She is a good person, not wanting to harm others, and we are inclined to excuse her for offences committed while she was a different moral character. Tam (1990) gives the example of a man who is hypnotized into not only wanting a glass of water but also wanting to satisfy his desire when others need the water more. Because he is not normally a selfish person, it would not be appropriate to blame him after he returns to normal.

> His brainwashed state can then be viewed as a lapse in relation to his central personality, or his permanent self. The personal quality reflected or manifested by this utterly selfish behaviour during the lapse is therefore not one to be found in John after the lapse, and for this reason it is inappropriate to adopt any personal attitude [of blame] towards John (after the lapse) for a personal quality which is not to be found in him.
>
> (Tam, 1990: 179)

A temporary change in moral character counts as an excuse.

In somnambulism, someone can act purposively, modifying her behaviour to take relevant factors into account. She might not take all relevant considerations into account, but then many voluntary actions performed under emergencies are like this too.

231

We might argue that someone who commits an offence during her sleep acts out of character. In this state, she is influenced by a different set of values and desires from the ones that operate in her conscious state. She is not her normal good self when she acts. If she commits an offence in this state, her normal good character does not deserve to be punished.

Finally, we have argued that if the principal self in a person with MPD is good, but has an evil *alter ego* who commits an offence, the principal self has an excuse. This is true even though the *alter ego* was aware and in control of his behaviour. The law argues that since the *alter ego* has responsibility for what he does, and there is only one person present, the principal self does not have an excuse. However, when the principal self is a good moral character (unlike the *alter ego*), we are inclined to excuse him because he was not his normal good self when he acted. Since he only committed the offence as a different character, he deserves to be excused on the basis of a change in moral character.

In all cases of automatism, it is when the person acts out of character that we are most inclined to excuse him. As long as a person acts in character, we have no reason to suspect he was swept away in some automatism. Some of the strongest evidence that automatism is present lies in the person acting out of character. If an evil person does something bad, acting perfectly in character, and claims he was suffering from an automatism, he is not convincing. Of course, it is possible for us to have evidence that an evil person did something evil during an automatism. For example, he may have a history of automatisms from childhood, when he did bad things while in a glazed expression, or while smacking his lips, suggesting he was suffering from temporal lobe epilepsy. But in cases of dissociation, where there are no such identifying features, we can only rely on uncharacteristic behaviour. Apart from professed amnesia, there are no tell-tale signs of automatism apart from the fact that the behaviour is out of character. This supports the view that, in dissociation at least, automatism excuses because of the excuse of a change in moral character.

CHARACTER CHANGE AS AN INSANITY DEFENCE

Reductionism assumes that ignorance and compulsion alone can account for the exculpatory power of mental illness. But there are many cases of mental illness that excuse (if any mental illness excuses) which do not satisfy either of these criteria. One example is the psychotically depressed mother who kills her children because she believes they are better off dead. Her ignorance does not satisfy the As-if Rule and does not excuse. But we still feel she should not be punished. Another case is the paranoid person who believes he is being persecuted and kills in retaliation. Even if he were being persecuted, this does not justify killing. Nevertheless, from M'Naghten onwards, such mentally ill offenders have been seen as paradigmatic cases of insanity. Rationalism argues that such patients are not reasoning clearly and that we should excuse them on this basis. Because M'Naghten and the depressed mother are not able to figure out all the options facing them, they should be excused. We saw that this excuse reduces to the excuse of exculpatory ignorance, and that while it might explain why some such cases should be excused, there are others that it cannot. The psychotic patient who kills because she believes that if she does not she will be tortured, does not have a complete excuse on the Rationalist view. But we do not feel inclined to punish her.

Let us start with neurological disease, which can cause a personality change, and this can lead to offences being committed. There need be no ignorance or compulsion, but we are still inclined to excuse such patients.

Lesions of the frontal lobe can produce a picture that simulates some facets of psychopathic personality. The main features are irritability, loss of initiative, lessening of the finer aspects of social adjustment, insensitivity to the feelings of others, and emotional lability . . . A 53-year-old hospital administrator gradually became irritable and apathetic in the course of 8–9 months. He had previously been a lively, vigorous, and socially popular man and affectionate father. In the 3 months before his admission he developed a cruel form of behaviour that was out of character. When his 15-year-old daughter was setting her hair in the evening, he would seize two or three of the curlers she had in position and twist them round and round until she

233

screamed in pain. He would then burst into loud and prolonged laughter. He proved to have a large meningioma on the convexity of the right frontal lobe.

(Roth, 1990: 441–2)

Do we punish the hospital administrator for his cruel behaviour after we have restored his normal character? Our intuitions suggest otherwise, and this can be explained by the excuse of a change in moral character.

Lishman (1987) documents that frontal lobe tumours frequently present with changes in character before intellectual impairment. Eleven of twenty-five patients reported by Direkze *et al.* (1971) presented with personality changes. A law-abiding greengrocer was charged repeatedly for speeding, a 53-year-old clergyman began telling smutty jokes, and a pharmacist uncharacteristically asked his wife to play Cowboys and Indians! All proved to have frontal astrocytomas. A tendency towards childishness, facetiousness, and a lack of concern for others are typical of these changes. If such patients commit offences when so transformed, and are restored to their normal characters by surgery, it would be perversely unjust to punish them for the evil done when they were not themselves. They have an excuse, not of ignorance or compulsion, but the excuse of a temporary change in moral character induced by neurological disease.

Radden (1985) gives the example of the PhD student from Austin University, Texas, who began to have thoughts that he should kill someone. After murdering his mother and wife, he climbed the university tower and shot forty-one people, killing seventeen of them. At autopsy, a cerebral tumour was found. The tumour did not appear to cause ignorance, compulsion, or an automatism. Suppose it induced a psychopathic personality change, making him indifferent to others. If he had lived to have the tumour removed and his normal character restored, should we punish him? No. But Radden thinks otherwise. She argues that if the sniper was aware of what he was doing and in control of his actions, then he would not have shot innocent people unless he was an evil person. But in this case he deserves to be punished. When a disease causes a gradual personality change, she argues: 'It does seem plausible to describe the criminal actions of sufferers from some slowly developing degenerative disease as done voluntarily and knowingly' (Radden, 1985: 38).

Such a person, she argues, is responsible.

This is wrong. Suppose Benedict, normally a gentle and considerate person, develops a frontal meningioma. This makes him psychopathic, and he stops caring about others. Consequently, when driving to work one day, he fails to stop at a pedestrian crossing and runs over an old lady. He knew what he was doing, and was able to resist the impulse to continue driving. But he just did not care. We operate on Benedict and restore his normal self. He experiences remorse for what he has done. Do we really want to say that he was responsible and that we should punish a good person?

> There is a good reason why we should be reluctant to excuse the criminal action of a person suffering from long-term personality change. It is because the element of knowledge would appear to enter critically into this case . . . Because with knowledge comes foresight and predictive and preventive powers, persons able to understand the disease's role in their motivation and action would be culpable in the same way as the alcoholic and drug addict. They could predict and thus would be held responsible for preventing the illegal actions by avoiding the occasion and means of criminality, or by actively seeking treatment and alleviation for that symptom of their condition.
>
> (Radden, 1985: 39)

But if the person undergoing a personality change becomes indifferent to others, then although he might know the consequences of his personality change, he will no longer *care* sufficiently to prevent his actions. It is all very well knowing he has changed, but if he has also undergone a change of moral character, he will not care to do anything about the change. If the person was originally a good person, we are inclined to excuse him because he acted out of character.

Mood disorders are another class of mental disorders which may excuse for none of the traditional reasons. In florid cases of mania, the patient is deluded and so high that he is unable to inhibit his impulses (Roth and Kroll, 1986). He has the excuses of ignorance and compulsion. But in milder cases (hypomania), the person changes character. If formerly unconfident, inhibited, and shy, he may become confident, adventurous, and outgoing. If he commits an offence, we are inclined to excuse him, but since he is neither ignorant nor compelled, the only grounds for excusing him is a temporary change in moral character.

Let me recount some of my cases. George, an inhibited man, became hypomanic. He found himself in such good spirits that he ceased to care whether he broke the law. He test drove a sports car, driving dangerously fast in a built-up area. He was charged with reckless driving. He knew what he was doing and was not overwhelmed by an impulse to speed. But speeding is uncharacteristic of him, and was induced by the temporary personality change. Mike was also an introverted man who became hypomanic. He was so high-spirited that he decided uncharacteristically to take a friend up on a dare and steal a car for a joy ride. He was caught and thought the whole thing was a huge joke. He knew what he was doing and was sufficiently in control to choose exactly the sort of car he had always wanted to drive. Nevertheless he only stole the car because his normal law-abiding character was replaced by a playful dare-devil character. Both men deserve to be excused because of a change in moral character. These cases are typical of offences committed by manic patients. Higgins (1990) reports that most offences committed by hypomaniacs are minor ones like drunkenness, traffic offences, simple assaults, damage to property, and indecent approaches: 'Courts have little difficulty in appreciating the significance of marked hypomania arising in a person of *good character* and will usually accept the suggestion of a medical disposal without demur [my italics]' (Higgins, 1990: 351). It is when such behaviour is seen as a break with the person's normal good character that the courts are most inclined to excuse. This is precisely what we have been arguing.

The excuse of a change in moral character enables us to explain why we are inclined to excuse those cases of mental illness that do not satisfy the traditional excuses of ignorance and compulsion. We excuse M'Naghten and the depressed mother even though both knew what they were doing and were in control. This is because the mental illness so disturbs them that they cease to be themselves. Their distress is so great that their values change. What becomes most important to them in such states is to end the distress, and therefore they act. Because their normal values do not incline them to behave in this way, we see them as having undergone a change in moral character, and for this reason deserve to be excused. It would be unjust to punish them because they are good people who undergo a change in moral character. Paranoid patients whose delusions do not satisfy the As-if Rule may still have excuses because they were not themselves when they acted. Similarly for those suffering from volitional disorders. If depression transformed McCullough from a law-abiding person to a person who no longer cared about the law, we would be inclined to excuse him even if he was not overwhelmed by his impulses. When illness makes a person act out of character, we are inclined to excuse him on the basis of a change in moral character. Conversely, when madness does not excuse, it is often because there is not the requisite change in moral character. The Neo-Nazi who kills what he takes to be a Jew does not have an excuse, even though psychotic, because he acts *in character*. When Deidre kills the casting director because she believes she has lost the part, we are not inclined to excuse her because she is a callous and ruthless person. The aim of excusing, remember, is to excuse good characters, and this explains why we are not inclined to excuse these cases.

Many jurists might object to this defence on the basis that it is difficult to determine whether someone acted out of character, and this will make the insanity defence unworkable. But moral character is not something hidden from view. We learn about someone's values by observing his behaviour. A pattern of behaviour indicating someone is caring, and the disruption of this pattern when he becomes cruel and indifferent to the needs of others, is something eminently observable, as the cases above demonstrate. Of course, there will remain problems of just where we draw the line between changes in character that excuse and changes that do not, but the same problem arises for beliefs and impulses that excuse and those that do not. There is no unique epistemological problem facing the excuse of a change in moral character. Either way, we need this defence to explain why many deserving cases of mental illness should be excused.

WHAT CHARACTER CHANGES EXCUSE?

Not all character changes excuse. Brian is a good person. He is kind and generous, caring for his family and the community. But tragedy strikes. His wife and two young children are killed by a drunken driver and he is unable to get over this loss. He becomes bitter and resentful. He cannot stand to see others happy and gets some solace from their misery. Eventually he sets about making them unhappy. Here a transformation of character develops through his inability to deal with a tragic loss. Suppose he deliberately spikes a colleague's drink in an attempt to make him crash. His colleague is killed. Should we excuse Brian because he has undergone a character change? No. We have certain expectations of Brian. We expect him to come to terms with the loss, preserve his good character, and continue to respect others. Because he could have avoided such a deterioration, he is responsible for what he does. People are responsible for such non-pathological changes to their character.

Mario is also a good man. But the economy fails and he and his family are forced into poverty. He becomes desperate. One day he is asked to deliver a package (containing drugs) for a sizeable sum of money. He chooses not to question what he is delivering, focusing on the fact that he will be able to feed his family. He delivers more packages, becoming used to ignoring the pricks of his conscience. He gets absorbed into the local mafia, doing more and more overtly illegal things. He gets so used to ignoring the needs of others that eventually he harms others without batting an eyelid. Should we excuse him because he was originally a good person, but difficult circumstances led to a gradual hardening of his character? No. He is responsible for these non-pathological changes.

Character changes can occur in different ways. They can be caused by diseases such as hypomania or frontal lobe tumours. They can also be caused by adverse life experiences. A person is regarded as responsible for some changes in his character. Mario had a choice about how he earned a living. It was through these voluntary actions that his character hardened. Similarly, Brian is responsible for not overcoming the loss of his family. He chose not to take up the challenge of making sense of his life and ending his resentment towards the happiness of others. Because such individuals are responsible for these changes to their characters, they do not have an excuse. Only if the person is not responsible for the character change, as in changes caused by disease, does he have an excuse. Only if changes are brought about by a disease will the person have an excuse.

Moreover, only changes in *moral* character excuse. Sid is a callous person. He has no qualms exploiting others, including the sexual abuse of children (as he is a paedophile). A brain tumour causes him to acquire a taste for violent sex with adults, but leaves his moral views unaffected. He rapes a woman. We remove his tumour, and consider whether to punish him. His having undergone a personality change (in that his sexual desires changed) does not excuse him – he remains an evil person deserving punishment. Now take Solly. He is a good person, but also acquires a brain tumour that similarly transforms his sexual desires. While he had never acted on his paedophilic desires, now the tumour also transforms him from a caring to a callous person. Thinking nothing of acting on his new sexual desires, he also commits a rape. After restoring his original character, do we punish him? This time, his personality change does provide an excuse. Solly is a good person, and so does not deserve punishment. Only if personality change leads to a change in moral character, does it excuse.

THE PARADOX OF EVIL

Up to this point we have concluded that those with a psychopathic personality disorder do not have an excuse – they know what they are doing and are in control of their actions. So why does a good person who acquires a disease (like a frontal lobe tumour) that makes him psychopathic have an excuse? If psychopathy is a disease, it must affect a person's character formation from a caring to an uncaring character. That is, the person with the disorder must undergo a personality *change*. So why not regard him as having the excuse of personality change? But if we excuse someone who has a personality disorder, we are in trouble. Retributivism tells us that we should be punishing evil characters who freely do evil. But those who are extremely evil – those who do not care sufficiently about others – usually suffer from a psychopathic personality disorder. We then face the paradox of evil: (1) we ought to punish evil characters (those who deserve it); (2) many evil characters have personality disorders that induce a character change; and (3) we ought to excuse those who suffer from a change in moral character. If being extremely evil is grounds (in those cases with personality disorders) for both an excuse and punishment, our moral system becomes incoherent.

239

Of course, many evil people (including many extremely evil people) suffer from personality defects rather than personality disorders. Many care about others, but not enough, and do evil because of this. When they do evil, they have to hide from themselves the truth about what they are doing because they do have some feelings for others. They suffer from personality defects like selfishness or narcissism that are not extreme enough to be classified as personality disorders. But we are not inclined to excuse someone just because of his personality defect. And hence this paradox does not force us to conclude that there are no evil people in the world. In fact, many people who do extreme evil may not suffer from any personality disorder. Simply doing extreme evil does not imply that the person is a psychopath.

If we are to resolve this paradox, one of the three propositions must be false. We argued, in the example of the transformation of Dr Jekyll into Mr Hyde, that when a person undergoes an irreversible personality change he does not have an excuse. This is because we excuse good characters, and the good character in this case no longer exists. But this applies only to non-pathological character changes. Let us consider unremovable frontal lobe tumours causing psychopathy. Do they really not provide an excuse? Or let us consider those with Huntington's Chorea. Oliver (1970) documented 100 cases, 38 of whom had psychopathic changes to their personality. This case is typical:

> A 54-year-old married woman, formerly noted for unusual intelligence and social poise, became lazy, quarrelsome and tactless. Somewhat later she began to cheat at bridge and on a shopping expedition stole a box of chocolates from the shop counter, showing no concern for the subsequent expostulations. During the next 4 years she was apprehended five times for similar blatant shoplifting. Finally language deterioration and memory impairment brought her to medical attention.
>
> (Toone, 1990: 386)

Victims of irreversible personality deterioration due to disease do not deserve to be punished.

One way to accommodate this intuition is to realize that when a good person is affected by a disease that irreversibly changes his character, we still think of him as a good person with a disease rather than simply an evil person. The disease is regarded as 'external' to his character – as something alien that can be conceptually separated from the affected personality. He is seen as a good character that is somehow 'inhibited' by the disease. If justice requires us to excuse good characters, we should excuse him. This allows us to avoid being inhumane by punishing those with Huntington's Chorea and other irreversible neurological disorders that induce character change.

If we excuse irreversible personality changes, we have reason to excuse those with a psychopathic personality disorder. Such people also suffer from irreversible changes to their characters, so why not excuse them? Note here that it would be a mistake to argue that we should not excuse them because we cannot talk about a *change* in character unless we can identify a previously existing good character, and that no such good character exists in those suffering from psychopathic personality disorder (because it is a developmental disorder). This argument fails because we would still be inclined to excuse a person who suffered from a slow-growing frontal lobe tumour that was present at birth and prevented the person from ever having a good character in the first place.

The case for excusing them is also supported by the fact that we might discover a cure for psychopathic personality disorder (Reznek, 1991). Suppose the drug Conzac reverses the autonomic defect, enabling psychopaths to feel sympathy. What should we do when a psychopath commits an offence? Should we treat him, reversing his evil character? Or should we withhold the treatment and punish him instead? Or should we treat him, turning him into a good person who experiences remorse, and still punish him? The existence of a cure allows us to see a good person trapped inside the personality disorder. But as soon as we can identify a good person within an offender, then justice requires that we should not punish him. A cure for psychopathy enables us to do this, and therefore we ought to excuse such offenders. This conclusion is supported by both Retributivism and Utilitarianism. Retributivism suggests that we should not punish a treated psychopath – even if his character was changed rather than restored, as he is not evil now. Utilitarianism agrees – there is little gained by punishing a cured or reformed evil character. He needs no deterrence, reform, or incapacitation. Therefore, we ought to excuse him.

This means that if we classify psychopathy as a disease, those with the disorder are seen as undergoing a character change, making them into evil characters. This means that they will be eligible for the excuse of character change. We seem to have arrived at the paradox of evil – those who are the embodiment of evil in that they care nothing for others turn out to have an excuse, and are not evil at all. Instead we see them as good characters inhibited by a disease making them do evil things.

IS PSYCHOPATHY A DISEASE?

Psychopaths are so constituted that they do not care about the well-being of others. We have argued above that those who care nothing for other people should be classified as evil. While they are not responsible for their characters, psychopaths commit awful offences against others in full knowledge of what they are doing and in full control of their actions. So how can we argue that they should be excused on the basis of a character change? Is there not a flagrant contradiction here?

Not really. We can avoid the contradiction by simply defining an evil character as someone who does not care sufficiently for others (in the pursuit of his own selfish interests) where this has not been brought about by a disease. On this amended definition, psychopaths will no longer qualify as being evil. But many, myself included, feel uneasy about excusing psychopaths. We can avoid this unpalatable consequence by resorting to a final dimension of the concept of disease. I have argued in *The Philosophical Defence of Psychiatry* that homosexuality satisfies many of the requirements for being a disease. The process causing it is both abnormal and without an obvious cause; it produces harm in that homosexual couples are precluded from reproducing (and in this sense are like infertile heterosexual couples); it cannot be reversed by an act of will, and so on (Reznek, 1991). But I argued that for political reasons we should not view homosexuality as a disease. At present, all we achieve by labelling homosexuality as a disease is stigmatizing a group of people who are not in a position to change and who do not want to change. All we create is a divisive society. We are better off not creating a stigma and not classifying the condition as a disease.

There is no fact of the matter whether or not homosexuality is a disease – it carries no disease label independently of our judgements, and how we see it is up to us. In fact, we should not be asking the question whether homosexuality or any other condition *is* a disease, but rather whether we *ought* to classify that condition as a disease. It is usually the well-being of the individual that influences whether we ought to classify a condition as a disease. But sometimes it is the social and political *consequences* of the classification that is crucial. With homosexuality, the decisive factor in classifying it as normal is the negative political consequences of labelling the condition as a disease.

For a similar reason, we should hesitate to classify psychopathy as a disease. There is, as with homosexuality, a fundamental choice here. The fact that psychopathy has an abnormal biological cause in no way settles the issue. Homosexuality also has an abnormal biological cause. But so too does high intelligence. For any unusual human trait, we should *expect* to find an underlying abnormal biological cause. Whether we classify them as diseases is up to us. Even if a disease is an abnormal involuntary process without an obvious external cause that produces harm, we are not forced to classify every such process as a disease. When the cost of doing so outweighs the benefits, we are entitled to decide not to classify it as pathological. I believe that, at the present time, the costs of classifying psychopathy as a disease are greater than the benefits. There is no cure in sight, and such offenders are better dealt with by the penal system. They are extraordinarily adept at fooling psychiatrists into thinking they have responded to treatment, and so should not be handled in the mental health system. Moreover, it is dangerous to think we can cure psychopaths, to seduce ourselves into thinking we can release them, when experience has told us they only re-offend again and again. We have more reason, then, not to see psychopathy as a disease at this time, but instead as the essence of evil. And by so classifying it, we remove the possibility of their excusing themselves on the basis that they suffer from a disease that has brought about a character change. By this choice, we are permitted to see them as evil rather than ill.

There is another reason why we should hesitate to excuse psychopaths. Radden argues that the need to distinguish mad from bad forces us to classify personality disorders on the side of bad.

Legal hesitation in classifying character disorders as criminal insanity (and thus as exculpating conditions) seems to rest on the impulse to separate mad from bad. A condition characterized by nothing but aberrant desires to harm others cannot be adequately distinguished from sheer evil. There seems no way to separate the case of Fish, for example, from paradigmatic cases of willful wickedness like that of Cesare Borgia.

(Radden, 1985: 116)

We need to persuade people to obey the law, and the institution of punishment serves to do this. However, if this is seen as fundamentally unjust, our rationale for obeying will evaporate. If we are not able to draw a natural line between those that are evil on the one hand, and those that are (psychopathically) personality disordered and not evil on the other, we have no non-arbitrary way of preventing everyone from claiming to have an excuse. As far as we currently know, those with personality disorders only differ by degree from those who are normal. These disorders are unlike brain tumours and Huntington's Chorea which are qualitatively distinct from normal. The reason why we classify them as disorders is that they are simply at the extreme of normality. Therefore there is no non-arbitrary way of drawing the line between those who are evil and those who have an excuse. To avoid this arbitrariness, it is more fair to withhold excuses from those suffering from personality disorders, and conclude that they are evil rather than ill.

If we are to explain the most central cases where mental illness excuses, we have to resort to the novel excuse of a change in moral character. This also explains why many cases of provocation, duress, and automatism excuse. This raises a problem for our drawing a line between the mad and the bad when considering personality disordered offenders. In general, where a disease (other than a personality disorder) changes a personality from a good to a bad moral character, we are inclined to excuse him whether the change is reversible or not. When a personality disorder produces an evil character, we are much less inclined to excuse him because there is no natural place to draw the line between the mad and the bad. Moreover, whether we classify psychopathy as a disease (and therefore grant psychopaths an excuse on the basis of character change) is a matter of choice, and at present there are good reasons for not doing so. The social and political cost of classifying psychopathy as a disease suggests at present that we should view it as the embodiment of evil instead.

12

THE CLASH OF PARADIGMS

HOW RATIONAL ARE WE?

We need to be rational to be responsible, because only if we are rational can we do otherwise in standard circumstances. If we are all irrational, no one will be responsible. But is it possible to discover that we are all irrational? There are some philosophers who believe we can never discover this. Cohen (1981) uses the competence/performance distinction proposed by Chomsky (1957) to argue that we cannot. According to this distinction, someone can know the rules of grammar, but still speak ungrammatically for other reasons – for example, he may forget the earlier part of a long sentence and fail to complete it grammatically. Similarly, if a subject fails to be logical, this need not imply that he lacks the rules of logic. Armed with this distinction, we can always interpret logical errors as performance errors, and conclude that everyone is perfectly logical. But this argument is flawed. If someone consistently makes errors in his reasoning, it looks decidedly empty to assume that he really possesses perfect competence in the rules of logic but that circumstances constantly bias his use of them.

Although any hypothesis can be held true come what may, the perfect competence account seems to gain epicycles too fast. Eventually, it amounts to saying that an agent accepts a metatheoretically adequate logic; he just usually misapplies it because, for example, in Cohen's words, eliciting conditions are 'rarely, if ever, ideal for the exercise of such a competence.' Rather than attempting a principled account, a classical competence/performance distinction must explain away a wide range of actual behaviour as 'mere' exceptions, as insignificant 'noise'.

(Cherniak, 1986: 144)

Making too many mistakes suggests eventually that we are irrational.

Cohen also argues that error is relative to a system of logic – a person making an 'error' may be reasoning correctly according to an alternative system of logic. But this objection is also flawed. There are some standards that all systems of logic must follow if they are to avoid error. For example, all systems of logic must obey the law of non-contradiction – no proposition can be both true and false. Similarly, in inductive logic, 'the law of large numbers is not simply a feature of standard statistical theory, it is a phenomenon readily demonstrated by empirical means. Hence I am quite happy to say that intuitive statistical judgments which take no account of sample size are in error. Much of our irrationality cannot be attributed to an adequate alternative logic' (Evans, 1989: 9).

Davidson (1984) also argues that it is logically impossible for others to be pervasively illogical. In order to understand or translate another's speech, we need to assume *inter alia* that he is logical. First, we must assume that most of his perceptual judgements are true:

> The method is not designed to eliminate disagreement, nor can it; its purpose is to make meaningful disagreement possible, and this depends entirely on a foundation – some foundation – in agreement. Since charity is not an option, but a condition of having a workable theory, it is meaningless to suggest that we might fall into massive error by endorsing it.
>
> (Davidson, 1984: 197)

If an alien calls red 'zeen' and green 'zed', I can only infer that we are disagreeing if I assume he means green by 'zeen' and red by 'zed'. But to reach this conclusion, he must apply 'zed' and 'zeen' to red and green most of the time. Even disagreement presupposes we mostly agree.

Second, we need to assume he is being logical. As Hollis (1979: 232) puts it:

In general we cannot first identify a native constant as

247

'if . . . then' and then go on to show that modus ponens does not hold, since, if modus ponens does not hold, then the constant has been wrongly identified. Native logic must either turn out to be a version of our own or remain untranslatable.

Sharing the same logic is a precondition for understanding others. Similarly, we cannot discover that others have a pervasive inductive irrationality. Newton-Smith (1982: 110) writes: 'R is a reason for believing that p just in case there is an appropriate truth linking R and p. That my typewriter case looks white to me is a reason for thinking that it is white just because things that look white in the sort of circumstances that obtain at the moment are or tend to be white.' If a person used the term 'zeason' when there was no truth linking the zeason and the conclusion, we would not translate the term as 'reason'. This means that others cannot be pervasively inductively irrational.

This seems to imply that we cannot discover that others have a pervasive practical irrationality. To understand someone's behaviour, we have to postulate a desire and a belief. If someone goes onto a rickety bridge, we might explain this by postulating that he wants to die and believes the bridge will cave in, or by postulating that he does not want to die but does not believe the bridge will cave in. We can only translate 'Zis zidge is zickety' if we have an idea of what he believes, and we can only do this if we can explain his behaviour. We can decide among these two hypotheses because we do not just have one piece of behaviour and one sentence to go on. We have other behaviours which indicate that he does not want to die. This helps us decide what he believes, and this helps us translate the sentence. But in all of this, we *assume* a minimal practical rationality – that an agent's behaviour is rationalized by a desire and a belief. If behaviour were not explicable in this way, we could never even get started.

Does this prove that we can never abandon the assumption that we are rational? No – this assumption is part of a testable empirical theory:

On the above picture of translation one will begin by hypothesizing a similarity between oneself and the [aliens] in regard to basic desires, low-level perceptual beliefs, and logic. If on this basis one is able to come up with a translation scheme which enables one to successfully predict

[alien] behaviour that will be evidence for both the translation and the initial assumption . . . But there is no reason to
elevate reasonable *a posteriori* conjectures into *a priori*
presuppositions.

(Newton-Smith, 1982: 115)

This means that we *can* have evidence that we are irrational. In
fact, we do have such evidence when behaviour is extremely
disorganized. In trying to explain bizarre behaviour, we look for
a pattern. If there is none, we accept that the presupposition of
rationality does not obtain. Laing (1965) argues that the
disorganized behaviour of schizophrenics is rational. He claims
they behave bizarrely to resist being explained by others because
they believe this will lead to their being controlled. The problem
with this is that we can make any behaviour appear rational – if
B describes the behaviour, all we need to assume is that the
person desires D and believes B will satisfy D. But such explanations lack empirical support. To sustain the idea that the person
really desires D, we need other evidence for it, and so too for the
belief. If there is none forthcoming, we cannot sustain the belief
that the bizarre behaviour is rational. We are therefore not forced
to conclude that all behaviour will necessarily be minimally
rational.

Similarly, while we might have to preserve the truth of most
perceptual statements and simple logical inferences in order to
understand another person, we do not have to conclude that all
his theoretical statements and more complex logical inferences
are correct. We could never translate others as rejecting the laws
of identity and non-contradiction, but we might find that they
are illogical in more complex reasoning. While we must assume
that others have minimal practical rationality, this does not
preclude discovering that they are irrational in a more substantive practical sense. Thus we can both understand others *and*
discover pervasive irrationalities. The existence of shared
perceptual truths and basic logic enables translation to get
started, but we can still arrive at pervasive falsehoods and illogicalities outside these shared truths and inferences by showing
that such a theory is the best explanation of that person's
behaviour. The possibility is open that there are widespread irrationalities in human beings.

And the evidence already shows this to be true. Evans (1989:

5) writes: 'The results of the many hundreds of such experiments that have been reported in the psychological literature indicate that subjects' responses very frequently deviate from the logically prescribed answers.' One such study by Watson (1966) demonstrates our Confirmation Bias. We have a tendency to seek information that is consistent with our current beliefs and avoid the collection of potentially falsifying evidence. Subjects were presented with four cards lying on a table, each card having a letter on one side and a number on the other (A, D, 3, and 7). The subject is asked which cards have to be turned over to find out whether the following rule is false: 'If there is an A on one side, then there is a 3 on the other.' Most say that the A and the 3 card should be turned over, but we need to choose those cards which will show that the rule is false, and it will only be false if there is an A on one side and not a 3 on the other. Other arrangements are consistent with the rule, and thus cards A and 7 should be selected. In one study of 128 university students, only 5 got the answer!

There is ample evidence we are inductively irrational. One consistent error we make is the Bias of Representativeness (Kahneman *et al.*, 1982). We are over-influenced by our stereotypes. For example, if asked whether a shy, retiring, person is more likely to be a nurse or a librarian, most people plump for her being a librarian in spite of the fact that there are far more nurses than librarians. This ignores the relative sizes of each class. Inductive logic also employs the law of large numbers. According to this idea, there is a small chance that 50 per cent of coin flips will be heads if we throw a coin a few times. But if we throw the coin hundreds of times, it is extremely likely that 50 per cent of the coin flips will be heads. Kahneman and Tversky (1972) showed how subjects ignored sample size. They gave them the following information: A certain town is served by two hospitals. In the larger one, about forty-five babies are born each day, and in the smaller about fifteen. Although 50 per cent are boys in each hospital, the exact percentage varies from day to day. Over one year, each hospital recorded the days on which more than 60 per cent of the babies were boys. Which hospital recorded more such days? Subjects showed no preference for the smaller hospital, which will clearly experience the deviant result more often. We also make the Fundamental Attributional Error. We explain things by attributing the source to persons rather than situations (Ross and Anderson, 1982). One study divided subjects into questioners, answerers, and observers. Questioners think up any questions, answerers try to answer them, and observers observe. Afterwards they rate the IQ and knowledge of the questioners and answerers. Both observers and answerers rate the questioners as much more intelligent and knowledgeable in spite of the fact they know they had an unfair advantage.

There is a wealth of evidence that people are far from consistent in their desires, attitudes, and beliefs. A national survey taken by *The New York Times* in the 1970s showed that a majority of Americans disapproved of government-sponsored welfare programmes, yet 81 per cent approved of the government assisting poor single-parent families, 81 per cent approved of the government helping poor people buy cheap food, and 82 per cent approved of the government paying for health care for poor people (Atkinson *et al.*, 1983)! There are other experiments (Tversky, 1969) which demonstrate that our preferences are far from transitive. In one study, subjects were asked to select college applicants with information about their intellectual ability, emotional stability, and social facility. They were told that intellectual ability was the most important trait to look for, but that the others had some value too. Intransitivity of preferences was demonstrated when subjects preferred applicant A to B on the basis of a certain mix of these three traits, B to C, but C to D, where D had the same mix of traits as A. Such intransitivities were far from uncommon.

When people do adjust their beliefs to be more consistent, they frequently do so in an irrational (but face-saving) way. The most dramatic example of this comes from the study of the cult that believed the world would come to an end (Festinger *et al.*, 1956). They believed they would be saved by a ship from outer space and gave up all their possessions. When the fateful day passed without the world being destroyed, they were shaken. Their response was not to give up their beliefs and return to their normal life – this would have exposed their sacrifice as futile. Instead, they argued that their faith had postponed the end of the world! In another study, Festinger (1957) induced subjects to tell waiting stooges that a dull task had been interesting. Subjects who had been paid $20 did not change their belief that the task was dull, but those paid only $1 did change their beliefs. They had acquired an inconsistent triad of beliefs: 'I am an honest person, I found the task boring, I told the next subject it was interesting.' This inconsistency creates cognitive dissonance – a disturbing state a person is motivated to reduce. The dissonance is worst when the person is provided with no good reason to be dishonest (given no monetary inducement). What is significant is that the adjustment made is not the one required by the evidence. Subjects do not conclude that they are dishonest. A face-saving adjustment is made and they conclude that the task was not dull.

In summary, there are no philosophical objections to our discovering that we are widely irrational. Moreover, we have substantial evidence that we *are* irrational in many ways. This means that responsibility cannot require the presence of (full) rationality. But we can (and should) continue to argue that rationality is required for responsibility. The fact that we are not ideally rational does not mean that we are not sufficiently rational to be responsible for our actions (in the sense required).

THE FATE OF FOLK PSYCHOLOGY

The Legal Paradigm depends on the truth of the Folk Psychology. Folk Psychology, remember, assumes that intentional behaviour is caused by desires and beliefs and that people are largely rational (in the practical sense). Do we now have sufficient evidence to undermine Folk Psychology, and, if so, are we forced to reject the Legal Paradigm? While we have significant evidence that we are not as rational as we supposed, this is not sufficient to undermine Folk Psychology. We might fall significantly below the ideal of rationality, but this does not imply we cannot (by and large) form rational beliefs, figure out available options, infer the consequences, and follow the maxim of minimal practical rationality. We might not be ideally rational, but we are rational enough to be responsible.

What of Folk Psychology's assumption that intentional behaviour is caused by desires and beliefs? We have abundant evidence that we act because of reasons. We frequently predict what someone will do from our knowledge of his desires and beliefs. As Cherniak (1986: 4) says: 'It seems an uncontroversial fact that we very commonly employ this procedure for predicting people's behaviour in everyday situations.' But in spite of this, Folk Psychology has come under attack. Patricia

Churchland (1986: 305) thinks 'it would be astonishing if folk psychology, alone among folk theories, was essentially correct.' On her view, Folk Psychology will be reduced to Neuroscience.

There are two sorts of reduction. In Eliminative Reduction, the entities from the old theory find no place in the new and are eliminated. When the theory of phlogiston was replaced by the theory of oxygen, there was no term in the new theory that occupied the same role that phlogiston did in the old. Phlogiston was the substance that Priestley and other eighteenth-century chemists believed was given off when metals like mercury were burned in air. The powder produced by this 'calcination' was supposedly due to the loss of phlogiston. But we see this process as oxidation – the *addition* of oxygen rather than the *removal* of phlogiston. In the new theory there is no entity that can be identified with phlogiston – there is no 'bridge law' identifying phlogiston and oxygen, and therefore we talk of the entities postulated in the old theory as being eliminated. Similarly, the medieval theory that women who behaved bizarrely were witches possessed by the Devil has been eliminated in favour of a theory that mental illness causes such behaviour. In Non-Eliminative Reduction, the entities in the old theory find a place in the new. The molecular theory replacing Boyle's theory of gases does not deny there are gases, or that they can exist at various temperatures – only that gases are collections of molecules in motion, and that temperature consists of mean molecular kinetic energy. 'Bridge laws' identify the entities and properties of the old theory with the entities and properties of the new.

Will Neuroscience eliminate Folk Psychology? Neuroscience assumes that behaviour is the consequence of brain events. We know that action consists of bodily movements, that this is caused by muscular contractions, and these, in turn, by activity in the motor cortex. Complex brain events cause behaviour. Paul Churchland (1989: 125) thinks such a theory will eliminate Folk Psychology:

> Neuroscience is unlikely to find 'sentences in the head', or anything else that answers to the structure of individual desires and beliefs. On the strength of this assumption, I am willing to infer that folk psychology is false, and that its ontology is chimerical. Beliefs and desires are of a piece with phlogiston, caloric, and the alchemical essences.

But accepting that our behaviour is caused by brain events does not mean we have to abandon Folk Psychology. We cannot deny that behaviour is goal directed, but if we accept this, we have to adopt some explanation in terms of possessing goals and having feedback from the environment. But then we can identify desires and beliefs with these theoretical entities, and we do not have to eliminate Folk Psychology. If we discover that our behaviour is caused by the firing of neurons from various areas, this does not mean that Folk Psychology is wrong. All it means is that desires and beliefs can be identified with these events.

If Churchland wishes to explain goal-directed behaviour, he is forced to accept that there are motivating factors and cognitive factors explaining behaviour. But once he does this, what reason does he have to deny that these factors do not have the 'structure of desires and beliefs'? Folk Psychology does not endow desires and beliefs with such exact properties that we cannot identify them with the explanatory factors of Neuroscience. If this is the case, Folk Psychology will not be eliminated. We are not forced into this even if the match between desires and beliefs and their neuronal counterparts is not exact. There might be two different neuronal systems mediating belief, and six different systems influencing motivation. Then there will be no neat correspondence between neuronal systems and psychological states. But this will not undermine Folk Psychology. All this means is that more than one neuronal system grounds our desires and beliefs. What if there are some systems that have both motivating and cognitive properties? We still need not abandon Folk Psychology. The fact that one neuronal system grounds both desires and beliefs does not show that our behaviour is not caused by desires and beliefs. Whatever theory we arrive at, it need not eliminate Folk Psychology.

Any attempt to eliminate Folk Psychology is also self-defeating. In order to state the position that there are no such things as beliefs, the Eliminativist must believe what he says. However, if there are no beliefs, then the Eliminativist cannot believe what he says. And if he believes what he says, then there really are beliefs. He can expect to be taken seriously only if his claim cannot, and hence he refutes himself. Of course, it might be objected that any claim to show that Folk Psychology is inadequate cannot be expressed in the terms of Folk Psychology. If the new term for possessing information about the world is to X, then the person can say that he Xs that there are no such things as beliefs. Then his position would not be self-refuting. But this will not help. If Xing is to achieve the function it purports to, it must have so many of the properties of believing that there will be no reason to deny that beliefs do not exist.

There is a school of thought that argues that there can be no psychophysical laws (Davidson, 1980; McGinn, 1978). If there are no such 'bridge laws', there can be no reduction. Davidson argues that psychological terms are applied holistically – we cannot attribute to a person the belief that the Eiffel Tower is in Paris unless we also attribute to him a whole set of other beliefs (about physical objects and geography), whereas if his belief is a physical state, it will be that physical state irrespective of the state of the rest of his brain. This is wrong. A physical state cannot be the realization of a belief unless it too has a causal connection to other states, and this causal connectedness is constitutive of that belief. But this makes it like beliefs, and hence there is no objection to the development of psychophysical laws.

McGinn argues that beliefs and desires are functional terms, and can be realized by different brain states. A brain state will be a pain if it has a certain causal relationship to behaviour – if it leads to the avoidance of the source of pain, and so on. This state might be different in different people (and species), and yet will still be pain if it has this causal connection to behaviour. This means that there can be no psychophysical laws. But this too does not follow. While psychological states may be functional kinds and brain states natural kinds, this does not mean that we cannot get some bridge laws going. Just as we cannot identify a functional kind other than via its causal role in a system, so we do not identify anatomical structures in the brain other than via their anatomical connections. Some structure of the brain is the visual cortex because of its connection to the eye; if it lacked this, it would not be the visual cortex. If it were connected to the olfactory nerve, it would not be the visual cortex (but the olfactory cortex). There is a parallel connectionism that affects our identification of physical systems too, and hence it is possible for psychophysical laws to hold. In either event, even if McGinn and Davidson are correct, all they show is that we cannot reduce Folk Psychology to Neuroscience, and if we cannot reduce it, we cannot eliminate it either.

Neuroscience will not eliminate Folk Psychology. Whatever the physiological explanation for our behaviour, we can identify beliefs with those neuronal systems involved in cognition, and desires with those systems involved in motivation, and our behaviour will still be caused by desires and beliefs. And since we have evidence that we are at least sufficiently rational, Folk Psychology and the Legal Paradigm can survive.

GUILTY BRAINS

Bernhard Goetz, the 'subway vigilante' who shot four teenagers threatening him, was charged with attempted murder. He claimed self-defence, but the 1986 ruling by New York State's Court of Appeals required him to show that his actions were objectively those of a 'reasonable man'. In the trial, the District Attorney argued that because Goetz had fired a second shot into one of the assailants when the immediate threat was over, he was not a reasonable man. The law expected Goetz to calm down immediately he perceived the danger was over. But is this a reasonable expectation?

> I believe the 'reasonable person' argument an illogical and outdated approach to fully understanding events in the Goetz case and other selective instances of violence. On the basis of what I know about the human brain, I'm convinced that no one acts reasonably when feeling threatened by death or severe bodily harm. Deep within every reasonable person's brain is the limbic system [the emotional brain] ... Under conditions of extreme duress the limbic system is capable of overwhelming the cerebral cortex, wherein many of the reasonable person's most reasonable attributes – like interpretation, judgment, and restraint, are formulated.
>
> (Restak, 1991: 52)

Is the 'reasonable man' standard unreasonable?

Restak (1992) argues that medical progress is leading to the use of what he calls the Neurological Defence: A person is excused when his behaviour is due to a brain disease – when he has a guilty brain and not a guilty mind. (This is, of course, none other than the Durham Defence in neurological terms.) We now know that impulsive violence is due to low serotonin levels

(Virkkunen, 1992), and that neurological damage can lower serotonin levels. What if such neurological damage so lowers the serotonin levels that the person commits a violent crime? Should he not be excused because his brain and not his mind is guilty? Fenwick (1993) relates the cases of an adolescent boy of good character who made an unprovoked, vicious and uncharacteristic attack on his neighbour's daughter, and of an 18-year-old of blameless reputation who impulsively attacked a barmaid following a period of depression. Medical evidence revealed neurological damage in both cases. Fenwick suggests we should use Neurology and not Folk Psychology to determine guilt (or innocence):

> A display of uncontrolled and uncharacteristic anger following minimal provocation can be explained in brain words – a decrease in brain serotonin manifesting as a depression of mood and interacting with a disordered hippocampal amygdala system in a damaged brain. Or it can be explained in mind words – he felt sad and depressed, did not understand why he got so angry, and is sorry for all the trouble he caused. At first glance, brain words seems less accessible. But it can be argued that they give not only a more precise but also a more useful description of what happened, because they enable the court to judge blameworthiness . . . It seems clear that, first, in the field of automatism, and second, in the area of diminished responsibility, the concept of a guilty mind belongs to a non-scientific era. There are clearly occasions when an act carried out will depend on a brain malfunction of which the person is not aware, or will depend on a brain malfunction of which he or she is aware, but cannot control (although this may not be understood at the time). As knowledge of brain functioning increases and imaging facilities become more available, it will become easier to detect minor degrees of brain malfunction, and the usefulness of the concept of *mens rea*, the guilty mind, may diminish even further.
>
> (Fenwick, 1993: 572)

Fenwick argues that we do not need *mens rea* or Folk Psychology to determine guilt or innocence because the discovery of a brain malfunction settles the issue.

We usually use Folk Psychology to determine guilt: A person is guilty if he knew what he was doing and was in control. These explanations use concepts like 'know' and 'control' which come from Folk Psychology. Fenwick's examples do not prove that we do not use Folk Psychology to decide a person's guilt. In both cases, the impulsive, uncharacteristic, and uncontrolled nature of the attacks suggests that the defendants were not in control of their actions, and it is only because of this that they deserve to be excused. These are not examples where neurological evidence suggests that the mind is innocent because the brain is guilty. The neurological argument only works by showing that the person lacked control. These are cases where we judge, on the basis of Folk Psychology, that the mind was innocent (because the person was not in control).

There is a fundamental flaw in the idea that the brain might be guilty but the person not. Whenever someone commits an offence, it is always his brain that has caused it. His desires, beliefs, deliberations and choices are, after all, events in his brain. But this does not mean that he is not guilty – that he has not done it. The question is whether the brain caused the behaviour without the person's knowledge or control. But if this is the critical question, then we have sneaked *mens rea* through the back door, and re-introduced a dependence on Folk Psychology rather than Neurology to determine guilt. The critical issue is not whether the brain has caused the behaviour, because the brain has always caused it. The issue is whether the person knew what he was doing and was in control, or whether he has undergone some personality change.

It does not help to argue that a class of criminal behaviour – acts of impulsive violence – is due to low serotonin. Acts of law-abiding behaviour in the face of temptation also have a neurological cause – normal serotonin levels. Why should we excuse the former and not the latter? One idea might be that low brain serotonin levels are due to a disorder while high serotonin levels are not. But this gets the conceptual cart before the horse. We judge that impulsive violence is part of a disease process because it is involuntary – we do not judge that it is involuntary because it is part of a disease process. We do not first judge that low serotonin is part of a disease process and then conclude that the person lacks control and should be excused. We decide that low serotonin is part of a disease process because we have already judged that the person is out of control – that the process is involuntary. Moreover, the whole argument is circular in a more pernicious way. We can only identify low serotonin as causing a loss of control if we have a way of identifying loss of control independently of low serotonin. But if we can do this, then we do not need anything other than Folk Psychology to determine guilt.

Nevertheless, Neuroscience *can* help us to determine responsibility in some borderline cases. Suppose we have used standard incentives to discover which sorts of acts constitute those over which agents lack control (such as the paradigmatic cases discussed above). We find that serotonin levels are low in such individuals. This may help decide borderline cases. Do those who are chronically (rather than uncharacteristically) impulsive lack control? If they cannot restrain themselves, they should be excused. If they are in control, they should be punished. How do we decide? They tell us they try to stop themselves, but are overwhelmed. Since they have much to gain from saying this, it is hard to believe them. If we found low serotonin levels in such individuals, this would constitute powerful evidence that such people were not in control and should be excused. The Neurological Defence can help because the brain, unlike the person, cannot 'lie'. But this does not mean that a Neurological Defence can replace the Insanity Defence – it can only extend and refine it.

Finally, we do not need to invoke the Neurological Defence to show that someone like Goetz is not guilty. This is because the law does set such unreasonable expectations. As Lord Morris said in the case of Lynch: 'If someone is forced at gun-point either to be inactive or to do something positive – must the law not remember that the instinct and perhaps the duty of self-preservation is powerful and natural? I think it must.' Again in Shannon, he ruled:

> A person defending himself cannot weigh to a nicety the exact measure of his necessary defensive action. If a jury thought that in a moment of unexpected anguish a person attacked had only done what he honestly and instinctively thought was necessary, that would be the most potent evidence that only reasonable defensive action had been taken.
>
> (Gordon, 1978: 431)

As Oliver Wendell Holmes put it: 'Detached reflection cannot be demanded in the presence of an uplifted knife.' By allowing people to be human rather than super-rational, the law rejects unreasonable standards.

THE CLASH OF CONCEPTUAL PARADIGMS

It is now time to evaluate the paradigms and decide which to adopt. Please refer to the assumptions of each paradigm listed in the Introduction. We noted there that the Legal Paradigm presupposes Folk Psychology, accepting that we act rationally on the basis of reasons, while the Medical Paradigm assumes we are irrational and act because of physiological causes. The first assumptions are not in conflict. Folk Psychology is correct to claim that we act for reasons, but our actions are also caused by physiological events. If we are to reconcile these two accounts, individual beliefs and desires must be identical to states of the nervous system. The second assumptions can also be harmonized: while there is widespread irrationality in human behaviour, this does not mean that we do not possess minimal practical rationality sufficient to make us responsible.

Both paradigms assume that if an agent is free and rational, he is responsible, but both draw different conclusions from this. The Legal Paradigm accepts we are responsible because we are free and rational, while the strong Medical Paradigm denies that we are free and rational, and therefore that we are responsible. We have argued in Chapter 7 that the fact that actions are caused does not mean that no one is responsible. Responsibility needs determinism. If our actions were random and uncaused by reasons, no one would be responsible. Moreover, there is a Utilitarian argument against the rejection of responsibility. If we encourage the idea that people are not responsible for their behaviour, we diminish the already tenuous control they have on their antisocial impulses. The most effective way to get people to behave the way we want is to attribute responsibility to them. Halleck (1986: 143) writes: 'In most societies a medical approach to crime has been rejected because it is believed to foster a model of responsibility that is incompatible with societal needs for law and order.' Even if we judge that crime is a disease, this does not imply we should adopt a treatment approach to it. The treatment of disorders like drug addictions (Fingarette, 1988) and eating disorders (Woodside, 1995) involve encouraging the patient to take responsibility for his or her behaviour. Encouraging the idea that the person is the helpless victim of some disorder may make the condition worse. As Halleck (1990: 310) puts it:

> The approach should be one in which the emphasis is on maximizing the patient's responsibility for undesirable conduct and one in which such conduct is never tacitly excused. By avoiding reinforcement of undesirable behavioural aspects, this approach would diminish iatro-genicity.

There are good Utilitarian reasons why we should not jettison our notion of responsibility.

The Legal Paradigm argues that ignorance or compulsion are excuses, while the strong Medical Paradigm excuses everyone. Here the Medical Paradigm is wrong, but the Legal Paradigm is incomplete – changes in moral character can also excuse. The weak Medical Paradigm adopts the Neurological Defence, but we have seen that this cannot dispense with Folk Psychology, *mens rea*, and the Legal Paradigm. The Legal Paradigm argues that lay people are best placed to decide guilt and disposition, while the Medical Paradigm argues that psychiatrists should decide the disposition – they know whether a mental illness was involved in the causation, whether the person is dangerous, and hence are best placed to decide on a safe disposition. But we have argued in Chapter 10 that matters of responsibility and insanity are moral issues – they are about whether we ought to punish a person. Thus the decision should be left to lay people. Moreover, to decide matters of responsibility, we need only decide whether the person knew what he was doing, whether he was in control, or whether he underwent a change in moral character. To decide this only requires a grasp of Folk Psychology, and no expertise in neurological matters is needed. Regarding disposition, both paradigms have something important to say. If a person is found guilty, then lay people should decide his disposition. If the person is judged NGRI, psychiatrists should decide how he should be treated.

The Legal Paradigm assumes that punishment serves the Utilitarian functions. There is some evidence that it incapacitates. Greenwood and Abrahamse (1982) used self-reports and other information about the careers of robbers and estimated that lengthening the sentences of 'high-rate robbers' would achieve a 15 per cent reduction in California's robberies. But punishment does not appear to reform. The Cambridge–Somerville Youth Study provides the best attempt to study reform, following up nearly 2,000 boys, half of whom had counsellors, half not. There was no evidence that the counsellors were able to do any reforming (Powers and Witmer, 1951). Punishment does not appear to be a Special Deterrent either. Data from the Bureau of Justice Statistics (in the USA) show that crime rates have not responded to 'get tough' approaches to incarceration. In 1970, there were 200,000 Americans in prison, in 1993 there were 900,000. In spite of this increase, violent crimes per 100,000 have climbed from 450 to 750 and murder rates and property crimes have remained constant (Woodbury *et al.*, 1995). In Britain during the early 1980s, a 'short, sharp shock' regime was introduced for young offenders that included strict discipline, drill, physical exercise and close supervision. Analysis of reconviction data showed that the tougher regimes did not produce any notable reduction in re-offending (Stephenson, 1992).

Punishment also does not seem to be a General Deterrent. The British Royal Commission on Capital Punishment collected evidence from many countries and concluded that there was no clear evidence that the death penalty affected the homicide rate (Kenny, 1978). In 1973 a Birmingham youth was sentenced to 20 years of detention for a particularly brutal mugging. This exceptional sentence received a lot of publicity, and in an attempt to see whether this had a General Deterrent effect, Baxter and Nuttal (1975) compared the rate of muggings before and after the sentence. There was no decrease. But the fact that tough punishments do not affect crime rates does not prove that they do not deter. It only shows that harsh punishment gives no *more* deterrence than a lenient one. Increasing punishment from a week in prison to life *would* affect the murder rate. The death penalty might not add to the deterrent effect of life in prison, but this does not mean that life in prison does not deter relative to a much lesser sentence. 'The only empirical way to study the deterrent effect of punishment would be to compare the effects of two laws in parallel jurisdictions on the same type of subject matter, one of which had a sanction attached and the other did not' (Kenny, 1978: 77).

Moreover, there might be two populations – the majority who are deterrable and the hardened minority who are not. Increasing the deterrence beyond the threshold that deters the majority will have no detectable deterrent effect on the hardened few who are going to commit the offence anyway. This suggests that we should develop two approaches to offenders. For normal individuals who will benefit from punishment, this should be administered. For psychopaths who are not effected by it, we should strive to develop a medical treatment. There are some treatments that have already proved effective against those who are impulsively violent (Sheard *et al.*, 1976), and we should pursue research into other treatments. This raises the issue of whether the treatment should be involuntary. I believe we should offer recidivists a choice – either they accept a lengthy imprisonment or opt for treatment, if it exists. Hobson's choice, but at least a choice. Deterrence has proved bankrupt with such offenders and the time is right for a different approach.

The Medical Paradigm also introduces the idea of the prevention of crime (primary treatment). Is this morally acceptable? Is it fair to identify someone whom we know is likely to become a criminal and subject him to treatment *before* he breaks the law? We can already identify future recidivists at age 11 or 12 with an accuracy of 75 per cent. And we know they will go on to commit 70 per cent of crimes. If we develop a treatment, we will have a choice of allowing them to grow up into offenders, or subjecting them to such treatment programmes. As children cannot give informed consent, would it be ethical to treat them without their consent? We subject children to education, vaccinations, and so on without their consent. We know they would avoid such interventions if they had the choice, but we treat them this way because we know it is in their best interests. Why should we not take someone with an autonomic disorder who is likely to become miserable (because he will be in and out of prison all his life) and subject him to treatment to enable him to live life to the full? Not only does this seem justifiable from his point of view, but also from the point of view of society. We already see ourselves as justified in treating adults like disease carriers against their will if they constitute a health risk to others. So why not treat potential recidivists to prevent the harm they will cause?

By allowing primary treatment the Medical Paradigm permits interference in a person's life before he has broken the law, which conflicts with the Retributivist principle that we are only entitled to inflict punishment on someone after he has committed a crime. Whether this conflicts with Utilitarianism depends on many factors. We do not as yet possess an effective treatment for potential recidivists, but suppose we did. By treating them, we would prevent crime but at some cost to our liberty. We value the freedom to lead the lives we wish, even if this includes being free to break the law, and offering punishment maximizes the amount of liberty we have by giving us this choice. Which paradigm is justified from the Utilitarian point of view will depend on the relative efficacy of treatment, as well as whether we value freedom more than the harms done by crime. If we value the reduction of suffering from crime more than liberty, we will embrace the Medical Paradigm's preventative programme.

In the end, we should accept a Mixed Paradigm:

1 Intentional behaviour is explained by reasons (and brain events).
2 Agents are sufficiently rational to be responsible (although irrational in many ways).
3 If an agent is capable of rationality and choice, he is responsible.
4 Agents who break the law but suffer from exculpatory ignorance, compulsion, or change in moral character should be excused.
5 Lay people are best placed to decide who is responsible, but experts are helpful in deciding disposition.
6 Punishment or treatment should be settled in part by matters of justice and also by what is effective in reducing crime.
7 Punishment has a general deterrent and incapacitating effect.

We are largely rational creatures who are responsible for our actions. If we break the law, we should be punished provided we do not have the excuses of ignorance, compulsion, and a change in moral character, and provided no greater harm is done by the punishment. Whether we should be excused is a moral matter, and one that must be settled by lay people with a grasp of Folk Psychology. With some actual and potential offenders, treatment may hold out more hope for crime prevention, but at some cost to liberty. The exact balance of punishment and treatment that is justified can only be settled by carefully weighing the consequences of any programme and making a choice between the values of welfare and liberty.

13

THE INSANITY DEFENCE IN PRACTICE

THE LAY CONCEPT OF INSANITY

The practice of the law often does not conform to its principles. When M'Naghten was tried, insanity was defined by the Wild Beast test – to be NGRI, a person's understanding had to be reduced to that of a 14-year-old. Although M'Naghten's under-standing exceeded this standard, the jury found him NGRI because they accepted Stephen's claim that he was so much in the grip of his delusions that he could not stop himself acting on them. The jury were instructed to follow a cognitive test of insanity but instead used a volitional one. Similarly, the jury found Hadfield NGRI using a more liberal cognitive test than the current Wild Beast test.

Juries seem to operate with their own concept of insanity. In 1881 William Davis, a 38-year-old labourer, attempted to murder his sister-in-law because 'the man in the moon told me to do it. I will have to commit murder, as I must be hanged'. Medical witnesses testified that he suffered from delirium tremens and that although he knew what he was doing, he was unable to control himself. Stephen summed up: 'Both the doctors agree that the prisoner was unable to control his conduct, and that nothing short of actual physical restraint would have deterred him' (Walker, 1968: 107). Davis knew what he was doing, but the jury was influenced by Stephen's claim that what was important was loss of control. When they judged he was NGRI, they were using the Irresistible Impulse test of insanity and not the M'Naghten Rules. Similarly, in the trial of Fryer, a soldier who had strangled his fiance, Mr Justice Bray explained the M'Naghten Rules to the Gloucester jury but then continued: 'If it

266

is shown that he is in such a state of mental disease or infirmity as to deprive him of the capacity to control his actions, I think you ought to find him what the law calls him – "insane" ' (Walker, 1968: 107). The jury took his advice. They ignored the M'Naghten Rules but instead used the Irresistible Impulse test.

In 1949 the Gowers Commission recognized that both judges and juries did not stick to the letter of the law – the M'Naghten Rules were widely stretched. The juries did not ask whether the defendant knew what he was doing or whether it was wrong, but whether he was psychotic, and if so, he was NGRI. The Commission reported that many psychiatrists felt that the Rules were so excessively restrictive that they made their own minds up whether the accused should escape the death sentence and testified accordingly, often with the connivance of the judge. Lord Cooper, Lord Justice General for Scotland, told the commission that whatever judges said to juries, the latter simply retired and asked themselves: 'Is this man mad [psychotic] or is he not?'

It is time to consider the concept of insanity that jurors (and judges) actually employ, irrespective of the current legal definitions of insanity. We will look at three different strands of evidence. First, we will examine the rates of acquittal in one place at different times. If the rates remain constant in spite of differences of legal definitions of insanity, this supports the idea that the man on the street has his own definition of insanity that stays constant. Second, we will look at whether mock juries are influenced by different definitions of insanity. If they are not, again this suggests they operate with their own concept. Third, we will look at the differences between those defendants who have been acquitted and those convicted. This too will tell us about the lay concept.

CHANGES IN LEGAL DEFINITIONS

The first important change in the legal definition of insanity in English law came when the M'Naghten Rules replaced the Wild Beast test. If juries had been influenced by legal definitions, more defendants would have been excused. But far from a flood of criminals being found NGRI, in the 10-year period following the M'Naghten Rules, 7.5 per cent of trials for murder resulted in acquittal on the grounds of insanity – the same percentage in the 10 years preceding the act (Walker, 1968). This strongly suggests that the jury operates with its own concept of insanity, independently of legal definitions.

The next change in English law came with the introduction of the Diminished Responsibility test in 1957. While this did not replace the M'Naghten Rules, it added a new test which was far more liberal than the cognitive test enshrined in the M'Naghten Rules. No longer did a defendant have to be suffering from a disease of the mind (he need only suffer from a mental abnormality), but he need not be ignorant of what he was doing or that it was wrong. The jury had only to judge that his responsibility for his behaviour was substantially impaired, and this meant that he could be found not guilty of murder if he satisfied the Irresistible Impulse test. The more liberal Diminished Responsibility test should have led to an increase in offenders found not guilty of murder on the basis of mental illness. But it did not. Gibson and Klein (1961) compared the percentages of murderers committed to trial who successfully used the defences of 'insanity on arraignment', 'NGRI', or 'Diminished Responsibility' in the years before and after the Homicide Act. The combined percentages totalled much the same. If the Diminished Responsibility test was influencing the judges and juries, more cases should have been excused after the introduction of the Homicide Act. Instead, judges and juries continued to operate with the same concept of criminal responsibility they had used before. Walker (1968) extended this study by comparing the percentages from 1946 to 1963. He found that although offenders found NGRI and those found unfit to stand trial (insane on arraignment) decreased after 1957, this was exactly compensated for by the cases excused on the basis of Diminished Responsibility. 'These trends suggest that section 2 of the Homicide Act has done no more than take over the sort of case which previously would have been accepted by courts as within the M'Naghten Rules' (Walker, 1968: 157).

Our common-sense expectations are wrong because they are based on the mistaken assumption that the courts are influenced by legal definitions of criminal responsibility. If they were, the more liberal rules embodied in the Homicide Act would have excused more cases than the M'Naghten Rules. Killers like Byrne would not have been found not guilty before 1957. Byrne brutally sexually assaulted and killed a young woman, and was found not guilty of murder because he was supposedly suffering from an irresistible impulse. But he was M'Naghten sane – he knew what he was doing and that it was wrong. More people (those with irresistible impulses) would have been excused by the Diminished Responsibility test. But this would only have happened if the Irresistible Impulse test had not been used prior to the Homicide Act. Yet we know from the above cases that it was – in fact, it was on this basis that M'Naghten himself was excused.

Turning to America, the John Hinckley verdict in 1982 led to a public outcry prompting many states to change their definition of insanity. In the next three years thirty-four states enacted reforms. Changes in NGRI verdicts were studied following these reforms. In 1982, California revised the test of insanity from the ALI test to a modified M'Naghten test – instead of the disjunctive 'or' a conjunctive 'and' was used. A person was now NGRI only if he was unaware of what he was doing *and* unable to control himself. This should have made the insanity defence more restrictive. McGreevy and her colleagues (1991) studied all individuals entering the insanity plea during a six-year period – three years before and three years after the reform. The acquittal rate was unaffected by the change in legal definition.

Between 1973 and 1979 Wyoming moved from a M'Naghten test to an ALI standard. Pasework *et al.* (1984) found no differences in the rate of NGRI verdicts. In 1979, Montana abolished the insanity defence and replaced it with a *mens rea* defence – someone was excused only if mental illness undermined *mens rea*. The acquittal rate three years before and three years after the reform was studied. Although NGRI verdicts markedly declined, dismissals based on incompetence to stand trial increased substantially. Packer (1985) studied Michigan's adoption of the ALI standard in place of a combined M'Naghten and Irresistible Impulse test, and found no difference in the rate of insanity acquittals. Steadman and his colleagues (1989: 360) report:

> [P]ersons who would have been found not guilty by reason of insanity under the old law have had their charges dismissed and been committed indefinitely to the same facility to which those acquitted by reason of insanity had been retained. This suggests that 'abolition' of the insanity defence may occur only in those jurisdictions where state regulations and facilities allow the maintenance of old ways under new states.

The new legislation excused the same number of offenders on the basis of mental illness albeit under a different name. 'If a person's mental status was seen as sufficient to warrant reduced criminal responsibility, they were found IST [incompetent to stand trial] and committed to the same hospital and the same wards where they would have been confined if they had been found NGRI' (Steadman *et al.*, 1989: 361).

All these studies show that juries ignore the legal definitions of insanity, operating with their own concept. This explains the constancy of acquittal rates in spite of changes in the legal definition of insanity.

JURY STUDIES

It is a feature of Anglo-American law that while the judge instructs the jury about matters legal, and expert psychiatric witnesses tell the juries whether the defendant is mentally ill, it is up to the jury to decide what this means. The following is a representative instruction by the court to the jury on how they should treat expert testimony:

> The important point of all this discussion of expert witnesses and opinion testimony is that you are not bound as jurors to accept the testimony of expert witnesses. You should certainly consider carefully the qualifications of the witnesses, their experiences, their observations of the defendant, their opportunity to observe, and all of the factors that they told you about in their lengthy testimony today. Then you are to give to their testimony as experts such weight as in your judgement it is fairly entitled to receive with full recognition of the fact that while you shouldn't arbitrarily disregard the testimony of any witness, yet, if you are satisfied that you don't accept the testimony of the expert witnesses you are not bound to do so.
>
> (James, 1967: 81)

In determining the application of the concept of insanity, the jury is king.

The vast majority of insanity pleas do not come to trial – only 15 per cent of serious offences reach that stage (Stephenson, 1992). Most insanity acquittals will be made by judges reviewing the case for the prosecution. Does this mean it is the judge rather than the jury that sets the boundaries of the concept? No. The judge makes the decision when the case is clear-cut, and it is clear-cut when the judge knows that most juries deciding such a case would grant the insanity plea. It is because of what any *jury* would say that the judge makes his decision, and therefore juries still implicitly decide such cases. But far more important for drawing the boundaries and establishing the meaning of a concept is looking at how the concept is applied to borderline cases, and it is borderline cases that come to trial. Either way it is the jury that determines the concept of insanity in practice.

James (1967) made her landmark study on juries using two trials based on actual cases. A transcript of these trials was edited to contain the lawyer's opening and closing statements, the judge's instructions to the jury, and witnesses' testimony. It was recorded and played before juries selected from local jury pools in a courtroom to make the procedure seem real. James varied the instructions she gave to the juries. Some were given the M'Naghten definition of insanity, some the Durham Rules, and others were simply told that they should find the defendant not guilty if he was insane. After the trial but before the juries deliberated, each juror was asked to fill out a brief questionnaire in which he was asked to state how he would decide the case. Then the jury was sent away to deliberate, having been told that their deliberations would be recorded. Finally, the jury was taken in front of the judge to report its verdict.

Of the 1,176 jurors involved in the study, 360 were exposed to the housebreaking trial and 816 to the incest case. The defendant in the housebreaking trial was described by two psychiatrists as a 'psychopathic personality with psychosis'. He had a long history of mental disturbance, previous hospitalizations and attempted suicides. He was unable to hold down a job and his testimony during the trial was incoherent. When psychiatrists were asked whether he was insane, in the M'Naghten version they testified they were unable to answer. In the Durham version they testified that the defendant had a mental disorder which 'did affect his capacity to control his conduct'. The defendant in the incest case was described by two psychiatrists as suffering from 'paraphiliac neurosis', but had never been psychotic. He had no history of hospitalizations or antisocial behaviour. He was efficient at work. When psychiatrists were asked whether he was insane, in the M'Naghten version both doctors answered that in their opinion the defendant could distinguish right from wrong. Under Durham, they answered that the defendant's behaviour towards his daughters was a manifestation of his mental disease.

In the housebreaking trial, 76 per cent of the uninstructed jurors judged the defendant NGRI, 65 per cent of those instructed under Durham judged him NGRI, and 59 per cent of those instructed under M'Naghten did. The difference between the juries acting under the Durham and M'Naghten Rules was not significant. The small difference might have been due to the fact that, in the M'Naghten version, psychiatrists were unable to say whether he was insane, while in the Durham version they concluded that he was. Since 74 per cent of jurors said the psychiatric testimony was helpful, we might hypothesize that this was responsible for the difference. In the incest trial, 34 per cent of the uninstructed jurors judged the defendant was NGRI, 36 per cent of those under Durham did so, while 24 per cent under M'Naghten did. The difference between those deciding under the Durham and M'Naghten Rules was significant, showing that the former is a more liberal definition of insanity, but the difference is relatively small. Again, this difference may be accounted for by the influence of psychiatric opinion – only in Durham did the psychiatrists conclude that the defendant was insane.

James analysed the discussions of the juries. Even when instructed under Durham, jurors adopted a cognitive definition of insanity:

> [I]f you break the law, because you have this quirk and still have the mental capacity to know what you are doing and go ahead and do it deliberately, then you are not insane . . . Now in his (the defendant's) mind he knew that it was wrong according to our society's teachings, and that doesn't make him insane . . . Everyone admits he's mentally abnormal; but did he know he was committing an act against society? That's the whole point.
>
> (James, 1967: 162)

Jurors instructed to ignore cognitive criteria took them into account! This explains why there is so little difference between these two groups.

This view is confirmed by the taped deliberations. Seven out of the fourteen Durham juries considered the issue of whether the defendant was able to distinguish right from wrong, as did seven out of the thirteen uninstructed juries. For most jurors, the defendant's admission that he knew what he was doing was wrong proved that he was not insane.

> Two points emerge from the discussion above. The first is that all jurors, those instructed under M'Naghten as well as those instructed under Durham, believed that cognition was the crucial factor in determining responsibility. The second point is that the Durham jurors appeared to have no more difficulty than the M'Naghten jurors in construing the instructions to suit their beliefs concerning the centrality of cognition.
>
> (James, 1959: 68)

Jurors ignore the judge's instructions and fall back on their own cognitive concept of insanity. James also examined the impact of the jurors' knowledge of the disposition after conviction on their judgement. The argument was that if jurors think an NGRI verdict will lead to freedom, they will not reach this verdict. What she found was that the presence of commitment information had no effect. When she tested the jurors' expectations of the court's disposition in an NGRI verdict, she found that jurors who did not receive the instruction assumed correctly that the defendant would be committed. This explained why the information made no difference – the jurors already knew what would happen.

A further study asked 132 college students to be mock jurors and pass verdicts on five written hypothetical cases using six different insanity tests (Finkel *et al.*, 1985). The insanity tests used were the Wild Beast test, the M'Naghten Rules, the M'Naghten Rules plus the Irresistible Impulse test, the Durham Rule, the ALI standard, and Fingarette and Hasse's (1979) Disability of Mind test. There were no significant differences among the tests in regard to the mock juror's verdicts on the five cases. There were no differences between the M'Naghten Rules (the cognitive test only) and the M'Naghten plus the Irresistible Impulse test (the cognitive plus the volitional test). This shows once again that the juries have their own concept of insanity and apply it irrespective of the legal definition.

Another study gave mock jurors four insanity tests: the Insanity Defence Reform Act (IDRA) of 1984 (a version of the M'Naghten Rules), the ALI test, the Wild Beast test, and no instructions, and asked them to provide their verdicts in written hypothetical cases (Finkel, 1989). After their verdicts, jurors were encouraged to give their reasons for their decisions, choosing from a number of categories: incapacity, impaired awareness and perceptions, distorted thinking, being unable to control her actions, non-culpable actions, no evil motive, and others at fault. The instructions given to the jurors did not produce any significant differences in the verdicts – jurors did not use the definition of insanity they were instructed to use. For example, mock jurors using the IDRA test did not use the cognitive test more, or the volitional test less, than the ALI jurors.

There have been few studies that have studied the layman's concept of insanity outside the paradigm of mock trials. One study made random telephonic contact with 434 subjects from New Castle County following the Hinckley verdict (Hans and Slater, 1984). Respondents were asked: 'In a few words, what do you think is the legal definition of insanity?' The answers were taken down verbatim and grouped into fourteen different categories. Forty-three per cent gave a broadly cognitive definition of insanity, defining insanity as not knowing what one is doing, or as not being able to tell right from wrong. Sixteen per cent said insanity consisted in not having control over one's actions. All in all, around 59 per cent used elements of the ALI definition of insanity. Only 5 per cent used the Durham definition. The researchers comment:

> The most frequent way people defined the legal test was *Don't know what you're doing*. This may represent on an intuitive level people's views of what is, or in any event should be, the condition under which an individual may be excused from responsibility ... Even if defendants are legally insane under the relevant test, unless they 'don't know what they're doing' some members of the public may hold them criminally responsible.
>
> (Hans and Slater, 1984: 111)

Jurors have their own concept of insanity and it is a cognitive test: A person is judged NGRI if he does not know what he is doing.

WHO ARE EXCUSED?

What is it about a defendant that induces the jury to pass a verdict of NGRI? By studying the differences between those excused on this basis and those not, we will get an idea of the concept of insanity employed by juries. Rice and Harris (1990) looked at those cases in Canada found NGRI and compared them to those who had not been found NGRI. Canada adopts a version of the M'Naghten Rules: 'No person shall be convicted of an offence, while he has disease of the mind to an extent that renders him incapable of appreciating the nature and quality of an act or omission or of knowing that an act or omission is wrong.' They found that insanity acquittees had been charged with more serious offences, had less extensive criminal histories, and were more likely to be psychotic (schizophrenic) and less likely to be personality disordered. When the insanity acquittees were matched for the same offences with those whose insanity plea had failed, being psychotic predicted 81 per cent of the acquittals. The authors conclude: 'The present results show that most decisions regarding insanity can be modelled by saying that insanity acquittees are those persons accused of murder or attempted murder who show clear evidence of psychosis (almost always schizophrenia) during a post-offence psychiatric examination' (Rice and Harris, 1990: 222). Being psychotic appears to be sufficient for the application of the lay concept of insanity.

In New York, Steadman and his colleagues (1983) did a similar study. The insanity defence in New York is a cognitive test: 'A person is not criminally responsible for conduct if at the time of such conduct, as a result of mental disease or defect, he lacks substantial capacity to know or appreciate either: (a) the nature and consequences of such conduct; or (b) that such conduct was wrong.' The major factor related to acquittal was the diagnosis of psychosis. Of the defendants found insane, 82 per cent were psychotic compared to 28 per cent of those found guilty. Jeffrey and his colleagues (1988) conducted a study in Colorado where a variant of the M'Naghten Rules are used. They found insanity acquittees were more likely to have a diagnosis of schizophrenia and less likely to have a history of drug abuse or personality disorder. They also found a high concordance (88 per cent) between the psychiatric evaluation and the eventual court decision, suggesting that the courts take the psychiatric testimony seriously. Janofsky and others (1989) examined all defendants pleading NGRI over a 12-month period in Baltimore City. These comprised 1.2 per cent of all defendants, and only 10 per cent of these were successful. The authors found marked agreement between the prosecution and defence, and again the psychiatric evaluation of insanity predicted the court's decision. Rogers *et al.* (1984) examined 316 Oregon cases where the defendant successfully pleaded NGRI. Prosecutors agreed to the insanity verdict in more than 80 per cent of cases. In most cases all examining experts diagnosed the defendant as psychotic. The smaller number of defendants who were diagnosed as personality disordered accounted for a disproportionately large percentage of the contested trials. Wettstein and Mulvey (1988) studied the characteristics of insanity acquittees in Illinois between 1982 and 1984. Acquittees had committed no previous offences, had previous psychiatric hospitalizations, and suffered from a psychotic illness (mostly schizophrenia).

These studies explode a number of myths. First, it is a myth that large numbers of ordinary criminals try to 'beat the rap' by pleading insanity, duping or bribing gullable or corrupt psychiatrists to support their claims, and persuading jurors bewildered by psychiatric jargon that they are mad and not bad. The insanity plea does not represent a threat to justice and deterrence – it is successful in under 1 per cent of felony cases (Pasewark, 1984). This gives the lie to the public outcry that the insanity verdict will result in a flood of criminals escaping punishment. Second, it is a myth that trials pit lawyers against psychiatrists. The eventual court decision usually coincides with the results of psychiatric evaluation. We must abandon the myth that successful insanity defences are characterized by defence psychiatrists convincing juries over the prosecutor's objections to acquit defendants. Studies show that most cases do not come to trial because of agreement among the prosecutor and the psychiatrists. Third, it is a myth that psychiatrists frequently disagree among themselves. While the adversarial system enables the defendant to search for a psychiatrist to support his case, there is still widespread agreement over diagnosis. For example, in the Yorkshire Ripper trial, all psychiatrists agreed he suffered from schizophrenia. For most diagnostic categories, there is 90 per cent inter-rater agreement (Helzer *et al.*, 1977). When there is disagreement amongst psychiatrists, it is over the 'ultimate issue' of insanity. But insanity is not a diagnosis – it is a moral judgement, and psychiatrists are *not* experts on this matter. Therefore, the fact they disagree does not undermine their expert status. All it shows is that they have strayed from their area of expertise. Moreover, as Quen writes:

> As for the 'battle of experts', I confess that I've never been able to understand why, when psychiatrists disagree, it is proof positive that they don't know what they're talking about and it demeans the profession; while, when our Supreme Court decides the law of the land by a disagreement of 5–4, they are scholars dealing with profound, difficult, and complicated issues and one must respect their differences in judgement.
>
> (Quen, 1990: 247)

In the case of Morgan, the judges voted 3:2 that someone who has sex with a woman in the honest belief that she is consenting is not guilty of rape. Hardly much agreement here.

The rule that best captures the practice of the law is this: Someone is NGRI if he was psychotic and this was causally responsible for his offence. This is the Butler Committee's recommendation:

> [W]e propose that the special verdict should be returned if at the time of the act or omission charged the defendant was suffering from severe mental illness or severe subnormality . . . A mental illness is severe when it has one or more of the following characteristics: (a) Lasting impairment of intellectual functions . . . (b) Lasting alternatives of mood of such degree as to give rise to delusional appraisal of the patient's situation . . . (c) Delusional beliefs . . . (d) Abnormal perceptions associated with delusional misinterpretations . . . (e) Thinking so disordered as to prevent reasonable appraisal of the patient's situation.
>
> (Home Office, 1975: 227–9)

This would accurately reflect the practice of the law. It also fits in with the lay person's concept of insanity which, as we have seen, is cognitive in nature.

EVIL OR ILL?

While the jury is inclined to excuse a person (find him NGRI) when he is psychotic, they are also heavily influenced by moral considerations. This is to be expected since the insanity verdict is a moral one – it is a matter of judging that the person deserves not to be punished. This is a question of judging that the person is basically of good character, and so we should expect that such considerations influence insanity verdicts. I hope to show that while jurors might ask themselves whether the person is mad or not, the fundamental question they ask is whether the person is good. They really ask themselves whether a person is evil or ill.

Williams (1983) suggests that it is sympathy for the defendant that inclines jurors to make a Diminished Responsibility verdict. If the jury recognizes the defendant as a good person who has only done something bad *in extremis*, they are likely to acquit him. The verdict is a moral one:

> The defence has been successfully raised on thin grounds in cases evoking sympathy although there were clearly no reasons for a hospital order ... A man who had been tormented for years by his neighbours (the worst neighbours you can possibly imagine) went berserk and shot dead the family of three; the psychiatrists, bless them, stated that he acted in a state of hysterical dissociation, and the jury returned a verdict of diminished responsibility ... A 'slave son' of 21 shot and killed his father and mother. He had been ill-treated by them all his life: horsewhipped, overworked without wages, and made to sleep in a dog-kennel. The jury returned a verdict of manslaughter ... In short, the defence of diminished is interpreted in accordance with the morality of the case rather than as an application of psychiatric concepts.
>
> (Williams, 1983: 693)

The jury first decides that the defendant is basically good, and then concludes that he suffers from Diminished Responsibility. Chiswick (1985: 977) agrees that 'the defence of diminished responsibility does not have its basis in any psychiatric theory. It was not introduced in response to psychiatric innovations but in response to social and political pressures to see some convicted murderers escape the death penalty.' For similar reasons, mercy killers have often been found not guilty of murder. Mercy killings more than any other serious crime are not committed by evil characters, but people motivated to enhance the well-being and end the suffering of others. Our sense of justice requires that we excuse them rather than punish them. And Wootton (1981: 224) argues:

> It was surely compassion rather than evidence of mental abnormality which accounted for the success of a defence of diminished responsibility in the case of the major who found himself the father of a Mongol baby and, after reading up the subject of Mongolism in his public library, decided that the best course for everybody concerned would be to smother the child.

When a jury decides a person is basically good, they are inclined to excuse.

The idea that character is central to a juror's verdict has some empirical support. Jurors appear to elaborate a narrative in arriving at their decision, and if this casts the defendant in a role as a good person, the verdict will be not guilty. In one study, twenty-six subjects watched a three-hour video-taped trial of a man called Johnson (Hastie *et al.*, 1983). The stories narrated afterwards had little in common apart from the facts that Johnson and Caldwell had been in a bar, Caldwell had hit Johnson, and Johnson had subsequently stabbed Caldwell. When Johnson was construed as a good person justifiably defending himself, he was found not guilty, and when he was construed as a bad person over-reacting to humiliation, he was found guilty. The perceived character of the defendant influences the verdict. Further studies support the thesis that defendant characteristics influence judgements of guilt. Dane and Wrightsman (1982) suggest that jurors operate with unwritten stereotypes. We expect villains to be unattractive, of low socio-economic status, of dubious moral character, from a powerless minority group, and to have attitudes that deviate from the norm. Thus, when attractive, high status, majority-group members of previously good moral character appear in the dock, the temptation for jurors is to elaborate a story illustrating their innocence.

This suggests that the verdict is influenced by jurors' perceptions of the moral character of the defendant. In order to test the hypothesis that what is important to the jury in insanity cases is the question of whether the person is evil or ill, I constructed a questionnaire providing four written trials which included the principal arguments from psychiatric experts. Psychiatrists for the defence and prosecution agreed on the diagnosis but not on the 'ultimate issue' of insanity. Subjects were asked whether they considered the person NGRI or guilty, but no definition of insanity was provided. Unbeknown to the subjects, pairs of cases were presented. In both, the nature and degree of mental disorder and the offence were equivalent – the only difference lay in the character of the defendant. One pair consisted of a schizophrenic suffering from the delusion that he was being attacked by the Devil, defending himself by killing his 'assailant'; and a Nazi with schizophrenia suffering from the delusion that the person next door was a Jew, proceeding with his plan to exterminate all Jews by killing him. Subjects found the first person NGRI, but with few exceptions judged the Nazi guilty. The other pair consisted of a woman of good character tormented by her abusive husband for years, being slapped, occasionally raped, and constantly humiliated until she had become depressed and lost control, assaulting him with a knife; and a mean and jealous woman who had abused her timid husband for years, belittling him in front of others, and who had become depressed after her best friend had married the man she secretly admired, making her lose her control with her husband and assault him. Significantly more subjects judged the first case NGRI.

This demonstrates that the good character of the defendant is critical in determining an NGRI verdict. Even when both members of the pair were psychotic, the character of the defendant was critical. If a juror judges someone to be evil, then he is not inclined to arrive at a verdict of NGRI even if the defendant is psychotic. Jurors were not adopting the simple rule: If the man is mad, he is NGRI. Instead, they adopted the As-if Rule, support for the idea that it is *good characters* they are trying to excuse. The As-if Rule helps differentiate those acts which would have been justified given the delusion is true from those that would not – that is, it helps us identify those who are not evil characters. Jurors see themselves as having to answer the question: 'Is this person evil or ill?' There is an inclination for them to assume that these categories are mutually exclusive and exhaustive, so that if a person is ill, he cannot also be evil, and if he is evil, he cannot also be ill. Jurors judge that if anyone is ill, a psychotic person is, and this inclines them to judge that he is not evil – that he is NGRI. This explains why psychotic offenders are mostly found NGRI. But when a delusion does not satisfy the As-if Rule, showing that the person is evil, this overrides their judgement that he is ill. This shows that jurors do operate with the rule: If someone is mad, he is not bad. If a juror has evidence that a defendant is good (as in mercy killings), he will be judged ill – that is, NGRI, even if there is no evidence of mental disorder. Again, what seems of overriding importance is the moral character of the defendant. But the assumption that 'evil' and 'ill' are mutually exclusive and exhaustive categories sometimes leads to error, as we shall see in the following cases.

THREE TRIALS

In the Bobbitt and Dahmer cases, we see how a person's character is critical in influencing the jury's decision. Both knew what they were doing, and were in control of their actions, but the verdicts were different because of the difference in character. In the Hinckley trial, the jury had some evidence he was psychotic, and because of their dichotomous thinking, erroneously concluded he was NRGI. In their different ways, these trials illustrate the moral nature of the NGRI verdict.

John Hinckley

Hinckley began isolating himself from adolescence – he did not date and had difficulty establishing relationships. After enrolling at Texas Tech in 1973, he spent two years reading, listening to music, playing guitar and watching television, but established no meaningful relationships. In the spring of 1976 he dropped out of school, going to Hollywood where he spent a futile six months pursuing a career as a songwriter. While there, he became intensely interested in the film 'Taxi Driver' which he saw about fifteen times! In this film Robert DeNiro plays the character Travis Bickle who becomes interested in Betsy, a woman working for a presidential candidate. Thwarted in his advances, he 'rescues' Iris, a young prostitute played by Jodie Foster, and becomes a hero when he kills her pimp. Hinckley identified with Travis, picking up many of his mannerisms (for example, he began wearing army fatigues and keeping a diary), and became obsessed with Foster. After time at home, he enrolled again in Texas Tech. However, he attended classes sporadically. He experienced sleeplessness, headaches, and weakness, and returned home. He persuaded his parents to let him enrol in a writing course in Yale, but instead pursued Foster, leaving her poems, letters, and trying to contact her by phone. Thwarted, he purchased some guns and decided to stalk President Carter. He followed Carter to Memphis, but could not bring himself to assassinate him. Having failed at everything, he went home and made a suicide attempt. At this time, his thoughts alternated between suicidal ideas and a grandiose identification with Travis Bickle. He criss-crossed the country trying to make contact with Foster, ending up in Washington. After writing a letter to her describing his assassination plan, he went to the Hilton where he shot President Reagan – a deed which he hoped would make him famous and unite him with the woman he loved.

At his trial, the question facing the jury was whether he knew what he was doing and that it was wrong, or whether he was unable to conform his behaviour to the law (the ALI standard). Dr Carpenter for the defence testified that Hinckley was deluded about his chances with Foster and about what would win her affections. The prosecution psychiatrist, Dr Dietz, showed that Hinckley recognized that Foster was unattainable and was not deluded about his expectations. Hinckley admitted he had not introduced himself in person because of 'insecurity. I mean, she was a pretty famous movie star and there I was, Mr Insignificant himself'. He also quoted from a poem of Hinckley's to her: 'Even a phone conversation seems to be asking too much, but I really can't blame you for ignoring a little twirp like me' (Low et al., 1986: 42). This strongly suggests that he appreciated the reality of his chances.

Psychiatrists for the defence and prosecution acknowledged that Hinckley knew what he was doing and that it was illegal. Dietz argued:

> He concealed successfully all of his stalking . . . including hiding his weapons, hiding his ammunition. This conceal-ment indicates that he appreciated the wrongfulness of his plans . . . In that letter to Jodie Foster, he indicated that he was going to attempt to get Reagan, and he indicates his

knowledge that he could be killed by the Secret Service in the attempt. That is an indication that he understood and appreciated the wrongfulness of his plans because the Secret Service might well shoot someone who attempted to kill the President.

(Low *et al.*, 1986: 63)

The reasoning here is based on Folk Psychology and not on technical psychiatric theory. You do not have to be a psychiatrist to figure out that a person who conceals a weapon, or who is aware that the police might shoot back, knows he is breaking the law. We only need Folk Psychology to explain his behaviour, and this tells us that he knew what he was doing was wrong.

Regarding the volitional prong, Dietz testified that Hinckley was not in the grip of an overwhelming impulse:

A man driven by passion, by uncontrollable forces, is not often inclined to take the time to write a letter to explain what this is about. He did. And he claims he spent 20 to 35 minutes writing that letter. He concealed the weapon ... That ability to conceal his weapon is further evidence of his conforming his conduct, that is, he recognized that waving a gun would be behaviour likely to attract attention, and did not wave the gun. He concealed it. His ability to wait, when he did not have a clear shot of the President on the President's way into the Hilton, is further evidence of his ability to conform his behaviour.

(Low *et al.*, 1986: 81)

These arguments do not depend on complex psychiatric theory. As Morse (1979: 294) comments, 'most of the evidence necessary to make the broad, social common sense judgement about responsibility can be easily based on lay testimony'. Folk Psychology tells us that someone who loses control does not plan carefully what he is going to do and take precautions to ensure that he is not interrupted. Since Hinckley did, he was in control.

There was a conflict over Hinckley's diagnosis. Carpenter argued that Hinckley had schizophrenia, while the prosecution experts denied he had any psychotic illness. Deciding when a belief is a delusion is often difficult:

He identified with and dressed like the protagonist, Travis

Bickle, he memorized the music, perhaps he lived out the plot. Are these behaviours evidence of psychotic identification problems (as the defence argued) or do they amount to something much less (as the prosecution psychiatrists said)? Was his obsession with Jodie Foster a delusion, or was it merely unrealistic and inappropriate? When does a fantasy become a fixed idea? When does a fixed idea become a delusion?

(Stone, 1984: 89)

In the end, the jury found Hinckley NGRI, agreeing with the defence summation: 'I submit these are the acts of a totally irrational individual, driven and motivated by his own world which he created for himself, locked in his own mind, without any opportunity to have any test of those ideas from the real world because of his isolation' (Low *et al.*, 1986: 103). This decision was strange: Hinckley knew what he was doing, knew that it was wrong, and was in control of his actions. The evidence of Hinckley's psychosis – his delusional thinking – was far from uncontroversial. But the jury felt otherwise. Stone argues this was the right decision:

There was certainly very good reason for the jurors to believe that Hinckley could have been psychotic, that he could have had a thought disorder, and that he could have lacked the substantial capacity to appreciate wrongfulness and to conform his behaviour. The psychiatric testimony leaves one in doubt on these matters, but the burden was on the prosecution to remove that doubt. Under existing law the Hinckley verdict was a just result, and psychiatry has no reason to go on apologizing for that result.

(Stone, 1984: 94)

The burden was on the prosecution to prove that Hinckley was sane beyond a reasonable doubt, and this created the difficulty. As President Reagan put it afterwards: 'If you start thinking about even a lot of your friends, you have to say, "Gee, if I had to prove they were sane, I would have a hard job!".' When the jurymen were interviewed, they cited this as the single most decisive factor in the outcome in this case. That this was important is supported by the fact that when states changed the burden of proof, there was a dramatic change in the acquittal rate. In Georgia and New York, shifting the burden of proof to the defendant led to a decrease in the overall number of NGRI verdicts (Appelbaum, 1994).

Why did the jury not use the As-if Rule? Even if the assassination had won fair lady, this does not justify it. As Hinckley himself said: 'I was found not guilty by reason of insanity because I shot the President and three other people in order to impress a girl.' Killing to impress a girl is the act of an evil person, and so he does not have an excuse. Why did the jury not see this? Here the dichotomous thinking of evil versus ill led the jury into error. They assumed the categories were mutually exclusive, and because they had evidence that Hinckley had a major psychiatric illness, they concluded he was not evil, that he was NGRI. As a juror testified before a Senate Subcommittee: 'If we all had had another choice, it would have been different now. It would not have been this way. Everyone knew beyond a shadow of doubt that he was guilty for what he did. But we had that mental problem to deal with. We just could not shut that out' (Finkel, 1988: 172). This illustrates how jurors think being ill precludes being evil.

Many saw the volitional prong as the reason Hinckley was found NGRI, and concluded the cognitive test is more scientific. Bonnie (1983: 195), a University of Virginia law professor, argued that the volitional prong was problematic because 'there is no scientific basis for measuring a person's capacity for self-control or for calibrating the impairment of that capacity'. He persuaded both the APA and ALA to remove the volitional prong from the Federal insanity defence. In a much-quoted phrase, the IDWG (1983: 685) contended that 'the line between an irresistible impulse and an impulse not resisted is probably no sharper than that between twilight and dusk'. However, they clearly did not study the trial carefully. As Stone (1984) has argued, the difficulty of deciding whether a person was suffering from exculpatory delusions is just as difficult as the question whether he was unable to resist his impulses. In contrast to this 'emotional' response, the American Psychological Association argued in favour of testing insanity standards empirically, and questioned the assumption that cognitive tests are empirical while volitional tests are not. Rogers (1987) supported this position by examining the reliability of insanity evaluations made by two experienced forensic psychiatrists, finding no evidence that judgements on the volitional prong were less reliable than judgements on the cognitive prong – the volitional prong is as 'scientific' as the cognitive one.

Lorena Bobbitt

This case illustrates how a jury may ignore obvious legal facts by excusing someone with whom they sympathize and judge as a good character. On 10 January 1994 Bobbitt went on trial in a Virginia courtroom for cutting off her husband's penis with an eight-inch kitchen knife. She did it, she said, after he had come home drunk on 23 June 1993 and raped her. The defence argued that she had been subjected to extreme brutality and violence at the hands of her husband – violence including rape, beatings, kickings, and chokings. He threatened that if she ever tried to leave him, he would find her and rape her any way he wanted. The defence argued that because of this relentless violence she had become clinically depressed and had been unable to resist the impulse to attack him. Dr Feister, psychiatrist for the defence, argued she was 'overwhelmed by the kind of flooding of emotions that she experienced and under the experience of these overwhelming emotions, she attacked the weapon which was the instrument of her torture, that is, her husband's penis' (Kane, 1994: 347).

The psychiatrist for the prosecution agreed she was depressed. But in his testimony, Dr Nelson referred to the 700-page deposition Bobbitt had made for the police. In it she describes how she felt after being raped:

> 'I was hurt, I went to the kitchen to drink water. I opened the refrigerator and I got out a cup of water. Then I was angry already.' She stated a feeling. Hadn't stated any other feelings or confusion about feelings at that point in time . . . 'And I turned my back and the first thing I saw was the knife. Then I took it and I was just angry . . . Then I took it and I went to the bedroom and I told him he shouldn't do this to me, why he did it. And then I said, I asked him if he was satisfied . . . I was just mad.' There's no indication of any confusion about her feelings . . . She says to him, 'I asked him if he was satisfied with what he did and he was just half-asleep or something. I was just mad.'

So when she goes to him and says 'Hey, you talk to me, do you like what you just did to me? Because I'm about to tell you how much I don't like it. And he says he doesn't care about feelings. He did say that and I asked him if he has an orgasm in me 'cause it hurt me – when he made me do that before he always has an orgasm and he doesn't wait for me to have an orgasm. He's selfish. I don't think it's fair. So I pulled back the sheets and I did it.'

(Kane, 1994: 411)

When asked whether she was suffering from an irresistible impulse, he commented:

It seems very unlikely that this would have been an irresistible impulse. For example, she picks up the knife, she goes into the bedroom, but she pauses. She stops long enough to have a conversation with him. So that clearly suggests that the impulse of whatever she's going to do with the knife – and in truth we don't really know what she's going to do – [is not irresistible].

(Kane, 1994: 411)

No technical psychiatric theory is needed to show that Bobbitt was not suffering from an irresistible impulse. Folk Psychology tells us that if she was able to pause in the midst of her crime, she was not overwhelmed by an irresistible impulse. No experts are needed, or any understanding of theoretical notions like serotonin levels or frontal lobe dysfunction. A jury can understand and make this decision themselves. The Butler Committee (Home Office, 1975: 242) noted that 'the idea that ability to conform to the law can be measured is particularly puzzling, and doctors have no special qualifications or expertise which fits them to undertake so puzzling a task'.

It is worth commenting that the psychiatrist for the defence also mentioned that Bobbitt suffered from 'battered woman's syndrome' (BWS). This is not currently classified as a disorder in DSM IV, and does not meet our definition of a disease. After being beaten repeatedly, a woman becomes demoralized, depressed, learns to be helpless, and acquires low self-esteem. While BWS makes a person worse off and is not reversible by an act of will, it has an obvious cause in the abuse. But we have seen that being a disease is not essential for a condition (like

287

emotional arousal) to excuse. So does BWS excuse? In the infamous trial of Paul Bernardo – accused with his wife, Karla Homolka, of abducting, torturing, raping, and killing two teenage girls – psychiatrists argued that Homolka was suffering from BWS and therefore had an excuse – it made her unable to refuse to comply with Bernardo. But is the abuse excuse valid? As Dershowitz (1994: 30) argues: 'The truth is that the vast majority of women (and men) who have been abused are entirely capable of controlling their behaviour and complying with the law.' Even if a person is abused, this does not absolve her of responsibility.

> Lisa B. Kemler, who successfully defended Lorena Bobbitt, offered a defence lawyer's variation on the 'naturalistic fallacy': 'The more we learn about how and why we act in a certain way, unless we rule out everything as psychobabble, the more we're able to offer viable defences.' The 'naturalistic fallacy' is a famous flaw in logic that makes the mistake of confusing the empirical realities of nature with the moral implications to be drawn from these realities.
>
> (Dershowitz, 1994: 35)

We make the Naturalistic Fallacy when we infer a moral conclusion (that someone should be excused) from a factual premise (that she has some condition or illness). Identifying a cause for the behaviour does nothing to excuse it. But the dichotomous thinking of jurors creates the real danger that they commit the Naturalistic Fallacy, and that 'for every bad act, there seems to be a made-to-order excuse'.

So why did the jury find Bobbitt NGRI? Both psychiatrists for the defence and prosecution agreed that she was depressed. But suffering from a mental illness is not sufficient for being insane. Neither did she behave like someone with an irresistible impulse. The reason for this odd verdict is that the jury asked themselves whether Bobbitt was evil or ill. They had evidence that she was a fundamentally good person brutalized until she had fought back. The fact that her husband was abusive, violent, arrogant, insensitive, unrepentant, and sexist supported their view that she was a good person fighting an evil husband. But if she was good, it followed that she had to be ill. Hence the verdict of NGRI. But clearly, Bobbitt's action was wrong. Even if she was abused, she had the opportunity to escape on many occasions, including the night in question. She knew what she was doing and was in control of her actions. But the jury was trapped within a dichotomous system, and given their assessment of her character as not being evil, they were forced to conclude that she was ill.

Jeffrey Dahmer

Dahmer was tried in Wisconsin which adopts an ALI standard of insanity. Testifying on his behalf, Dr Becker argued that Dahmer suffered from necrophilia such that he was unable to control his impulses to have sex with dead bodies. She used the common-sense notion that if someone can stop what he is doing with a policeman at his elbow, he is in control of his impulses, and pointed to the fact that Dahmer had been interrupted once by police but had carried on with the murdering straight afterwards: 'I mean that comes as close as you can get to a policeman at your elbow, and it kind of frightened him, of course, that they were there but that didn't stop him.' This is a strange use of the argument. Dahmer *did* interrupt what he was doing when the police intervened, but this interruption showed he *was* in control of his impulses. By (temporarily) stopping what he was doing and continuing only when it was safe, he demonstrated he was in control. In fact, under cross-examination, Dr Becker was forced to acknowledge that Dahmer had released one victim with the agreement to meet the next day because he lacked the drugs necessary to render him unconscious. He had purchased a mallet to do the job the next day. This is not the behaviour of a man overwhelmed by a murderous impulse.

Dr Dietz, testifying for the prosecution, also relied on common-sense notions:

> I asked him once again starting with Mr. Doxtater, whether if at the time he was killing Mr. Doxtater, his grandmother had walked in or some other witness, would he have killed him nonetheless and he said no . . . [I]f detection were imminent, he would have stopped, or that if he could have obtained the company of these men and sexual contact with them with less drastic means, he would have stopped. There was no force pushing him to kill. There was merely a desire to spend more time with the victim and had that

been possible through some other means, the killing would have become irrelevant to him.

(Transcript, 4 February 1992: 44)

Here again we see the employment of the simple concept of being able to do otherwise – if ordinary changes in the circumstances (like the presence of a witness) would have inhibited his behaviour, then Dahmer was in control. No psychiatric concepts are needed to see this.

In addition, Dietz argued that if Dahmer had been overwhelmed by an impulse to kill, he would not have prepared in advance for the deed:

And all of that preparation, from preparing the tablet in advance, having the equipment handy that he would need, finding the attractive victim, bringing him back, whatever preparations he made with them once they were with him, all of that is an indication that these behaviours were not impulsive. The killing was never an impulsive act. It was always a planned and deliberate act.

(Transcript, 4 February 1992: 46)

Once again, only Folk Psychology is needed to grasp that Dahmer's action was not the result of an overwhelming impulse. Dietz also pointed to the fact that Dahmer always killed at the beginning of weekends, showing how the murder was planned to give him time with the body and time to dispose of it without missing any work. He also argued 'the distribution spatially of where the killings occurred is an indication of his ability to conform his behaviour to the requirements of the law and to delay this process until it meets his practical needs for doing this privately'. All this uses only common-sense explanatory notions, and no psychiatric expertise is needed to understand this.

In general, Dietz pointed out that necrophilia does not compel someone to break the law:

The paraphile [person with a disorder of sexual preference] is as free as any other human being to choose whether to commit a crime to gratify his wishes or to not commit a crime to gratify his wishes, just as an individual who would like to have money fast and lots is in our society free to choose to commit a crime to get that money or go about it the hard way and earn it . . . Paraphilia is a description of what is sexually exciting. Whether one acts to seek out that image in varying ways is not determined by the paraphilia but by other aspects of one's life; one's morals, one's character, whether one drinks, all these other things, but I think it is important to point out that acquiring a paraphilia is generally not a matter of choice . . . We don't generally choose what we will find sexy. What humans do choose is whether they will act on their sexual interests or not.

(Transcript, 4 February 1992: 87)

Most necrophiliacs never break the law, though this does not imply that there are not a few who are unable to stop themselves breaking the law. But the fact that Dahmer could plan to commit his offences on the weekend when he had more time to enjoy the bodies suggests very strongly that he chose to break the law. Dietz argued that this 'is as much a matter of his choice as it is for any individual who makes a decision whether to satisfy sexual urges in some lawful way, including masturbation, or in some illegal way'. Interestingly, the trial debated whether Dahmer was suffering from a mental disease. As we have argued, this is irrelevant to whether Dahmer was not responsible. Dietz agreed:

It doesn't change my opinion on whether he appreciated the wrongfulness of his conduct or whether he could conform his conduct because my opinion on those issues isn't based on a consideration of diagnosis or what may be wrong with him, but rather on evidence concerning the behaviour at the time of the crimes.

(Transcript, 4 February 1992:64)

In the end, Dahmer was found guilty of the murders. The jury might have been influenced by the fact that had Dahmer been found NGRI, psychiatrists might have judged him well within a few years and released him. (In most American States, if someone is found NGRI, he is committed to a mental institution until a review panel is satisfied that he is no longer suffering from a mental illness.) But more importantly, Dahmer was clearly an evil character. Like Bobbitt, he suffered from a mental disorder and was able to resist the impulses arising from that disorder. But unlike her, he was clearly an evil character –

the jury was aware that he needed an evil character to express his necrophilia by killing. But if he needed an evil character to commit the offences, then he was not NGRI.

Summary of trials

These trials illustrate a number of important points. First, there is a logical gap between a psychiatric diagnosis and the judgement of insanity. In some of these trials (Dahmer and Bobbitt) there was agreement over diagnosis (necrophilia and depression respectively), but this agreement did not entail an agreement over the issue of insanity. Psychiatric diagnosis is distinct from insanity, and no diagnosis entails insanity. Second, and this follows from the first point, assessing responsibility does not require expert psychiatric testimony. Anyone who understands the rudiments of Folk Psychology can explain the behaviour and judge whether the person knew what he was doing, whether he knew it was wrong, whether he was in control of his actions, and whether his actions arose from his evil character. As Chiswick (1985: 976) puts it:

> The law continues to assume that these traditional concepts [of insanity] are proper subjects for psychiatric deliberation. The assumption has a certain face validity but little more and it might be argued that moral philosophers, behavioural scientists, or ministers of religion have an equally valid view on the mind and questions of individual responsibility.

Third, the jury makes the decision it does because it is forced to choose between two ostensibly exclusive and exhaustive options – whether the person is evil or ill. When the jury has evidence that the person is a good character (as with Bobbitt), they are inclined to conclude that she is NGRI. On the other hand, when they have evidence that the person is evil (as with Dahmer), they are inclined to conclude that he cannot be NGRI. The jury asks themselves one question: 'If we take away the disease, do we have a good character?' If they conclude that they do, they will be inclined to arrive at an NGRI verdict, and conversely. This is exactly what we have argued is the essence of the insanity defence: it is there to excuse those who are fundamentally good characters, and who would not have done evil were it not for the mental illness. Sometimes, however, this dichotomous thinking can lead to error, as in the Hinckley case.

Fourth, the notion of being unable to control one's conduct is no more obscure than the notion of not knowing what one is doing. On the contrary, the question whether Dahmer suffered from an irresistible impulse and should be excused was much clearer than the question whether Hinckley was deluded and suffered from exculpatory ignorance. The APA and ABA are simply wrong to think that the latter makes the insanity test more scientific. We do not make the insanity defence any the less empirically decidable by removing the volitional prong. Fifth, the law calls upon psychiatrists to deliver their views on the 'ultimate issue' of insanity. Not only do they have to diagnose what illness the defendant has but also whether he was insane. But insanity is a moral category and not a medical one. A psychiatrist might be best placed to decide whether someone is mentally ill, but he has no special training in judging whether that mental illness provides him with an excuse. This should be left to the jury to decide. Having an excuse is a moral notion, and something that we are all qualified to judge. As the Butler Committee (Home Office, 1975: 242) remarked: 'It seems odd that psychiatrists should be asked and agree to testify as to legal or moral responsibility. It is even more surprising that courts are prepared to hear that testimony.'

Sixth, the critical factor in such trials is the good character of the defendant, which is what we would expect given our understanding of the notion of excuses. Excuses are there to exempt good characters from blame and punishment. Bobbitt and Dahmer were both in control of their impulses, and yet only Bobbitt was found NGRI. This was because only Bobbitt was considered to be of good character. The verdict is ultimately a moral one, as one of the written opinions of the appellate courts put it:

> The application of these tests [M'Naghten and Irresistible Impulse test], however they are phrased, to a borderline case can be nothing more than a moral judgment that it is just or unjust to blame the defendant for what he did. Legal tests of criminal insanity are not and cannot be the result of scientific analysis or objective judgment.
>
> (Halpern, 1980: 155)

Laymen have a concept of insanity that is broadly cognitive: a person is NGRI if he is psychotic. But this reflects a deeper conception of insanity: Someone is NGRI if the person's underlying character is good. Jurors in insanity trials really ask themselves: 'Is this person evil or ill? If we take away the disease, do we have a good character?' That this is so is shown by the fact that even if a defendant is psychotic, he is not judged insane if he is seen as evil. In general, those who are psychotic are judged NGRI and those personality disordered as guilty because a psychotic illness more than any illness can make a good person do something bad, and a personality disorder more than any disorder cannot be distinguished from an evil character. In both cases, the moral verdict of the defendant's character is critical: If a story can be elaborated showing he is basically good, jurors will conclude he must have been ill. On the other hand, if the person is seen as evil, he is judged guilty. But being forced to fit decisions into two categories not mutually exclusive can sometimes lead to error.

CONCLUSION
Psychiatric justice

THE CASE FOR ABOLITION

A growing number of abolitionists argue for the abolition of the insanity defence (Szasz, 1965; Wootton, 1959, 1981; Halpern, 1977; Morris, 1982). Conservative abolitionists argue for abolition on the grounds that if we retain the principle of *mens rea*, we do not need the insanity defence. Radical abolitionists argue that we should jettison the whole notion of *mens rea*, including the insanity defence.

The case for conservative abolition is simple: with the excuses of ignorance and compulsion already enshrined in the law, the insanity defence is redundant. Those who do not know what they are doing lack the *mens rea* to be convicted of the offence. As Kadish (1968: 280) puts it:

> A total inability to know the nature and quality of the act quite plainly precludes convicting a defendant of any crime whose definition requires that he have that knowledge. If it were not for the special pre-emptive defence of legal insanity, therefore, the defendant would have a complete defence on the merits to any such crime – namely, the lack of *mens rea*.

And those who cannot control themselves are behaving involuntarily, and therefore not performing the *actus reus*. Morris (1982: 65) argues: 'Manifestly, the epileptic in a grand mal whose clonic movements strike and injure another commits no crime; but we need no special defense of insanity to reach that result, well established *actus reus* doctrines suffice.' We do not need cognitive and volitional insanity tests because these tests are already embodied in the principles of *mens rea* and *actus reus*. But this position is flawed. We have seen that most cases excused on the basis of insanity knew what they were doing and had control over their actions. Even Morris concedes that cases like Hadfield and M'Naghten would not be excused without an insanity defence because they possessed *mens rea*.

Radical abolitionists argue we should get rid of *mens rea* altogether, adopt the Medical Paradigm, and live in what Kittrie (1971) calls the Therapeutic State. Here the only function of the law would be the prevention of socially harmful acts. Since intent is unnecessary for an act to cause harm (negligent, careless and indifferent acts do more harm than acts done with deliberate intent), all crimes must be of strict liability. Wootton thereby jettisons the distinction between mad and bad:

> We end with the hope that in the fullness of time the present distinction between the wicked and the sick will be regarded as largely irrelevant to the classification of anti-social behaviour: that the boundary between penal and medical territory will be obliterated, along with the consequential distinction between the punitive and remedial institution. Then we shall no longer feel bound by court decisions as to whether or not what degree a criminal act is the result of mental disorder. Only then shall we escape from the paradox that, at a certain degree of gravity or irrationality, a crime ceases to be wicked and becomes merely a medical symptom. Once that is accomplished, we could look to every offender's future, not to his past record, concentrating on the search for whatever method (medical or other) of dealing with each individual case looked most promising.
>
> (Wootton, 1981: 532)

Let us review her position.

Her main argument is epistemological. She believes we are not able to differentiate between the mad and bad because we are unable to know the mental states of offenders:

> [N]either medical nor any other science can ever hope to prove whether a man who does not resist his impulses does not do so because he cannot or because he will not. The propositions of science are by definition subject to empir-

ical validation; but since it is not possible to get inside another man's skin, no objective criterion which can distinguish between 'he did not' and 'he could not' is conceivable.

(Wootton, 1981: 78)

She argues that juries struggle to distinguish irresistible impulses from impulses not resisted, and arbitrarily assume that bizarre desires are more difficult to resist than familiar desires. In support, she points to the fact that in two-thirds of cases where the defence of diminished responsibility succeeds there is evidence of mental illness, whereas less than half of those cases where the defence fails have a history of mental instability. She concludes that juries erroneously infer lack of responsibility from the presence of mental illness. But her arguments are too cavalier.

First, if juries adopted a simplistic view of the relationship between mental illness and responsibility, then 100 per cent of cases excused on the basis of diminished responsibility would have a history of mental illness compared to 0 per cent of those not excused. The percentages show that this is far from the case. Second, juries do not automatically excuse those with bizarre desires. They convicted Peter Sutcliffe, the 'Yorkshire Ripper', in spite of the fact that he had sadistically mutilated and murdered thirteen women. Similarly, they convicted Nilsen who confessed to killing fifteen men, having sex with the dead bodies, and keeping them in his apartment 'for company' before cutting them up and disposing of them (Masters, 1985). Third, it is unclear that ordinary folk cannot make the distinction between irresistible desires and desires not resisted. A grasp of Folk Psychology tells us that someone struggling to resist a desire will express the desire to resist it, will expend energy trying to resist it, will take precautions to prevent acting on it, will have good reasons not to act on it, and will express regret and experience remorse after acting on it. A jury can use such observations to get 'inside another man's skin'. Fourth, while it is true that we cannot literally get inside a person's head, we cannot get inside an atom either, but this does not stop us from having evidence for nuclear theories. Moreover, if we can never get inside a criminal's head, it would seem that we could never understand his everyday conduct. But we frequently do.

297

Fifth, strict liability creates a 'utilitarian nightmare', making it difficult to decide who among all those causally contributing to a crime should be punished or treated. As Fuller (1964: 93) asks:

> A man in a drunken rage shoots his wife. Who among those concerned with this event share the responsibility for its occurrence – the killer himself, the man who lent the gun to him, the liquor dealer who provided the gin, or was it perhaps the friend who dissuaded him from securing a divorce that would have ended an unhappy alliance?

If we do away with the notion of *mens rea* and concentrate on whoever caused the harm (no matter what his mental state), there will be too many to punish. We usually direct punishment at those evil characters who intended to commit the crime for the reason that this will be the most effective way of preventing re-offending. But we need *mens rea* to help us direct the 'treatment' in the right place, which is something Wootton (1978: 146) herself acknowledges: 'The presence or absence of guilty intention is all-important for its effect on the appropriate measures to be taken to prevent a recurrence of the forbidden act.' The reason is simple: Those who have the characters that make them intend such actions are most likely to do them again.

Wootton also argues that we cannot draw the line between mad and bad because we are unable to define mental illness in objective terms:

> If mental health and ill-health cannot be defined in objective scientific terms that are free of subjective moral judgments, it follows that we have no reliable criterion by which to distinguish the sick from the healthy mind. The road is then wide open for those who wish to classify all forms of anti-social, or at least of criminal, behaviour as symptoms of mental disorder . . . to obliterate the distinction between criminality and illness altogether . . . to treat all offenders as 'patients', and to dispense with the concepts of responsibility altogether.
>
> (Wootton, 1959: 227)

The distinction between disease and health is not objectively discoverable because disease is a value-laden notion. In this sense, the distinction is invented. But this does not mean that we invent the line between mad and bad. I have argued that in order to be excused, a person must be ignorant of what he is doing and be unable to do otherwise. Since there are objective ways of deciding these issues, the distinction between the mad and the bad is not invented.

Halpern (1977) argues there are three good reasons to get rid of the insanity defence. He enumerates the first two:

> 1. There is no morally sound basis to select a mental disease or defect as a justification for exculpability while excluding other behavioural determinants, such as heredity, poverty, family environment, and cultural deprivation . . . 2. There is neither a scientific nor an effective way in which the degree of mental disease or defect can be measured so that a defendant can be fairly and reasonably found to be lacking in criminal responsibility on that account.
>
> (Halpern, 1977: 46)

We have answered the first objection: Not all causes excuse – only those that affect his knowledge, control, or moral character do. The second objection is also flawed. We have argued that Folk Psychology can help us to objectively decide when someone like Dahmer is responsible: he is responsible when he knows what he is doing, is in control, and does not suffer from a change in moral character.

Halpern's third argument is Utilitarian – abolition removes the danger of the premature release of insanity acquittees. To recall, the need to detain those who were mentally ill but dangerous led to the creation of the special excuse of insanity and an appropriate disposition. Without it, dangerous mentally ill offenders would have been released. Insanity acquittees were initially detained indefinitely 'at Her Majesty's Pleasure'. But over time things changed. In England, someone found not guilty of murder on the grounds of Diminished Responsibility receives a lesser sentence than life imprisonment (Dell, 1984). A defendant killing in the course of a depressive illness can be released as soon as he recovers, which may be in months. In America, civil libertarianism produced reforms preventing insanity acquittees from being detained longer than they would have been had they been civilly committed. In Michigan 55.6 per cent of patients found NGRI were discharged following a 60-day diagnostic assessment (Criss and Racine, 1980). Halpern infers from this that the insanity defence is dangerous, and cites examples like the man who killed his aunt and uncle after being released a few months after discharge from Buffalo State Hospital. He had been found NGRI and detained there after killing his parents. Halpern has a point here – if this were the current practice, Halpern would be right about the insanity defence.

But currently there is a move away from the early release of insanity acquittees. The IDWG argues: 'In our view, it is a mistake to analogize such insanity acquittees as fully equivalent to civil committees who, when all has been said and done, have not usually already demonstrated their clear-cut potential for dangerous behaviour because they have not yet committed a highly dangerous act' (IDWG, 1983: 686). Civil commitment is justified if the person is suffering from a mental illness making him dangerous (to himself or others). The usual civil committee has not committed any offence nor will he – most psychiatric patients are not dangerous. But the dangerousness of the insanity acquittee has already been demonstrated, and since past behaviour is the best guide to future behaviour, the insanity acquittee should not be treated in the same way as the civil committee. He is more dangerous and should be detained longer. If the insanity defence is used properly, it will not be dangerous.

Halpern believes that the insanity defence is also dangerous because it allows those who feign mental illness to elude the law. This assumes psychiatrists are easily fooled, and there is some evidence of this. In the early 1970s Rosenhan (1973) and seven colleagues from the Stanford University Psychology Department presented themselves to twelve different psychiatric hospitals complaining they were hearing voices saying 'empty', 'hollow', and 'thud'. They were all admitted and diagnosed schizophrenic! But there is good inter-rater agreement over when someone is suffering from a psychiatric illness (Helzer *et al.*, 1977; Spitzer *et al.*, 1979). There is also good evidence that diagnostic categories are valid. For example, once a diagnosis of schizophrenia is made, a prediction of a deteriorating course can be reliably made (Helzer *et al.*, 1981). Together these studies imply that psychiatrists are not easily fooled. If they were, diagnoses would not carry reliable predictions. This squares with the evidence that even in the adversarial legal system, psychiatrists for the prosecution and defence are mostly in agreement over diagnosis (Phillips *et al.*, 1988; Janofsky *et al.*, 1989). If psychiatrists simply do their job in the legal system, which is to make diagnoses and prognoses, they will not be fooled, and the insanity defence will not be dangerous.

Thus the case for abolition is weak. The insanity defence is not redundant – we need it to excuse such cases as Hadfield and M'Naghten. In addition, we should not get rid of *mens rea* altogether (together with the insanity defence). The consequences of this will be unacceptable.

THE MORAL FOUNDATION OF THE INSANITY DEFENCE

The most important argument supporting anti-abolitionism is a moral one (Hart, 1968; Bonnie, 1983; Goldstein, 1967; Kadish, 1968). A woman who kills her children believing they face a life of torture, the man who kills his parents believing they have been replaced by hostile aliens, and the man who kills his father believing he is the Devil are not evil. Retributivism argues that a person must be evil before we can justify punishing him, and such individuals are not evil. Hart (1968: 35) writes:

> [T]he importance of excusing conditions in criminal responsibility ... derives from the more fundamental requirement that for criminal responsibility there must be 'moral culpability', which would not exist where the excusing conditions are present. On this view the maxim *actus reus est reus nisi mens sit rea* refers to a morally evil mind.

This applies to the insanity defence. As Bonnie (1983: 194) puts it: 'The moral core of the defence must be retained because some defendants afflicted by severe mental disorder who are out of touch with reality and are unable to appreciate the wrongfulness of their acts cannot justly be blamed and do not therefore deserve to be punished. The insanity defence, in short, is essential to the moral integrity of the criminal law.' A cognitive test of insanity is justified because someone who harms others only because he does not know what he is doing is not evil and deserves no punishment.

Someone who offends only because he cannot stop himself is also not evil. As Hart (1968: 39) argues: 'One necessary condition of the just application of a punishment is normally expressed by saying that the agent "could have helped" doing what he did.'

301

Bonnie (1983: 195) sees this as justifying a volitional test: 'Proponents of the [insanity] defence believe that it is fundamentally wrong to condemn and punish a person whose rational control over his or her behaviour was impaired by the incapacitating effects of severe mental illness.' As the IDWG (1983: 683) argues:

[D]efendants who lack the ability (the capacity) to rationally control their behaviour do not possess free will. They cannot be said to have 'chosen to do wrong.' Therefore, they should not be punished. Retention of the insanity defence is essential to the moral integrity of the law.

The same moral principles that preclude punishing sane people who are ignorant or out of control, also justify us excusing those who are insane (and satisfy cognitive and volitional tests). Retributivism argues that we are not entitled to punish a good person, and this justifies the cognitive and volitional standards. It also justifies excusing those who only offend after undergoing a reversible change in moral character. The insanity defence is a microcosm of the law, embodying the requirements of knowledge and voluntariness for guilt, and embodying the idea that a person is only responsible for his evil acts if he acts in character. Only if a person knows what he is doing and is in control of his actions does he have a fair opportunity to avoid punishment, and is it fair to punish him when he breaks the law. As such, the insanity defence is an extension of the doctrine of *mens rea*, and we cannot get rid of the former without undermining the latter.

Does Utilitarianism support this justification? If someone is insane, he cannot be deterred by the threat of punishment (because he either does not understand what he is doing or is out of control). Therefore we should not punish him. Utilitarianism also justifies the detention of insanity acquittees who remain ill. If someone is found NGRI, this means that we judge him to be a good character who has only done something bad because of his illness. However, if he remains ill, he constitutes an ongoing danger to others, and Utilitarianism justifies his detention. Thereby, the deterrent effect of the law is not weakened because such offenders may be detained indefinitely. It also justifies the release of those whose illness has been treated. If a good character only does something bad because of an illness, and his illness is treated, he will not constitute a danger if released. Moreover, it justifies monitoring acquittees once they have been released by such devices as PSRBs to ensure that they remain well.

Other Utilitarians argue that the insanity defence reminds others that they are responsible for their actions, and is therefore a deterrent:

> The insanity defence is critical to the criminal law itself. Its purpose is to insure that the criminal law has moral authority . . . What is a court to do when it confronts a case so bizarre and so incongruous that all the premises of criminal law, including free will, seem inappropriate? Should the court simply grit its teeth and go on? . . . If so, the criminal law risks demeaning itself, risks demonstrating that its language is not universal, its moral comprehension not encompassing. How much wiser for the criminal law instead to have an escape hatch, not only to avoid embarrassment, but also because by obverse implication every other defendant does have free will. Thus the insanity defence is in every sense the exception that proves the rule. It allows the court to treat every other defendant as someone who chose 'between good and evil'.
>
> (Stone, 1984: 222)

The idea is that 'if we can identify a group of individuals (the "insane") who are not responsible for their actions, we shall induce in the remainder of the population the belief that they are responsible' (Monahan, 1973: 730). This is a difficult argument to evaluate. What is true is that the law loses its moral authority when its verdicts and sentences are perceived as unjust. But it is unclear that convicting insane defendants will be seen as unjust. In fact, the reverse is sometimes true. In the case of the Yorkshire Ripper, there would have been moral outrage had he been found not guilty, as there was in the Hinckley case.

Ultimately, if someone with a good character does something bad because he is suffering from a mental illness, excusing him on the grounds of insanity will be the right thing to do. Not only will it be right from the Retributivist point of view, which requires we should only punish evil characters, but Utilitarianism supports this position too, because if the acquittee is treated, his early release will not constitute a danger to the public (because a good character is not dangerous), but if he cannot be treated, his lengthier detention will ensure the safety of the public. Should we find those who are not insane, but who are good, NGRI? For instance, there would be no virtue in detaining the person who kills a horribly abusive father or husband, or the person who kills his wife suffering terribly from terminal cancer. A Hybrid theory of excuses would excuse them. As the evidence from the Diminished Responsibility trials indicates, this is in fact what frequently happens. When the jury sees the defendant as a person of good character who does not deserve punishment, they are inclined to use the NGRI verdict to achieve an acquittal. This is just. Should we find the person who is not insane, but who is very dangerous, NGRI if this is a way he could be detained for a longer period? Again, the Hybrid theory suggests we should.

Utilitarian and Retributive theories are not opposed because the notion of an evil character, which is central to any Retributivist theory, is also central to any Utilitarian one. Those who are not evil characters but who break the law (because of ignorance, compulsion, or change in moral character) are unlikely to re-offend (unlike those who break the law because of their evil characters). This makes *mens rea* central, and we jettison it at our peril. But once we accept the idea that punishment should be directed at those who have the ability and a fair opportunity to avoid it, that is, at evil characters, then we are committed to excusing those who are insane. And once we accept the Utilitarian argument that we need to avoid releasing dangerous mentally ill offenders, the matter is settled. The insanity defence is justified.

DIMINISHED CAPACITY

Prosenjit Poddar was a lonely foreign student from India studying at the University of California. He fell in love with Tatiana Tarasoff who rejected him. He became depressed, neglected his appearance and studies, and began speaking disjointedly. He finally shot and stabbed her to death. At his trial, four psychiatrists agreed that he was suffering from schizophrenia, but the jury found him sane. While he had no delusion in terms of which his act was justified, and was not overwhelmed, there is some reason to think that he was not as guilty as a sane killer. He was not thinking or reasoning properly, and his mood was depressed, making it likely that his abilities to appreciate what he was doing and control his actions were diminished. If lacking understanding and control count as complete excuses, why deny that having reduced understanding and control count as a partial excuse? Morse (1979: 290) writes:

> The underlying rationale for defences based on mental abnormality is an impairment in free choice ... Where choice is lacking, blame and punishment can not justly be imposed. That mental abnormality is a matter of degree is well recognized. Consequently freedom of choice must also be a matter of degree.

It follows that responsibility too will be a matter of degree.

The principal argument for introducing the defence of diminished capacity is a moral one. The insanity defence excuses only those whose mental disorder exceeds a certain threshold of impairment. Those who are less incapacitated are judged by the same standard as those who are completely normal, and this is unjust. Halleck (1986: 140) argues: 'Imposing equal or similar prison sentences upon offenders who have committed the same crime, but who have different capacities to have chosen otherwise, violates a fundamental sense of fairness.' Once we grant that insanity excuses, and that mental illness comes in degrees, then we should accept that responsibility comes in degrees too, and that less severe psychological abnormality should partially excuse. It would be unjust not to punish those with diminished capacity less than those committing the same offences with a sound mind.

In spite of this, there are some good reasons why we should not introduce a diminished capacity defence into the law. First, the jury will be faced with four verdicts: Guilty, Not Guilty, NGRI, and Partly Guilty Because Partially Responsible. This makes the decision bewilderingly complex, and there will be a tendency for juries to opt for the intermediate verdict each time on the assumption that, at worst, it can only be half-wrong. Second, the moral argument only works if the standard for responsibility is very exacting. But the law sets a very minimal requirement which everyone except the most disturbed is able to satisfy. If this is the case, being mentally ill but still sane should not count as an excuse.

> Although it may be harder for some persons to conform to law, the criminal law does not set an enormously high standard for persons to obey . . . There may be significant differences among legally sane offenders in terms of their ability morally to evaluate or control their conduct, but all responsible offenders are capable of meeting the law's low threshold requirements for full responsibility for the crimes they have committed as defined by the strict elements. We should not conclude that the moral turpitude of an offender is not great simply because the moral turpitude of others may be even greater.
>
> (Morse, 1979: 298)

While justice requires that we accept degrees of responsibility, given that there is a very minimal standard expected by the law, everyone who is not insane can meet it. Therefore we should do away with the diminished capacity defence.

Third, a diminished capacity defence would seriously diminish the deterrent effect of the law. If we persuade everyone that we all have excuses (to a greater or lesser degree), we are not delivering a message that we are responsible and should take care of what we do. If we allow everything from battered woman's syndrome to child abuse to excuse, we will encourage those who are just looking for an excuse to hit at their victimizers (Dershowitz, 1994). As Halleck (1986: 140) argues: 'Holding those who are gravely impaired to this same standard of accountability as those who are more generously endowed might, in theory, discourage all potential offenders.'

Fourth, if we allow diminished capacity as a defence, all trials would become impossibly protracted.

> It would require consideration of complex biological, psychological, and sociological factors in every determination of criminal liability. Excuse-giving would be enormously expanded but the process would be much more cumbersome than it is in medicine, since each excuse would have to be litigated under some legal theory or doctrine. The ordinary trial might become as complicated as a contested insanity defence trial. Our courts could not tolerate such a burden.
>
> (Halleck, 1986: 143)

The solution is to allow only the insanity defence, but also have flexible sentences so that degrees of blameworthiness are reflected in the sentence rather than the verdict (Halleck, 1986; Dell, 1984; Chiswick, 1985).

THE NATURE OF INSANITY

The notion of an evil character is central to the idea of excuses. Ignorance, compulsion and automatism are all excuses because they are ways in which a good person comes to do something bad. We want to punish evil characters, and want our excuses to exempt good ones. Hence these are excuses. This hypothesis is tested (and in fact suggested) by cases of insanity. There are dramatic cases where a disorder changes the person's character, and where he deserves to be excused on this basis. In addition, ignorance, compulsion, and automatism frequently fail to excuse deserving cases of insanity. The only way to justify why they excuse is to accept the idea that a change in moral character excuses. This enables us to excuse deserving cases of insanity as well as to support the idea that excuses are designed to exempt good characters from punishment. Far from being peripheral, insanity shows us what is central about excuses. By showing how character change can excuse, insanity illuminates the central role of character in our moral system, suggesting that the whole system of excuses is based on the idea of punishing evil characters and excusing good ones. This idea is justified by Retributivist and Utilitarian principles – only evil characters deserve punishment, and only evil characters need motivation to behave otherwise. The insanity defence, then, illuminates the whole institution of excuses.

Someone has an evil character if he does not care sufficiently about the well-being of others, and has a willingness to ignore their welfare in pursuit of his own selfish interests. A person's actions reflect his character when he freely and knowingly acts. If a person ignores someone's interests but does not know he is doing so, his action does not reflect an underlying evil nature. If someone is unable to control himself harming others, his actions do not reflect his underlying willingness to harm others. Obviously, if the person acts out of character, his harmful act will not reflect his underlying good character either. Only when it does, do we feel the person deserves punishment. The notion of

307

a good character lies behind our impulse to excuse. Whenever someone does something bad, but has a good character, we excuse him. This is why sympathy lies behind the jury's impulse to excuse – if the defendant is a good person who is a victim of circumstance or illness, he is found not guilty. Mental illness frequently makes a good person do something bad. Psychosis may make a good person do evil because it undermines his understanding of what he is doing. Impulse disorders may make a good person do evil because he is unable to control himself. Automatisms may make a good person commit an offence because he is unaware of and unable to control what he is doing. Frontal lobe tumours may make a good person do evil because they change our characters. In all cases, it is the person's underlying good character that inclines us to excuse him.

Insanity is not a technical notion requiring the knowledge and expertise of psychiatrists. Being insane implies being worthy of exemption from punishment, and as such is a moral concept and not a scientific one. In addition, someone has an excuse only if he acts in ignorance, or is overwhelmed, or acts without conscious control, or acts out of character. This means that we do not need to know anything about serotonin levels or repressed Oedipal desires to judge whether someone has an excuse. In order to decide such matters, we need to explain the person's behaviour in terms of his desires, beliefs, rational deliberations and choices. The critical questions for responsibility are: Did he know what he was doing? Was he in control of his actions? Was he acting out of character? To answer these questions we only require Folk Psychology and not complex psychiatric theory. Our concepts of responsibility, desert, excuse, good, and evil, all depend on our explaining behaviour in a particular way within Folk Psychology. Whether some behaviour is good or evil depends on how we explain it within this theory. To be evil, behaviour must be explained by a person's indifference to the needs of others in the pursuit of his own selfish interests, and his acting freely. Since laymen are as expert at employing this theory as anyone, they are as qualified as psychiatrists to reach insanity verdicts.

We do not have to accept Wootton's paradox. If a man does extreme evil, it does not follow by definition that he is not responsible. But it suggests that there is something different about him, and if we find an abnormality that we judge we are better off without, then we may conclude he is ill. But Wootton is wrong to think this implies he is not responsible and not evil. Being ill does not exclude being evil. In fact, those who are sadists do have an illness, but are evil because they are not overwhelmed by their desires. They are evil, rather, if they choose to act on their deviant desires. Moreover, not every extremely evil act need be committed by someone who is ill in some way, and so extreme evil does not disappear.

We are left with a moral paradox. If someone has an excuse because he undergoes a change in moral character (from good to evil), someone with a personality disorder will deserve to be excused because he too has undergone a change in moral character. This means that the distinction between mad and bad is threatened. Of course, it is not completely threatened – there are many criminals who are not psychopaths and who cannot be excused on the basis of personality change. However, if there is no natural division between those with character defects (and responsible) and those with personality disorders (and excuses), the arbitrariness of concluding that those with personality disorders are not responsible (because of the excuse of character change) threatens to precipitate us down the slippery slope towards concluding that no one is responsible. To avoid this, we should conclude that those with personality disorders are responsible (where there is no natural line demarcating them). We do this by arguing that psychopaths are not ill – we may judge that some condition is not a disease if the political consequences of classifying it as a disease are too costly. This is the case with psychopathy – we are better off viewing psychopaths as evil and dealing with them in the penal system.

Aristotle argued that there were two excuses: Ignorance ('I did not know what I was doing') and Compulsion ('I lost control'). However, there is a third: Change in Moral Character ('I was not my normal good self'). These should be embodied in a new definition of insanity:

> Someone is NGRI if he is suffering from a mental illness at the time of the offence such that (1) he was unable to appreciate what he was doing or whether it was wrong, or (2) he was unable to control his actions, or (3) he was transformed from a good character into an evil one.

Exploring the concept of insanity has led us to discover a new excuse, and enabled us to see more clearly that the notion of an evil character lies at the heart of our concept of excuse and our whole moral and legal systems.

BIBLIOGRAPHY

Ackerknecht, E. (1982) *A Short History of Medicine*, Baltimore, Johns Hopkins University Press.

Appelbaum, P. (1994) *Almost a Revolution*, Oxford University Press.

Aristotle (1955) *Ethics*, Harmondsworth, Penguin.

Atkinson, R., Atkinson, R. and Hilgard, E. (1983) *Introduction to Psychology*, New York, Harcourt.

Austin, L. (1970) *Philosophical Papers*, Oxford University Press.

Ayer, A. (1954) *Philosophical Essays*, London, Macmillan.

Bavidge, M. (1989) *Mad or Bad?*, Bristol, Bristol Classical Press.

Baxter, R. and Nuttal, C. (1975) 'Severe sentences no deterrent to crime', *New Society*, 31: 11–27.

Bayer, R. (1987) *Homosexuality and American Psychiatry*, Princeton University Press.

Benn, S. (1992) 'Wickedness', in J. Deigh (ed.) *Ethics and Personality*, University of Chicago Press, pp. 191–206.

Bentham, J. (1982) *An Introduction to the Principles of Morals and Legislation*, London, Macmillan.

Bloch, S. and Reddaway, P. (1977) *Psychiatric Terror*, New York, Basic Books.

Bloom, J. and Williams, M. (1994) *Management and Treatment of Insanity Acquittees*, Washington, American Psychiatric Press.

Blumenfeld, D. (1972) 'Free action and unconscious motivation', *Monist*, 72: 426–43.

Bonnie, R. (1983) 'The moral basis of the insanity defence', *American Bar Association Journal*, 69: 194–7.

Boorse, C. (1976) 'What a theory of mental health should be', *Journal for the Theory of Social Behaviour*, 6: 61–84.

Brandt, R. (1992) *Morality, Utilitarianism, and Rights*, Cambridge University Press.

Butler, S. (1970) *Erewhon*, Harmondsworth, Penguin.

Cadoret, R. (1978) 'Psychopathology in adopted-away offspring of biological parents with antisocial behaviour', *Archives of General Psychiatry*, 35: 176–84.

311

Carroll, L. (1972) 'What the tortoise said to Achilles', in I. Copi and J. Gould (eds) *Readings on Logic*, New York, Macmillan, pp. 117–20.

Chapman, L. and Chapman, J. (1988) 'The genesis of delusions', in T. Oltmanns and B. Maher (eds) *Delusional Beliefs*, New York, Wiley, pp. 167–83.

Cherniak, C. (1986) *Minimal Rationality*, Cambridge, MIT Press.

Chiswick, D. (1985) 'Use and abuse of psychiatric testimony', *British Medical Journal*, 290: 975–7.

Chomsky, N. (1957) *Syntactic Structures*, The Hague, Mouton.

Christiansen, K. (1977) 'A review of criminality among twins', in S. Mednick and K. Christiansen (eds) *Biosocial Bases of Criminal Behaviour*, New York, Gardner Press, pp. 89–108.

Churchland, Patricia (1986) *Neurophilosophy*, Cambridge, MIT Press.

Churchland, Paul (1989) *A Neurocomputational Perspective*, Cambridge, MIT Press.

Clark, W. and Marshall, W. (1952) *A Treatise on the Law of Crimes*, Chicago, Callahan.

Cleckley, H. (1982) *The Mask of Sanity*, St Louis, Mosby.

Cohen, L. (1981) 'Can human irrationality be experimentally demonstrated?' *Behavioural and Brain Sciences*, 4: 317–70.

Cohen, M., Liebson, I., Fallace, L. and Sigvardsson, W. (1971) 'Alcoholism: controlled drinking and incentives for abstinence', *Psychological Reports*, 28: 575–80.

Criss, M. and Racine, D. (1980) 'Impact of change in legal standard for those adjudicated NGRI', *Bulletin of American Academy of Psychiatry and the Law*, 8: 261–71.

Cross, R. (1975) *The English Sentencing System*, London, Butterworth.

Crowe, R. (1975) 'An adoption study of antisocial personality', *Archives of General Psychiatry*, 31: 785–91.

Culver, C. and Gert, B. (1982) *Philosophy in Medicine*, Oxford University Press.

Curling, T. (1856) *A Practical Treatise on the Diseases of the Testis*, London, Churchill.

Dane, F. and Wrightsman, L. (1982) 'Effects on defendants' and victims' characteristics on jurors' verdicts', in N. Kerr and R. Bray (eds) *The Psychology of the Courtroom*, London, Academic Press, pp. 83–115.

Davidson, D. (1980) *Essays on Actions and Events*, Oxford, Clarendon Press.

—— (1984) *Inquiries into Truth and Interpretation*, Oxford, Clarendon Press.

Dell, S. (1982) 'Diminished responsibility reconsidered', *Criminal Law Review*, 809–19.

—— (1984) *Murder into Manslaughter*, Oxford University Press.

Dell, S. and Smith, A. (1983) 'Changes in the sentencing of diminished responsibility homicides', *British Journal of Psychiatry*, 142: 20–34.

Dershowitz, A. (1994) *The Abuse Excuse*, Boston, Little, Brown & Co.

Devlin, P. (1959) *The Enforcement of Morals*, Oxford University Press.

312

Diamond, B. (1962) 'From M'Naghten to Currens and beyond', *California Law Review*, 50: 189–205.

Dickens, B. (1986) 'The sense of justice and criminal responsibility', in S. Hucker, C. Webster and M. Ben-Aron (eds) *Mental Illness and Moral Responsibility*, New York, Butterworth, pp. 33–61.

Direkze, M., Bayliss, S., and Cutting, J. (1971) Primary tumours of the frontal lobe', *British Journal of Clinical Practice*, 25: 207–13.

Dubos, R. (1965) *Man Adapting*, Yale University Press.

Duff, A. (1977) 'Psychopathy and moral understanding', *American Philosophical Quarterly*, 14: 189–200.

Duff, R. (1990) *Intention, Agency and Criminal Liability*, Oxford, Blackwell.

Edwards, P. (1958) 'Hard and soft determinism', in S. Hook (ed.) *Determinism and Freedom*, New York, Macmillan, pp. 117–25.

Elliott, C. (1991) 'Moral responsibility, psychiatric disorders and duress', *Journal of Applied Philosophy*, 8: 45–56.

—— (1992) 'Diagnosing blame: responsibility and the psychopath', *Journal of Medicine and Philosophy*, 17: 199–214.

—— (1994) 'Puppetmasters and personality disorders', *Philosophy, Psychology and Psychiatry*, 1: 91–103.

Elliott, C. and Gillett, G. (1992) 'Moral insanity and practical reason', *Philosophical Psychology*, 5: 53–67.

Engelhardt, T. (1974) 'Explanatory models in medicine', *Texas Reports on Biology and Medicine*, 32: 225–39.

Enoch, D. (1990) 'Hysteria, malingering, pseudologia fantastica, Ganser syndrome, prison psychosis and Munchausens's syndrome', in R. Bluglass and P. Bowden (eds) *Principles and Practice of Forensic Psychiatry*, London, Churchill Livingstone, pp. 3805–18.

Eysenck, H. (1977) *Crime and Personality*, St Albans, Paladin.

—— (1985) *Decline and Fall of the Freudian Empire*, Harmondsworth, Penguin.

Evans, J. (1989) *Bias in Human Reasoning*, London, Lawrence Erlbaum.

Fenwick, P. (1990) 'Automatism', in R. Bluglass and P. Bowden (eds) *Principles and Practice of Forensic Psychiatry*, London, Churchill Livingstone, pp. 271–86.

—— (1993) 'Brain, mind, and behaviour', *British Journal of Psychiatry*, 163: 565–74.

Feinberg, J. (1970) *Doing and Deserving*, Princeton University Press.

—— (1986) *Harm to Self*, Oxford University Press.

Festinger, L. (1957) *A Theory of Cognitive Dissonance*, Stanford University Press.

Festinger, L., Riecken, H. and Schachter, S. (1956) *When Prophecy Fails*, University of Minnesota Press.

Fingarette, H. (1972) *The Meaning of Criminal Insanity*, Berkeley, University of California Press.

—— (1988) *Heavy Drinking*, Berkeley, University of California Press.

Fingarette, H. and Hasse, A. (1979) *Mental Disabilities and Criminal Responsibility*, Berkeley, University of California Press.

Finkel, N. (1988) *Insanity on Trial*, New York, Plenum Press.

—— (1989) 'The Insanity Defence Reform Act of 1984', *Behavioural Sciences and the Law*, 7: 403–19.

Finkel, N., Shaw, R., Bercaw, S. and Koch, J. (1985) 'Insanity defences: From the jurors' perspective', *Law and Psychology Review*, 9: 77–92.

Fletcher, G. (1978) *Rethinking Criminal Law*, Boston, Little.

Flew, A. (1973) *Crime or Disease?*, London, Macmillan.

Foot, P. (1978) *Virtues and Vices*, Oxford, Basil Blackwell.

Frankfurt, H. (1982) 'Freedom of the will and the concept of a person', in G. Watson (ed.) *Free Will*, Oxford University Press, pp. 81–95.

Freud, S. (1975) *The Psychopathology of Everyday Life*, Harmondsworth, Penguin.

Fuller, L. (1964) *The Morality of Law*, New Haven, Hillhouse Press.

Gelder, M., Gath, D. and Mayou, R. (1989) *Oxford Textbook of Psychiatry*, Oxford University Press.

Gibbs, W. (1995) 'Seeking the criminal element', *Scientific American*, 272: 100–7.

Gibson, E. and Klein, S. (1961) *Murder: a Home Office Research Unit Report*, London, HMSO.

Glover, J. (1970) *Responsibility*, London, Routledge.

Goldstein, A. (1967) *The Insanity Defence*, Yale University Press.

Goosens, W. (1980) 'Values, health and medicine', *Philosophy of Science*, 47: 100–15.

Gordon, G. (1978) *The Criminal Law of Scotland*, Edinburgh, Green & Son.

Gray, J. (1971) *The Psychology of Fear and Stress*, London, Weidenfeld & Nicolson.

—— (1975) *Elements of a Two-Process Theory of Learning*, New York, Academic Press.

—— (1976) 'The neuropsychology of anxiety', in I. Sarason and C. Spielberger (eds) *Stress and Anxiety*, Washington, Hemisphere, pp. 3–26.

—— (1981) 'A critique of Eysenck's theory of personality', in H. Eysenck (ed.) *A model of personality*, New York, Springer, pp. 246–76.

Greenwood, P. and Abrahamse, A. (1982) *Selective Incapacitation*, Santa Monica, Rand.

Gross, H. (1979) *A Theory of Criminal Justice*, New York, Academic Press.

Gunn, J. (1991) 'Trials of psychiatry', in K. Herbst and J. Gunn (eds) *The Mentally Disordered Offender*, London, Butterworth–Heinemann, pp. 17–36.

Halleck, S. (1986) 'Responsibility and excuse in medicine and law: a utilitarian perspective', *Law and Contemporary Problems*, 49: 127–46.

—— (1990) 'Dissociative phenomena and the question of responsibility', *The International Journal of Clinical and Experimental Hypnosis*, 38: 298–314.

Halpern, A. (1977) 'The insanity defence: a judicial anachronism', *Psychiatric Annals*, 7: 41–63.

—— (1980) 'Uncloseting the conscience of the jury – a justly acquitted doctrine', *Psychiatric Quarterly*, 52: 144–57.

Hamilton, J. (1990) 'Manslaughter: assessment for the court', in R. Bluglass and P. Bowden (eds) *Principles and Practice of Forensic Psychiatry*, London, Churchill Livingstone, pp. 205–14.

Hans, V. and Slater, D. (1984) 'Plain crazy: lay definitions of legal insanity', *International Journal of Law and Psychiatry*, 7: 105–14.

Hare, R. (1963) *Freedom and Reason*, Oxford University Press.

—— (1970) *Psychopathy: Theory and Practice*, New York, Wiley.

—— (1982) 'Psychopathy and physiological activity during anticipation of an aversive stimulus', *Psychophysiology*, 19: 266–71.

Hare, R., McPherson, L. and Forth, A. (1988) 'Male psychopaths and their criminal careers', *Journal of Consulting and Clinical Psychology*, 56: 710–14.

Hart, H. (1968) *Punishment and Responsibility*, Oxford, Clarendon Press.

Hastie, R., Penrod, S. and Pennington, N. (1983) *Inside the Jury*, Harvard University Press.

Healy, D. (1990) *The Suspended Revolution*, London, Faber & Faber.

Heather, N. and Robertson, I. (1981) *Controlled Drinking*, London, Methuen.

Helzer, J., Robins, L., Taibleson, M., Woodruff, R., Reich, T. and Wish, E. (1977) 'Reliability of psychiatric diagnosis', *Archives of General Psychiatry*, 34: 136–41.

Helzer, J., Brockington, I. and Kendell, R. (1981) 'Predictive validity of DSM-III and Feighner definitions of schizophrenia', *Archives of General Psychiatry*, 38: 791–7.

Henggeler, S. (1989) *Delinquency in Adolescence*, Newbury Park, Sage.

Higgins, J. (1990) 'Affective psychoses', in R. Bluglass and P. Bowden (eds) *Principles and Practice of Forensic Psychiatry*, London, Churchill Livingstone, pp. 345–52.

Hilgard, E. (1965) *Hypnotic Susceptibility*, New York, Harcourt.

Holborow, L. (1971) 'Blame, praise and credit', *Proceedings of the Aristotelian Society*, 54: 34–56.

Hollin, C. (1992) *Criminal Behaviour*, London, Falmer Press.

Hollis, M. (1970) 'The limits of irrationality', in B. Wilson (ed.) *Rationality*, Oxford, Blackwell.

—— (1979) 'Reason and ritual', in B. Wilson (ed.) *Rationality*, Guildford, Billing & Son, pp. 221–39.

Home Office (1975) *Report of the Committee on Mentally Abnormal Offenders*, London, HMSO.

Honderich, T. (1993) *How Free are You?*, Oxford University Press.

Horai, J. and Bartek, M. (1978) 'Recommended punishment as a function of injuries intent, actual harm done, and intended consequences', *Personality and Social Psychology Bulletin*, 4: 475–8.

Hospers, J. (1958) 'What means this freedom?', in S. Hook (ed.) *Determinism and Freedom*, New York, Macmillan, pp. 126–44.

—— (1973) 'Freewill and psychoanalysis', in P. Edwards and A. Pap (eds) *A Modern Introduction to Philosophy*, New York, Free Press, pp. 70–93.

Hume, D. (1962) *Enquiries Concerning Human Understanding*, Oxford University Press.

Hutchings, B. and Mednick, S. (1977) 'Criminality in adoptees and their adoptive and biological parents', in S. Mednick and K. Christiansen (eds) *Biosocial Bases of Criminal Behaviour*, New York, Gardner Press, pp. 70–88.

Insanity Defence Work Group (IDWG) (1983) 'American Psychiatric Association Statement on the Insanity Defence', *American Journal of Psychiatry*, 140: 681–8.

James, R. (1959) 'Jurors' assessment of criminal responsibility', *Social Problems*, 7: 58–67.

—— (1967) *The Jury and the Defence of Insanity*, Boston, Little & Brown.

Janofsky, J., Vandewalle, M. and Rappeport, J. (1989) 'Defendants pleading insanity', *Bulletin of the American Academy of Psychiatry and Law*, 17: 203–11.

Jeffrey, C. (1993) 'Biological perspectives', *Journal of Criminal Justice Education*, 4: 291–306.

Jeffrey, R., Pasewark, R. and Bieber, S. (1988) 'Insanity plea: predicting Not Guilty by Reason of Insanity adjudications', *Bulletin of the American Academy of Psychiatry and Law*, 16: 35–9.

Jellinek, E. (1960) *The Disease Concept of Alcoholism*, New Haven, Hillhouse Press.

Kadish, S. (1968) 'The decline of innocence', *Cambridge Law Journal*, 26: 273–85.

Kahneman, D. and Tversky, A. (1972) 'Subjective probability', *Psychological Review*, 80: 237–51.

Kahneman, D., Slovic, P. and Tversky, A. (1982) *Judgment under Uncertainty*, Cambridge University Press.

Kane, P. (1994) *The Bobbitt Case*, New York, Pinnacle Books.

Kant, I. (1959) *Foundation of the metaphysic of morals*, New York, Bobbs Merrill.

Kaplan, H. and Sadock, B. (1991) *Synopsis of Psychiatry*, Baltimore, Williams & Wilkins.

Katz, L. (1987) *Bad Acts and Guilty Minds*, University of Chicago Press.

Kendell, R. (1976) 'The concept of disease', *British Journal of Psychiatry*, 128: 508–9.

Kenny, A. (1978) *Freewill and Responsibility*, London, Routledge.

King, L. (1982) *Medical Thinking*, Princeton University Press.

Kittrie, N. (1971) *The Right to be Different*, Baltimore, Johns Hopkins Press.

Kleinig, J. (1973) *Punishment and Desert*, Hague, Mouton.

Kohlberg, L. (1976) 'Moral stages of moralization', in T. Lickona (ed.) *Moral Development and Behaviour*, New York, Holt, Rinehart & Winston.

Kripke, S. (1980) *Naming and Necessity*, Oxford, Basil Blackwell.

Laing, R. (1965) *The Divided Self*, Harmondsworth, Penguin.

Lange, J. (1931) *Crime as Destiny*, London, Unwin.

Leng, R. (1990) 'Mens rea and the defences to a criminal charge', in R. Bluglass and P. Bowden (eds) Principles and Practice of Forensic Psychiatry, London, Churchill Livingstone, pp. 237–250.

Lewis, D. and Bard, J. (1991) 'Multiple personality and forensic issues', Psychiatric Clinics of North America, 14: 741–56.

Lidberg, L. et al. (1984) 'Urinary catecholamines, stress and psychopathy', Psychosomatic Medicine, 40: 116–25.

Link, B., Andrews, H. and Cullen, F. (1992) 'The violent and illegal behaviour of mental patients reconsidered', American Sociological Review, 57: 275–92.

Lippert, W. and Senter, R. (1966) 'Electrodermal responses in the sociopath', Psychonomic Science, 4: 25–6.

Lishman, W. (1987) Organic Psychiatry, Oxford, Blackwell.

Low, P., Jeffries, J. and Bonnie, R. (1986) The Trial of John W. Hinckley, Jr., New York, Foundation Press.

Lunde, D. and Sigal, H. (1990) 'Multiple-victim killers', in R. Bluglass and P. Bowden (eds) Principles and Practice of Forensic Psychiatry, London, Churchill Livingstone, pp. 625–30.

Lykken, D. (1957) 'A study of anxiety in the sociopathic personality', Journal of Abnormal and Social Psychology, 55: 6–10.

McCloskey, H. (1968) 'A non-utilitarian approach to punishment', in M. Bayles (ed.) Contemporary Utilitarianism, New York, Macmillan.

McGinn, C. (1978) 'Mental states, natural kinds, and psycho-physical laws', Proceedings of the Aristotelian Society, 67: 40–78.

McGreevy, M., Steadman, H., and Callahan, L. (1991) 'The negligible effects of California's 1982 reform of the Insanity Defence Act', American Journal of Psychiatry, 148: 744–50.

Mackie, J. (1977) 'The grounds of responsibility', in P. Hacker and J. Raz (eds) Law, Morality and Society, Oxford, Clarendon Press.

Marks, I. (1969) Fears and Phobias, London, Heinemann.

Martin, G. (1981) 'Mental disorder and criminal responsibility in Canadian Law', in S. Hucker, C. Webster and M. Ben-Aron (eds) Mental Disorder and Criminal Responsibility, Toronto, Butterworth, pp. 15–32.

Masters, B. (1985) Killing for Company, London, Hodder & Stoughton.

Mednick, S. and Finello, K. (1983) 'Biological factors and crime', International Journal of Law and Psychiatry, 6: 1–15.

Menninger, K. (1968) The Crime of Punishment, New York, Viking Press.

Merskey, H. (1995) 'Multiple Personality Disorder and false Memory Syndrome', British Journal of Psychiatry, 166: 281–4.

Milliken, D. (1985) 'The insanity defence', Canadian Journal of Psychiatry, 30: 323–8.

Mitchell, C. (1988) 'The intoxicated offender – refuting the legal and medical myths', International Journal of Law and Psychiatry, 11: 77–103.

Monahan, J. (1973) 'Abolish the insanity defence? – not yet', Rutgers Law Review, 26: 719–40.

Moore, G. (1903) Principia Ethica, Cambridge University Press.

Moore, M. (1984) Law and Psychiatry, Cambridge University Press.

Morris, H. (1973) 'Persons and punishment', in J. Murphy (ed.) *Punishment and Rehabilitation*, Belmont, pp. 40–64.

Morris, N. (1968) 'The dangerous criminal', *Southern California Law Review*, 41: 514–20.

—— (1982) *Madness and the Criminal Law*, Chicago University Press.

Morse, S. (1979) 'Diminished capacity: a moral and legal conundrum', *International Journal of Law and Psychiatry*, 2: 271–98.

Nagel, T. (1979) *Mortal Questions*, Cambridge University Press.

Newton-Smith, W. (1982) 'Relativism and the possibility of interpretation', in M. Hollis and S. Lukes (eds) *Rationality and Relativism*, Oxford, Basil Blackwell, pp. 106–22.

Norris, J. (1988) *Serial Killers*, London, Arrow Books.

Nowell-Smith, P. (1954) *Ethics*, Harmondsworth, Penguin.

Oliver, J. (1970) 'Huntington's Chorea in Northamptonshire', *British Journal of Psychiatry*, 116: 241–53.

Olweus, D. (1987) 'Testosterone and adrenaline: aggressive antisocial behaviour in normal adolescent males', in S. Mednick, T. Moffitt and S. Stack (eds) *The Causes of Crime*, Cambridge University Press, pp. 262–83.

Orne, M. (1984) 'On the differential diagnosis of multiple personality in the forensic context', *International Journal of Clinical and Experimental Hypnosis*, 32: 118–69.

Packer, H. (1969) *The Limits of the Criminal Sanction*, Stanford University Press.

Packer, I. (1985) 'Insanity acquittals in Michigan 1969–1983: the effects of legislative and judicial changes', *Journal of Psychiatry and Law*, 13: 419–34.

Parsons, T. (1951) *The Social System*, London, Routledge.

Pasewark, R. (1984) 'Insanity plea: a review of the research literature', *Journal of Psychiatry and Law*, 8: 357–401.

Pasewark, R., Randolph, R. and Bieber, S. (1984) 'Insanity plea: statutory language and trial procedures', *Journal of Psychiatry and Law*, 12: 399–422.

Peck, M. (1983) *People of the Lie*, New York, Simon & Schuster.

Phillips, M., Wolf, A. and Coors, D. (1988) 'Psychiatry and the criminal justice system: testing the myths', *American Journal of Psychiatry*, 145: 605–10.

Piaget, J. (1948) *The Moral Judgment of the Child*, New York, Free Press.

Powers, E. and Witmer, H. (1951) *An Experiment in the Prevention of Delinquency*, New York, Columbia University Press.

Prins, H. (1986) *Dangerous Behaviour, the Law, and Mental Disorder*, London, Tavistock.

Pritchard, J. (1835) *A Treatise on Insanity*, London, Sherwood Gilbert & Piper.

Pritchard, M. (1974) 'Responsibility, understanding, and psycho-pathology', *Monist*, 58: 630–45.

Putnam, H. (1975) *Mind, Language and Reality*, Cambridge University Press.

Quen, J. (1981) 'Anglo-American concepts of criminal responsibility', in S. Hucker, C. Webster and M. Ben-Aron (eds) *Mental Disorder and Criminal Responsibility*, Toronto, Butterworth, pp. 1–10.

—— (1990) 'The history of law and psychiatry in America', in R. Bluglass and P. Bowden (eds) *Principles and Practice of Forensic Psychiatry*, London, Churchill Livingstone, pp. 111–18.

Quine, W. (1960) *Word and Object*, Cambridge, MIT Press.

—— (1969) *Ontological Relativity and Other Essays*, Columbia University Press.

Quinton, A. (1971) 'Views', *The Listener*, 98: 750–69.

Radden, J. (1985) *Madness and Reason*, London, George Allen & Unwin.

Raine, A. (1993) *The Psychopathology of Crime*, San Diego, Academic Press.

Raine, A., Venables, P. and Williams, M. (1990) 'Relationships between central and autonomic measures of arousal at age 15 and criminality at age 24', *Archives of General Psychiatry*, 47: 1003–7.

Rawls, J. (1971) *A Theory of Justice*, Oxford University Press.

Reid, J. (1960) 'The working of the New Hampshire Doctrine of Criminal Insanity', *University of Miami Law Review*, 15: 14–58.

Restak, R. (1991) *The Brain has a Mind of Its Own*, New York, Crown Publishers.

—— (1992) 'See no evil', *Sciences*, 45: 16–21.

Reznek, L. (1987) *The Nature of Disease*, London, Routledge.

—— (1991) *The Philosophical Defence of Psychiatry*, London, Routledge.

Rice, M. and Harris, G. (1990) 'The predictors of insanity acquittal', *International Journal of Law and Psychiatry*, 13: 217–224.

Robinson, P. (1984) *Criminal Law Defences*, St Paul, West Pub. Co.

Rogers, J., Bloom, J. and Manson, S. (1984) 'Insanity defences: contested or conceded?', *American Journal of Psychiatry*, 141: 885–8.

Rogers, R. (1987) 'APA's position on the Insanity Defence', *American Psychologist*, 42: 840–8.

Rogers, R. and Mitchell, C. (1991) *Mental Health Experts and the Criminal Courts*, Scarborough, Thomson Publishing.

Rosenhan, D. (1973) 'On being sane in insane places', *Science*, 179: 250–8.

Ross, L. and Anderson, C. (1982) 'Shortcomings in the attribution process', in D. Kahneman, P. Slovic and A. Tversky (eds) *Judgment under Uncertainty*, Cambridge University Press, pp. 129–52.

Roth, M. (1990) 'Psychopathic (sociopathic) personality', in R. Bluglass and P. Bowden (eds) *Principles and Practice of Forensic Psychiatry*, London, Churchill Livingstone, pp. 437–50.

Roth, M. and Kroll, J. (1986) *The Reality of Mental Illness*, Cambridge University Press.

Ryle, G. (1967) 'On forgetting the difference between right and wrong', in J. Walsh and H. Shapiro (eds) *Aristotle's Ethics*, Belmont, Wadsworth, pp. 70–9.

Schachter, S. and Latane, B. (1964) 'Crime, cognition, and the autonomic nervous system', in M. Jones (ed.) *Nebraska Symposium on Motivation*, University of Nebraska Press, pp. 221–75.

Schopp, R. (1989) 'Depression, the insanity defence, and civil commitment: foundations in autonomy and responsibility', *International Journal of Law and Psychiatry*, 12: 81–98.
—— (1991) *Automatism, insanity, and the psychology of criminal responsibility*, New York, Cambridge University Press.
Schwartz, A. (1992) *The Man who could not Kill Enough*, New York, Birch Lane Press.
Shapere, D. (1974) *Galileo*, University of Chicago Press.
Sheard, M., Marinin, J. and Bridges, C. (1976) 'The effects of lithium on impulsive aggressive behaviour in man', *American Journal of Psychiatry*, 133: 1409–13.
Sims, A. (1990) 'The phenomenology of neurosis', in R. Bluglass and P. Bowden (eds) *Principles and Practice of Forensic Psychiatry*, London, Churchill Livingstone, pp. 369–80.
Smart, J. and Williams, B. (1973) *Utilitarianism: For and Against*, Cambridge University Press.
Smith, R. (1981) *Trial by Medicine*, Edinburgh University Press.
—— (1983) 'Scientific thought and the boundary of insanity and criminal responsibility', *Psychological Medicine*, 10: 15–23.
Spitzer, R., Forman, J. and Nee, J. (1979) 'DSM-III field trials: interrater diagnostic reliability', *American Journal of Psychiatry*, 136: 815–7.
Steadman, H., Keitner, L., Braff, J. and Arranites, T. (1983) 'Factors associated with a successful insanity plea', *American Journal of Psychiatry*, 140: 401–5.
—— (1989) 'Maintenance of an insanity defence under Montana's "abolition" of the insanity defence', *American Journal of Psychiatry*, 146: 357–60.
Stephen, J. (1883) *A History of the Criminal Law of England*, London, Macmillan.
Stephenson, G. (1992) *The Psychology of Criminal Justice*, Oxford, Blackwell.
Stone, A. (1982) 'The insanity defense on trial', *Hospital and Community Psychiatry*, 33: 636–40.
—— (1984) *Law, Psychiatry, and Morality*, Washington, American Psychiatric Press.
Swanson, J., Holzer, C., Ganju, V. and Jono, R. (1991) 'Violence and psychiatric disorder in the community', *Hospital Community Psychiatry*, 41: 761–70.
Szasz, T. (1960) *The Myth of Mental Illness*, New York, Harper and Row.
—— (1965) *Psychiatric Justice*, New York, Macmillan.
—— (1973) *The Second Sin*, London, Routledge.
Tam, H. (1990) *A Philosophical Study for the Criteria for Responsibility Ascriptions*, Lampeter, Edwin Mellen Press.
Ten, C. (1987) *Crime, Guilt, and Punishment*, Oxford, Clarendon Press.
Thomson, J. (1986) *Rights, Restitution, and Risk*, Cambridge, Harvard University Press.

Thornton, D. (1988) 'Moral development theory', in B. McGurk, D. Thornton and M. Williams (eds) *Applying Psychology to Imprisonment*, London, HMSO.

Thorp, J. (1980) *Free Will*, London, Routledge.

Toone, B. (1990) 'Organically determined mental illness', in R. Bluglass and P. Bowden (eds) *Principles and Practice of Forensic Psychiatry*, London, Churchill Livingstone, pp. 385–92.

Tversky, A. (1969) 'Intransitivity of preferences', *Psychological Review*, 76: 31–48.

van Praag, H. (1991) 'Serotonergic dysfunction and aggressive control', *Psychological Medicine*, 21: 15–9.

Virkunnen, M. (1992) 'Brain serotonin and violent behaviour', *Journal of Forensic Psychiatry*, 3: 171–4.

von Hirsch, A. (1985) *Past or Future Crimes*, Manchester University Press.

Wadsworth, M. (1976) 'Delinquency, pulse rate and early emotional deprivation', *British Journal of Criminology*, 16: 245–56.

Walker, N. (1968) *Crime and Insanity in England*, Edinburgh University Press.

—— (1987) *Crime and Criminology*, Oxford University Press.

—— (1991) *Why Punish?*, Oxford University Press.

Watkins, J. (1984) 'The Bianchi case: sociopath or multiple personality?' *International Journal of Clinical and Experimental Hypnosis*, 32: 63–101.

Watson, G. (1982) 'Free agency', in G. Watson (ed.) *Free Will*, Oxford University Press, pp. 96–110.

Watson, P. (1966) 'Reasoning', in B. Foss (ed.) *New Horizons in Psychology*, Harmondsworth, Penguin.

Wettstein, R. and Mulvey, E. (1988) 'Disposition of insanity acquittees in Illinois', *Bulletin of the Academy of Psychiatry and Law*, 16: 11–24.

Whitlock, A. (1990) 'Criminal responsibility', in R. Bluglass and P. Bowden (eds) *Principles and Practice of Forensic Psychiatry*, London, Churchill Livingstone, pp. 265–70.

Williams, B. (1973) *Problems of the Self*, Cambridge University Press.

Williams, G. (1983) *Textbook of Criminal Law*, London, Stevens & Sons.

Wilson, J. (1993) *The Moral Sense*, New York, The Free Press.

Wolfgang, M., Figlio, R. and Sellin, T. (1972) *Delinquency in a Birth Cohort*, University of Chicago Press.

Woodbury, R. *et al.* (1995) 'The state of the Union', *Time*, 145: 42–52.

Woodside, B. (1995) 'A Review of anorexia nervosa and bulimia nervosa', *Current Problems in Pediatrics*, 25: 57–96.

Wootton, B. (1959) *Social Science and Social Pathology*, New York, Macmillan.

—— (1978) *Crime and Penal Policy*, London, Macmillan.

—— (1981) *Crime and the Criminal Law*, London, Macmillan.

INDEX